HUGH BRODY

MAPS AND DREAMS

**INDIANS AND THE
BRITISH COLUMBIA FRONTIER**

Douglas & McIntyre
Vancouver/Toronto

Copyright © 1981, 1988 by Hugh Brody

02 03 04   14 13 12 11

First Douglas & McIntyre paperback edition, 1988

Douglas & McIntyre Ltd.
2323 Quebec Street, Suite 201
Vancouver, British Columbia V5T 4S7

Canadian Cataloguing in Publication Data
Brody, Hugh, 1943 —
  Maps and dreams

  Bibliography: p.
  Includes index.
  ISBN 0-88894-593-0

  1. Tsattine Indians. 2. Indians of North
America — British Columbia I. Title.
E99.T77B76   970.004'97   C81-091269-4

Maps by Karen Ewing
Printed and bound in Canada by Friesens.

FOR THOMAS

". . . because a thing that is dreamed in the way I mean is already an accomplished fact. All our great West has been developed from such dreams; the homesteader's and the prospector's and the contractor's. We dreamed the railroads across the mountains, just as I dreamed my place on the Sweet Water. All these things will be every-day facts to the coming generation, but to us —" Captain Forrester ended with a sort of grunt. Something forbidding had come into his voice, the lonely, defiant note that is so often heard in the voices of old Indians.

WILLA CATHER
A Lost Lady

It is not down in any map; true places never are.

HERMAN MELVILLE
Moby Dick

Are we supposed to be nice and give you our traplines so that you can put your pipeline and benefit other people? . . . These traplines are for us, so we keep them. Why cannot you guys understand that? . . . I guess you don't really understand that this is our way of life and always will be.

CLARENCE APSASSIN
Blueberry River Indian Reserve
Public Hearings, December 1980

Contents

List of Maps

List of Tables

List of Figures

Introduction to
the 1988 edition

Maps and Dreams has been blamed and praised for being quiet in tone. But this book is dedicated to an old man whose gentleness of manner never got in the way of his persistent demand for an end to the war against his people. He also knew that to win in the white man's way would be another, and perhaps final, defeat. And I have tried to remain true to the atmosphere of one particular Indian world—that of the Beaver people of the eastern foothills of the Rocky Mountains.

The history of North America is anything but gentle. Indians have suffered attempted genocide, dispossession on a mass scale, the white man's persistent blindness to injustice, and our dismaying indifference to the possibilities for radical change that now stare us in the face. The victims themselves, however, including the peoples of the North, are inclined to be gentle and self-effacing. Many of their elders regard displays of anger, noisy confrontation or polemical hyperbole as infantile and self-defeating. They prefer to speak quiet truths. Politicians and bureaucrats whose entire way of life is dulled by clamorousness have no difficulty in smiling down with benign indifference on the nice and peaceful natives. Of course, these "nice and peaceful" peoples could blow up pipelines, burn down remote mines, and create guerilla mayhem in utterly vulnerable isolated white outposts. But many Indians' response to attack has in recent times been cautious and muted: wherever possible, they keep out of the way.

The political arguments that can, and in some form must, be assembled in support of American Indians, Australian Aborigines, the Tribals of the Indian sub-continent, and many other native peoples' demands, *are* large and loud. I shall try here to outline the wider, grimmer drama within which the people whose lives are the subject of the book itself are a single scene. I feel my own need to be clamorous on behalf of Indians—indeed, of all the peoples of what the great Indian leader George Manuel called the Fourth World.

"Indians," "Aborigines," "Tribals," "Native Peoples"— these and similarly colonial labels have long been used to lump together the original occupants of Europe's new-found lands, obscuring the real names of the cultures against whom European colonists have waged a war killing millions. That some of the colonized themselves now use these terms is a measure of the extent of the invasions. And the undeclared objective of this war has always been to deprive the indigenous inhabitants of their resources: territory, water, wildlife, fish, language, religion, even their children.

In the nineteenth century, mass death and dispossession were taken as a necessary price for progress. In the twentieth century, murder by and large gave way to quieter ways of dying—from new diseases, poverty, and hopelessness. Many still try to justify these calamities as inevitable or ultimately in the best interests of us all. Meanwhile, some urge the preservation of pure forms of tribal life in forest sanctuaries, where our idea of "tradition" is the formaldehyde in which to preserve what *we* like about *them*. Others lament the passing of the native as a misfortune that must be cured by more "progress." What does this progress mean for aboriginal peoples? More dispossession, more separation from the supposed millstone of the original cultures. Toxaemia is to be cured by more of the same poison.

The poison of "progress" continued even in the rich, fat 1950s. The war went on: more land was stolen, children were pressed into alien schools, and a job in the white man's world was offered as a panacea for all ills. By the late 1960s, the aboriginal peoples of the United States, Australia, Scandinavia and Canada—the fourth world inside the first world—lived in varying degrees of destitution or hid themselves in some remote margin of territories we said were not theirs.

Then Indian politics re-emerged (they had been clear and forceful in western America throughout the 1800s). "Red-power" caused a sudden flurry of excitement, the American Indian Movement appeared, and there arose an ever increasing number of native rights organizations—some autonomous, many funded by anxious or co-opting federal governments. Greenlandic Inuit fought for Home Rule independent of Denmark. Lapps agitated against Swedish, Norwegian and Finnish incursions on to their reindeer herding economies. Australian aborigines argued in the courts that their system was on a legal par with any other, and that ownership of their lands must therefore be fully acknowledged. Alaskan groups began a battle for settlement of their claims. The Dene and then the Inuit of northern Canada demanded recognition of their social and economic systems. Indians in every part of North America began to argue for their rights. Some groups, whose grandparents had signed treaties, showed that those treaties were fraudulent or had repeatedly been violated by settlers and industrial interests. Groups who had never signed treaties began actions in defence of an aboriginal title to their lands.

Since this book was first published, the people of northern Canada have continued to press their claims for lands and new jurisdictions. These claims take many different forms. In the far north, Inuit and Dene are pressing for a division of the Northwest Territories on new political lines, with a Dene jurisdiction in the western arctic and an Inuit region in the east. This has been the subject of a referendum arranged by the Northwest Territories government (which is now dominated by Inuit and Dene members) and is a matter of intense and complex negotiation. Similar negotiations pertain to an Innu district in the Labrador-Quebec Peninsula.

In British Columbia an aboriginal group has chosen to take a legal initiative where attempts at negotiation have, from their point of view, proved impossible or ineffective. In this action, hereditary chiefs of the Gitksan and Wet'suwet'en argue that their form of authority, ownership and management—in effect, their jurisdiction—has never ceased to be the legally relevant and appropriate system of government for their lives, lands and resources. It is possible that the legal action brought by the Gitksan and Wet'suwet'en against the Province of British Columbia will result in the Supreme Court of Canada making a ruling on the whole vexed question of aboriginal right in Canada, a ruling that could have many implications for both the theory and application of inter-cultural relationships in first world countries.

Meanwhile, the economies of the first world are losing a vital element in their credibility: belief in ever more growth, newer and better opportunities for all, has weakened. In particular, with too much, instead of too little, oil and gas available to the industrial nations, the energy crisis has moved into reverse. The developers' rush into Arctic and Subarctic wildernesses has abated. This means that the opportunity for a new justice in the North is stronger than ever before, Indians and Inuit want their territories for themselves, their rights to their own cultures acknowledged, control of their own resources left in their own hands.

But it appears that the moral atmospheres of this century contaminate our judgements. After all, we say, compared to those who starve in central Africa, or endure oppression by South African apartheid, or live with the limitations to autonomy imposed by the Soviet Union in central or northern

Asia, North American, Australian or Scandinavian aboriginals might be said to be prosperous. So we need not be too concerned: after all, the genocide (which is not admitted) has no modern equivalent inside our own societies. You see, it might all be far, far worse...

In Canada, many whites express outrage at the suggestion that their claim to the country is any different from the claim of the original populations, the pre-Canadians whose land has been stolen. Until 1969 Prime Minister Trudeau refused to acknowledge that there could be any such thing as aboriginal title, and declared treaties between different parts of the one country to be an absurd anomaly. In Australia the idea that aboriginal inhabitants have a right to prevent uranium mining on ancestral lands has been greeted with incredulity and fury. In the empire of the immigrant, new lands must be thought of as empty, and every human being as an equal newcomer— equal before the absence of law. Or, where there is law, it consists in the imperious fiats of the newcomers.

The problem here is a denial of the past, or a narrowness of vision that sees the arrival and then spread of immigrants as the very purpose of history. Debate spawned by fourth world politics has been intense. Many have sought to lay out the scale of both past and present injustices. In the case of North America, Dee Brown and, more recently, Peter Matthiessen have described in the most poignant terms something of that continent's monstrous history. But even after almost twenty years, the debate has not managed to establish in the public consciousness the nature of the past. The genocide—not against one people, but against hundreds of different cultures—is not acknowledged. Fourth world leaders who do speak of genocide are regarded as wildly intemperate, in the grip of absurd rhetoric. The facts about what has been done to aboriginal peoples just do not seem to penetrate a twentieth-century consciousness.

Is "genocide" what was attempted against the Jews alone? Is it not applicable to the extermination of other peoples? As if some indifference to the holocaust might be implied simply by the suggestion that it was not unique. Or are images of recent mass murder—this century's bequest to the imagination—so clear and irrefutable that events in "the wild west" or some old frontier or some wild outback are too remote to be real? Has the cowboy-and-Indian motif clouded in some insane romantic mist the murder and dispossession of aboriginals? Or has the crime been committed against peoples who do not quite qualify as human—men, women and children whose sadnesses and deaths are not part of any relevant moral reckoning? Is the scalping of Indians a small extension of trophy hunting? Is the shooting of Australian aboriginals an aspect of kangaroo killing in the outback? Is the taking and pollution of native peoples' resources an incidental part of unalterable human history? Somehow our consciousness of good and evil in this century blinds us to the scale of the genocide attempted against the original inhabitants of some of our most precious lands.

If we refuse to acknowledge the past, we conceal the nature of suffering, and therefore cannot understand demands in the present. Moreover, denial of the past obscures the way in which fourth world cultures have adapted to their histories. So people of the fourth world have to struggle against a double ignorance. It is as if modern Jews could persuade the world neither of the reality of the holocaust, nor to accept that Jewish culture is anything but a form of desert nomadism.

The original inhabitants of the Americas, Australasia and many other huge areas of the world have suffered an appalling and vicious colonialism. The surviving aboriginal societies, however, are not frozen in some archaic condition, but are our contemporaries. Their existences may be different, but they are modern; they live now, and—like us, like everyone—have to make accommodations between their pasts and their present. And if only we could break out of our political and imaginative constraints, if only we could shed the monopolistic belief in what might be called United Soviet Man, then we would see, hear and accept the peoples of the fourth world as modern societies with their own histories.

There are regions where this may be impossible: land made over to agriculture or industry cannot easily be restored in a form that meets tribal needs. And there are native organizations led by men and women who have accepted first world purposes, and seek to make claims based on aboriginal title in order to become rich in the white man's way. In surprisingly many places, however, the demands for justice are neither impossible to fulfil nor subordinate to cynical materialism.

In some of the semi-developed parts of North America, native societies struggle against dams that should never be built and pollution that could readily be prevented. In areas of Australia and Canada, comparatively remote groups argue against development projects that squander precious lands in order to develop resources that, even from what we call the rational economic point of view, would serve us best by being left in the ground. In Brazil and India, tribal peoples attempt to defend their forests against predacious, short-sighted developers. And these are forests upon which our very climates may depend. Throughout the Arctic, the Inuit and Dene uphold a concern for a fragile habitat whose destruction could have dire consequences for everyone in the world. In many regions indigenous peoples seek to re-enforce forms of government that have evolved over many centuries to be deeply egalitarian and committed to both a careful protection of resources and the well-being of all people—including the very old and the very young. In these places, such groups act on behalf of all of us. Indeed, there are—as I hope this book goes some way to show—strong reasons for saying that in North America it is the Indian interest that will often come closest to a best compromise between the pragmatic and the ideal. The first Americans, perhaps, are the truest upholders of the common good.

In northern Canada, as in much of Alaska and Australia, an astonishing upheaval could well take place. Throughout Australia aboriginal organizations insist that their sacred places, their cultural systems, be recognized. The 1971 Alaska Native Claims Settlement Act is under remorseless attack by native people who say their way of life and their kind of jurisdiction is still not acknowledged. At least a third of Canada is now in the grip of some form of native legal or political action. These demands will not go away; a final genocide is not going to be achieved.

We are surrounded by visible suffering we do not really see. And we are inured to its insidious forms—the stifling of other societies, cruelty to children, indifference to the elderly and the killing of our own environment. One hope for us all is that the Indian voice, while continuing to remain unlike our own, be heard.

Preface

I arrived in northeast British Columbia in September. I travelled along the Alaska Highway surrounded by infinite forests of evergreen splashed with pale yellows and reds — poplar, birch and willow in their early autumn colours. Turning west to follow thirty miles of dirty road to find the Reserve, the foothills of the Rocky Mountains rose ahead of me. A low sun lit the snow on distant peaks.

I was driving a pick-up truck that had come with the job. This vehicle — large, roomy, and powerful — was well suited to life in northern British Columbia. With the help of chains it could negotiate autumn mud and could nearly always be kept on roads covered with soft snow or meltwater. It would serve as a means of getting to the nearest shop (twenty-five miles away), making day trips and the occasional emergency dash to the nearest large town and hospital (eighty miles distant), and going hunting. The Indian Reserve where I had come to live, and with which a large part of this book is concerned, had only one other functioning vehicle. A researcher with a pickup had something to offer.

But after my first weeks on the Reserve there were times when the pickup seemed to be more of an obstacle than a help. Too many days were spent on errands and too few doing anything that would normally qualify as research. As the only driver of such a useful vehicle I had little time and less energy left over for thinking and learning, still less for making maps. As driver I met everyone, but the pickup defined what we did together, and therefore — I increasingly thought — placed close limits on what I could learn. My worst fear was that the pickup had instantly become far more important than work that any of us might try to do. Suggestions about the research were met with plans for driving. Yes, the people wanted to explain their economic system, but with the help of the pickup. It seemed to become harder and harder to disentangle the success of the pickup from that of the research project.

So I decided to take a chance: I gave the pickup to a colleague in town, got a lift back to the Reserve, and stayed there without a vehicle. The first hours were frightening. I had no easy escape from the difficulties that I feared would arise. I also knew that the research itself might now be declared unwelcome. Both my stay and the project were perhaps about to amount to very little.

The first people who spoke to me seemed to confirm the worst of these fears. "How are you going to eat?" asked one, apparently regarding a white man without a pickup as quite helpless. "What are you going to do now?" asked someone else. I said that I wanted to be without a vehicle, that because I was without it I hoped to see more of the land nearby, and that there would be many ways in which the work could proceed. I thought that I glimpsed looks of incredulity as well as dismay. But apprehensiveness can cause one to misinterpret everything. I waited.

On the day after my return to the Reserve, I visited an old man who had been especially interested in showing me the land, and who had from time to time made use of the pickup. With much of the awkwardness that is born of saying what you suspect others do not want to hear, I tried to explain to him and his household why I had now left it with someone else, and talked again about the work. I emphasized the extent to which map-making, and other kinds of inquiry, were ways of doing what Indian people of the region had said they wanted to do. Despite language difficulties, I felt that my fumbling statements were kindly received. Then, rather abruptly, the old man said: "Go to your house. Maybe we'll talk again later." It seemed that the whole endeavour had failed: I was being sent away. Confused and troubled, I did as I was told, and walked the quarter mile or so from their house to mine. The pickup had been nearly as big as my cabin and its absence now, as I approached, made the cabin seem a very vulnerable little place. Again I waited.

I sat inside for an hour or two and wondered what it all meant and what it was best to do now and how, if necessary, to get back to town. Then I heard the sound of a horse's hooves on the trail, and a bang on the door. Outside was a boy leading a horse. He said simply, "Old man says this is yours. Go to his house." And a few minutes later two men rode up, saying that I had better go with them — there were important places that could not be reached by pickup. On the way we called in at the old man's house. In answer to my thanks, he told me that he would fix some food for me that night, for without a pickup I would never be able to manage. A week later I went to town and collected the pickup. Eighteen months later I was still on the Reserve.

The odd-numbered chapters of this book are about those eighteen months, and they attempt to do justice to the way that the Indians of one reserve answered questions about a research project. Their response was to take me on a series of journeys. Along the way much was shown and explained, far more than I could see or understand. The people tried to demonstrate how their economic system worked, and showed me many facets of their way of life, on their own terms. Sometimes they addressed social problems and social ills, but these also were placed in the people's own terms of reference. In this way I, the researcher, was taken away from research schemes and agendas, and sometimes very far away from familiar kinds of inquiry. The odd-numbered chapters try to follow a route selected by the people.

In those chapters I have chosen to use fictitious names and have in other ways sought to conceal the identities of both people and places. I refer to the community as the Reserve, intending thereby to suggest that it has a general as well as a specific significance. The reasons for choosing the title — *Maps and Dreams* — should become obvious. Dreams collide; new kinds of maps are made. It is for this reason that the book is dedicated to a man whose gentle and dignified affirmations of all that is best, yet threatened, are totally alien to frontiers and frontiersmen.

It may also become obvious that there is a prospect in northern British Columbia for a replay of injustice, ruthlessness, and indifference to human well-being that is all too familiar in the history of white dealings with Indians and the land in the New World. Among simple societies, the hunters' has seemed the simplest; among flexible and non-industrial economies, theirs has seemed the most flexible, the ultimately non-industrial. When adventurers, missionaries, traders, or administrators encountered man-the-hunter, they were sure that here were people whose lives were bare of all comfort, without security, and below morality; people whose prospects for truly human achievement were minimal. Would-be civilizers concluded that hunters never had, or had lost, the means to achieve a decent way of life; should welcome the benefits of trade, wage employment, and proper religion; should allow their lands to be differently used; and must accept whatever changes are brought to them, however the changes are brought. This is a death sentence that colonialists issue to the hunters.

European ideas about the Far North have added to more general stereotypes of hunters' simplicity. The European imagination was appalled by the prospects of lands of eternal winter and intolerable extremes of cold. These uninhabitable places, however, turned out to be inhabited — by small nomadic bands. Their existence was then deemed to be particularly bereft of all human comfort and without the possibility of real human culture. So we think we must help them by changing them.

How strange it is, then, to find that the condemned have somehow repeatedly escaped their execution. Are the hunters of the world still caged on some benign death row, sustained there by merciful administrators? Are their economies deceased and the peoples now able to live thanks to handouts or a degree of participation in our real economy?

In 1955 and 1967 two studies of Indian life — totalling five volumes — were published by the government of Canada. The first of these centred on the 191 bands of British Columbia. The second treated the economic, social, and cultural conditions of the 580 Indian communities throughout the country. These books, thick with details and rich in all manner of social and economic statistics, say almost nothing about the reserves that are situated in the foothills, muskeg, forests, and prairie between the Rocky Mountains and the Albertan and Yukon borders. The peoples of this area are excluded from one of the studies; in the other, one group appears in two tables, where figures are based on guesses by local white officials. Apart from a Ph.D. dissertation and a scattering of articles, these two government publications are part of a long history of scholarly neglect.

Indians who have endured anthropological or other scrutiny might envy the people of northeast British Columbia for having had a fortunate escape from intrusive questioners and their mysterious, even dubious, purposes. It is never easy to know why research is being done, or whose interests in the end will be served. The accumulation of knowledge about colonial or tribal populations is often a facet of control and exploitation — even when the researchers firmly believe otherwise. To be neglected by science might well be a blessing.

But in 1978, with the growing likelihood that the Alaska Highway natural gas pipeline would cut directly through Indian lands, both government officials and representatives of Indian bands insisted that some consideration must be given to how Indians and their economic lives were going to be affected. Yet no outsider knew enough about the Indian economy in that area to say what the impact of any new development would actually be upon.

In September 1977, the Union of British Columbia Indian Chiefs had already begun to call for a public inquiry into the social and economic consequences of the northern British Columbia frontier. In the following March, Chiefs and Councillors of seven of the northeast's Indian bands made a series of presentations to a Select Committee of the Canadian House of Commons. They expressed their fears about the scale and pace of industrial development in their hunting and trapping lands. In particular, they stated their opposition to construction of the Alaska Highway natural gas pipeline. Partly as a result of these presentations, and partly because of intensive follow-up work by the Union of Chiefs, the Canadian government funded a land-use and occupancy study. This book has grown from, and in its way is a part of, that study. The even numbered chapters give the detailed, at times technical, findings. Above all, they seek to show the extent to which Indian economic life is modern, resilient and viable.

It was impossible not to feel apprehensive about the advantages of such research work to the people themselves. Even the best political organizations, happy to have secured government funding for their research, might find that they are unconsciously working against their constituents' own interests. In this case, the Canadian government gave money because of its wish to benefit from the construction of a system to deliver Alaskan energy to the American midwest. This alone was enough to give rise to doubts. Was the research a sop to the people who might stand to lose most? Might it be a way of overcoming possible opposition from those who could, if not appeased, threaten a radical and even violent disruption of the best-laid plans? Would it be a source of information that could then be translated into dollar compensation for the destruction of cultures? Or was it merely a salve to the developers' troubled consciences? As the research got under way, these thoughts were never far from mind. When I set out in the summer of 1978 on a first exploratory trip to northeast British Columbia, I was haunted by a thought that must have bothered many researchers: you might find out five or even ten years later whom you were really working for.

Maps and Dreams thus presents both findings and the way in which a project was shaped by a group of Indians. It is a book of anecdotes as well as a research report, its structure being the result of an attempt to meet two different needs. The problem is one of audience; or an awkward tension between a wish to maintain a sense of universal concern without losing a feeling for a particular place. For writings that grow out of resistance to colonialism, this problem can be overwhelming. There is a need for scientific detail, evidence that must stand the test of scrutiny by academics and cross-examination in uncomprehending or hostile courtrooms; yet it is also essential to bring to life unfamiliar points of view.

Land use and occupancy projects were pioneered in the Canadian Northwest Territories. Their primary aim is to map and explain all the ways in which Inuit and Indian peoples have used their lands within living memory. Since I had worked on the Inuit studies in both the Northwest Territories and Labrador, the Union of British Columbia Indian Chiefs asked me to help design a similar study of the northeast corner of their province. On first hearing of the study, I was both sceptical and apprehensive: many people had told me that the region had been so devastated by frontier developments as to make any work with its Indian peoples a thoroughly disheartening experience. Having come to share the most widespread stereotype of the area, I agreed to go to northeast British Columbia for no more than five weeks, in a purely advisory capacity. What is more, and of a piece with the way the region has been viewed and treated, I went there thinking it would be a convenient steppingstone to the Pacific Coast and the Yukon. The fact that three years later I was writing this book is an indication of just how much I had to learn — and how much prejudice and misconception I had to shed.

I owe thanks to all those who fought for, funded and then carried out the research that made it possible to see beyond frontier appearances. Indeed, it is necessary both to acknowledge a very large number of persons and to say at the same time that their roles are understated by the very idea of acknowledgement. All the work, which was often hard, uncomfortable, and nothing if not protracted, was shared.

In this process of learning and unlearning I was helped by and worked along with Martin Weinstein and Rick Salter. They contributed to every part of the work in northeast British Columbia, as well as giving me every help and encouragement they possibly could. In particular, I have relied heavily on Martin Weinstein's field work in and extensive biological understanding of northern British Columbia. He and Dinah Schooner also worked on the maps and mapping of Indian land use. Jim Harper, Richard Overstall and Paddy Wejr planned and executed the mapping of white uses of the region. Lilian Basil and Barbara Kuhn tirelessly advised at every stage of the work. Throughout, George Manuel and the staff at the Union of British Columbia Indian Chiefs gave their advice and support; Violet Birdstone and the Union's Energy and Resources team, in particular, bore a heavy administrative load. Arlene Laboucane was endlessly helpful as the regional field worker. Karen Ewing designed and then worked indefatigably on base maps for assembly of the data and, finally and painstakingly, has drawn or redrawn all the maps in this book.

At the beginning of the project each band in the northeast region selected a mapper and field worker, who helped band members to draw their own maps. They were: Bernie Metechea (Halfway), Robert Dominic and Jack Askoty (Doig), Eddie Apsassin

(Blueberry), Rubie Dokkie (West Moberly Lake), Amie Gauthier, Jim Gauthier, and Bud Napoleon (East Moberly Lake), Mary Murray (Prophet River), and Ken Burke and Mary Dickie (Fort Nelson). Bud Napoleon, Clarence Apsassin, and Eddie Apsassin also made immense contributions to the details of the domestic economy given in Chapter 12. *Maps and Dreams* does not even seek to do justice to the massive body of findings that resulted from all these individuals' work. Presentations by Martin Weinstein, Jim Harper, Michael Jackson, and Richard Overstall to the Northern Pipeline Agency's hearing at Fort St. John (December 1979) are major contributions to any discussion of northern British Columbia. I have drawn heavily on their work, but some of their more extensive results can be found in the publicly available transcript of the hearings, volumes 16 and 17. Also, only a small proportion of the maps are published here.

In preparation of this manuscript, the work of Heather Jarman, Alan Cooke, and Tom Engelhardt was invaluable. They, together with Miranda Tufnell and Michael Ignatieff, read successive drafts and made innumerable comments and suggestions. Bud Napoleon, Arnold Cragg and Steven Basil also offered detailed and valuable advice. The British Columbia regional office of the Department of Indian Affairs and Northern Development generously provided financial support.

When living and working a long way from home, and when writing, there are individuals who give help that is not easily described — who somehow manage to encourage, remain silent, or urge caution at just the right moments. I owe a very special debt of this kind to Fran Cameron and Rick Salter. No amount of thanks, however, can do justice to the support, help, and hospitality that the people of the northeast British Columbia reserves gave to me for eighteen months. They showed me their skills in the bush, taught me to ride in the right way, and worked hard to have me speak and understand a little of their language. Their patience, tried to extremes though it must have been, was unending. The weaknesses of this book can only be mine.

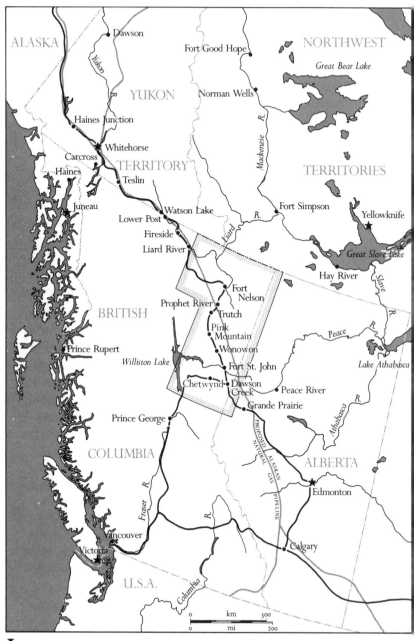

I NORTHWEST NORTH AMERICA

Joseph Patsah's Agenda

The oldest man at the Reserve is Joseph Patsah. He lights a fire in the woods with all the precision and attention to detail that is the untroubled self-consciousness of those who, with age, are resolved that what they represent be respected. He selects each piece of wood, pauses before placing it in the flame; pauses to look at it, frozen for an instant in some thought about its suitability or texture or species. It is easy to feel impatient with this pace and attentiveness to detail, with its touches of zeal, even fanaticism. Easy to be impatient, that is, until you remember what fire signifies to hunters of the sub-Arctic forest: fires and walking are the two ways to keep warm — clothes are light — and the old cannot always walk long enough or fast enough to keep out the cold. Excellence with fires is essential. Joseph Patsah does not flaunt his skill.

No one could fail to notice Joseph's standing in his community. Dealings with him (as with the elderly in many societies) are marked by a jocular respect, a celebration of an old man's importance and authority. To tease the elderly is to show that you are on terms of happy intimacy with your own heritage. It shows that you are glad to be a part of your society. Everyone, except his own children, calls Joseph by his nickname "Callan." And from time to time the young men call on his authority: Is this as far as the fence rails should extend? Is this the line along which to cut a horse's hooves? Do you ever find lynx on such and such a hillside?

I first met Joseph Patsah at his home on the Reserve. It was a cool but sunny day in late summer. The Reserve is sited in a wide valley, and the houses have been built on flat lands that abut a wide and fast-flowing river. In the far distance I could see the Rocky Mountains. Thick stands of mixed woodland covered a succession of ridges that rose above the houses and shaped the wide river valley below. The poverty and violence so widely associated with northern Indian reserves were, at this first impression at least, eclipsed by the beauty of the setting.

Brian Akattah, the young man whom the Reserve had chosen as their local research worker and mapmaker, insisted that we should go and talk to Joseph. Everyone who comes here with any questions, with any concerns that are taken seriously, is soon taken to see Joseph Patsah. So we went to his home as the starting point of our work.

His house stands at the far end of the Reserve, near two other houses and a tiny dilapidated cabin. It is about a quarter of a mile from the main cluster of homes often referred to as "the village," or — with a sardonic grin — as "downtown." Joseph's place is a prefabricated, three-bedroom standard-issue government house. It sits a short distance from the edge of a small bluff, whose face is eroded by trails. The regular scurries of children on their way from home to the wide, scrubby bank of the river keep pebbles and small earth slides loose and shifting on it. Below the bluff the children hunt birds and rabbits with slingshots and borrowed .22 rifles and, in summer and early fall, pick basketfuls of berries. The slopes and bank are also marked by horses that roam towards the river and must be herded home when they are needed. The firmer trails on the bluff have side paths. Some lead nowhere in particular, others to springs that now spurt out of two- or three-inch pipes jammed into fissures where water once seeped out of the ground. None of the houses has running water. Trips to the piped springs are a recurrent task, mainly for women and children.

Beside Joseph's house is all the paraphernalia of an encampment, so much so that the house itself is diminished, and becomes a far less dismaying sight than if it were a home as such, a place to which domestic life is restricted. The appearance of poverty has its place in a more complicated system of life; Joseph's Reserve home is one of several camps, cabins, and accumulations of equipment that together are far more important than the condition, size, or furniture of the house we were now visiting.

As Brian Akattah and I approached, it was impossible not to be both apprehensive and impressed. A welcome from the Patsahs would amount to a welcome from most, if not all, of the community. We also knew that maps drawn by Joseph and his household members would represent the most significant account of the whole region's hunting and trapping patterns. Contact with him was going to be a test of the validity of the work. If Joseph thought it was a good idea to represent the needs and claims of the people as land-use maps, then the whole project would be endorsed.

The approach to the household is impressive because of the curious mixture of pleasure, surprise, and familiarity that flickers through the mind when suddenly you see evidence of ways of life that are supposedly survivals from ancient times, that resemble old photographs or ethnographic films. You think immediately of the word "traditional," which so quickly and easily blinds the eye with mythical images that prevent your seeing gun scabbards hung ready for use by the door, the sharpness of the axes, the bags of dried meat, a box of new beaver traps — the means of satisfying present-day cultural and economic needs. To look for and find the traditional at Joseph Patsah's home is to imply that it is an intriguing relic that does not serve real life — and that is far from the truth.

Joseph was sitting with two middle-aged men in the partial shelter of a tarpaulin stretched over a tent frame. At one side were the barely smoking ashes of a fire; and around the fireplace were spruce boughs on which people could sit or lie, warm and dry on the ground. No more than twenty yards from this sheltered area was a teepee, about ten feet high, with its irregular upside-down funnel of frame poles rising out of a covering of overlapped pieces of canvas and plastic. To the left of the shelter blazed a large fire over which was set a very simple frame for drying and smoking meat. This fire had been laid in such a way as to heat a large drum of water, behind which were three women using the hot water to wash clothes. These (I learned later) were Joseph's wife Liza, her mother Reza, and her daughter Shirley. On the boughs in front of the fire lay a middle-aged man, stretched on his back, his head resting on his cupped hands, his elbows slightly raised from the ground. Beyond the fire, in a small oval corral fenced with long, thin wooden rails, were several horses, squat, barrel-chested, and powerful looking: three browns, two greys, and a sandy-coloured colt.

Between the front of Joseph's house and the fire was a wide area littered with odds and ends of equipment and supplies. An amazing profusion: a pile of green poplar firewood felled in late summer when it is wet with sap, then cut into large blocks and left to dry; three or four upturned saddles, their horns to the ground and stirrups flopped sideways; blankets and canvas casually draped over pieces of gear as protection against weather; more saddles on a rail fixed between two trees; pails; axes; a pile of clothing ready for the wash; coils of rope; long ends of fraying string; empty oat sacks, which hunters hang across their shoulders or tie behind a saddle to make a lightweight pack; a shovel, interesting for its large homemade handle. Almost merged with the grass lay another level of less obvious and identifiable items, bits and ends and things. Initially, these were noticeable only in a cumulative way as a kind of texture or fuzz, part of an overall appearance. On closer to the ground inspection, it was possible to discern slivers of wood shaped to some purpose, fragments of metal or plastic, jettisoned close by but later to be found and used again, and scraps or strips of leather that can be turned into thongs to fix bridle lines and stirrups. It is this blur of stuff, this texture, that causes visitors to see dirt and untidiness where there is often in reality a minor store of all manner of spare parts. A combination of these odds and ends with the larger equipment, with the complex of shelters and buildings, with the fires, with the frames and spruce boughs — all these create the extraordinary and indefinable qualities of a camp, the combination of permanence and transience, the reconciled contradiction with which hunting, trapping, and fishing peoples confront and confound us.

In the centre of all this sat Joseph. As we approached, the man lying by the washing-water fire raised his head and turned with the least of movements to look at us. His face was wide and deeply lined. Even from a distance the lines were remarkable — great bands of parallel creases that ran from temple to jawbone. His expression was watchful but not unwelcoming. As we came closer, he rolled into a half-kneeling position, then, with a decisive precision, got up and walked towards Joseph as if to warn or consult or find some shelter — at least to be prepared for our intrusion. This was Atsin, one of Liza's older brothers.

Joseph himself seemed hardly to notice our arrival. Even when we were within a few yards he no more than glanced at us, then turned to rekindle the fire. Brian spoke about the maps he had undertaken to draw for his people. Joseph seemed not to hear. His face was impassive, almost rigid; his occasional looks hardly more than quick, sharp glances. Had it not been for these movements I might have thought him deaf or merely indifferent to our presence.

Suddenly, he jumped up and hurried from the shelter to the house. It seemed that Joseph Patsah had rejected our visit. But Brian sat down by the fire, as at ease as could be, either impervious to rejection or content that all was well. Atsin meanwhile took up the axe that Joseph had been using and began to split firewood, first into narrow pieces and then along about four inches of their length, until every piece bore a splayed fringe that would burn with all the quick heat of so many matchsticks. The speed and precision with which he could wield a large axe to such intricate effect was spellbinding. As Atsin used the fringed kindling to blaze the fire, Joseph reappeared with a table. They had turned the shelter into a work place, and I was told to unroll the maps we carried with us and to lay them out on the table. Large topographical map sheets are cumbersome and difficult to align. With their maze of contour lines and streams, they are also hard to decipher. As I arranged and rearranged the sheets, Brian and I explained the work and the maps as best we could. I was uncertain about both Joseph's and Atsin's reactions to us, and wished to be as reassuring and clear as possible.

But there was little need for explanations. Joseph had his own agenda and his own explanations to give. He stood by the table, looked at the map, and located himself by identifying the streams and trails that he used. Periodically he returned to the map as a subject in its own right, intrigued by the pattern of contours, symbols, and colours and perhaps also by his recognition of the work that had brought us to his home. But if the map had any real importance for him, it seemed to be through its evocation of other times and other places. He looked at it with an intent silence, as if poised with a weapon to strike some prey.

Joseph's eyes, softly opaque with age, were startlingly attentive. He had not only the expertise but also the authority of his eighty-some years. But his composure and eloquence were not those of an old man; they expressed the completeness and distinctiveness of a culture. Joseph Patsah has always lived by hunting, trapping, and fishing, and has always depended upon the demanding conventions of an oral tradition. He had many things to say about his way of life, his society's needs, and he said them with graceful and cautious circum-locutions. His presence and manner caused the map to fade into the background.

It is difficult, perhaps impossible, to render Joseph's speech into written English. It is so firmly rooted in oral and Athapaskan modes as to defy a written version. As if this were not a source of enough difficulty, he also likes to speak to outsiders in English — an English that comes with a richness of unexpected rhythms, an ungrammati-cal shape, and with hesitancies and gestures that wonderfully overcome limitations of vocabulary. It is difficult, therefore, to do even remote justice to all he said as he looked at the map, while we sat on the spruce boughs by the fire, drinking mugs of tea.

He spoke first of all about his Daddy — the incongruity of the word made extreme by the unselfconscious and strong emphasis Joseph gave to it. "Daddy, he first came here nineteen-twelve. First comes to this place, way down Ospika. Nineteen-twelve up this river, pretty hard that time. I bet you not many people then. Sometime Daddy work like white man, panning gold. I learn all that, pan gold . . . ." The reminiscence thus spoken, and accompanied by an occasional search on the map for Ospika, the creeks tributary to the Midden River, or perhaps the mountains through which the family had travelled, slowly established his way of life. Since such poor justice to the power of the spoken word is done by the writing of it, especially verbatim, I give here only the main outline of Joseph's narrative.

For twenty or thirty years, around the turn of the century, moose populations in northwestern Canada were low. Moose, like caribou and many other herbivorous mammals, experience a long-term population cycle that is little understood. In years when other resources were not readily available, the scarcity of moose used to bring extreme hardship to many Indian hunting bands. (The buffalo, whose northern range once brought them into lands hunted by the Patsah family, had by the 1880s been more or less exterminated.) After several years of struggle and near starvation, Joseph's family moved north and west, higher into the foothills of the Rockies. Patsah's people had long regarded these higher foothills as a sort of meat bank on which they could draw when the usual game resources or hunting patterns failed. Now they hoped that moose, along with sheep, mountain goats, and caribou, would provide a more substantial and perhaps a permanent subsistence base.

So Joseph — then about fourteen years old — went with his family up the Midden River, then along the creeks and streams that cut routes through the edges of the mountains. They moved with their horses, hunting and fishing as they travelled, until they came to the Bluestone River. Here they camped with as much sense of permanence, as clear an idea of having arrived, and with as complete a feeling of change as are consistent with a way of life that depends on a perpetual readiness to move. They had arrived, they felt, because here they imagined they would be able once again to establish the whole year's round of camps and trading journeys in a new hunting territory. The family looked at the Bluestone and adjacent creeks, the Midden valley, the sharp and thinly wooded foothills not far beyond with confidence, hope, and determination. Within these valleys, forests, and uplands, surely there must be moose and mule deer. Higher still, within a day's walk or ride, there would be caribou, sheep, marmots — to say nothing of the rainbow trout, Dolly Varden, grayling, and Rocky Mountain whitefish (Joseph likes to recite names in lists) to be caught in many of the eddying elbows and pools of all those creeks. This area and its resources were new, but not entirely unknown. The Patsahs were still at the edge of the family's old hunting territory, their fallback, their bank vaults. They had moved from a centre to a periphery; but what was for them a periphery was for other Beaver Indian families the centre. They would now share resources, because they already shared a system that made it possible to move without fear of conflicts.

Yet Joseph's Daddy, along with the others, sought a confirmation of the new area's potential. This was done by means of dream prophecy and the erection of a medicine cross. They stripped a tall straight pine of its bark and affixed a crosspiece about four-fifths of the way along its length, then attached smaller crosses to the crosspiece — one at each end. They nailed a panel, also in cross formation, close to the base of the pole. Even when its base was sunk into the ground, this cross, or set of crosses, was twice the height of a tall man. When it was in place, Patsah and others hung skin clothing and medicine bundles from the main crosspiece, and on the panel near the base they inscribed "all kinds of fancy" — drawings of animals that had figured in the people's dreams, animals of the place that would make themselves available for the hunt.

The night the cross was completed, an augury came to one of the elders in a dream. A young cow moose, moving to the Patsah camp from the Bluestone Creek area, circled the base of the cross, then went off in the direction from which she had come. Two days after this dream, hunters discovered the tracks of a young cow moose, and, following these, recognized them to be the tracks of the dream animal. The tracks led to the cross, circled it, then returned to the Bluestone. The dream prediction had been auspiciously fulfilled. The new area would provide abundantly.

Despite this sign, after a while Joseph's father decided to return to the old heartland of his hunting area, and he moved once again towards the Ospika River. Joseph, along with some others, was opposed to the return and remained for the rest of his life in the lands where the cross had been set. However, Bluestone Creek and the location of the cross itself — a low, level stretch of woodland between the Bluestone and the Midden — did not come to be the most productive and evocative of the several locales that comprised this new territory. About ten miles northwest of the cross is another tributary of the Midden — the Sechin River. Sechin is a Beaver word, and means "to make a kill when hunting." This small, beautiful stream flows out of the very edge of the Rockies in a succession of bends and rapids. Both the Indians and local Whites know it by an English name — Quarry — a name that spills over to include the land around it. This area is a source of plenty and strength. To Joseph, his family, and many others of the Reserve, Quarry means home.

As Joseph Patsah told his story, he searched the map until he found a particular bend in a river. Here a hunter, standing on a steep bank, can look out onto open flats and easily spot moose and beaver, and sometimes, with a long shot from above, can even make a kill. He sought the exact place where, in September or October, it is easy to catch fat rainbow trout. He traced the length of a trail that each year he and others used to travel from a spring beaver-hunting camp to the trading post at Hudson's Hope. He satisfied himself that we understood the exact distance between the Reserve (a spot where he used to camp for part of each summer) and the best of his winter cabins. And at times, as he talked, Joseph made use of the map in the most general, even abstract way: with no more than a slight flutter of a gesture he established Quarry as his. At different times he said, "This land, all this my country"; "I bet you every place this country my country"; "No white man this place."

It was often not clear, perhaps not even intended to be clear, whether or not his words floated back to some former time or were addressed to the realities of Quarry now. It was too soon to understand the subtleties of Joseph Patsah's sense of time. But at least, in this first conversation, centred on his own arrival and his claim to the place, he had introduced us to Quarry. He had brought us as far as the cross.

Every now and then, Joseph broke into his story and, by way of a parenthesis seemingly at odds with the story's place in the past, remarked that we should go to Quarry. With a gesture towards the northwest he said, "Sometime we go up Quarry. Maybe tomorrow. Someday." Such a statement was an invitation and a recognition that the place, with all its importance and meaning, is still there. Joseph emphasized this in one of his asides by adding, "It's no good in these flats. Better go up Quarry. Live up there, die up there. No damn good here. Home in that place."

He had established Quarry and had located the whole Quarry area on a map. Mapping as such was now completed, and Joseph made this clear by a decisive movement. He stood up, pushed back his shoulders a couple of times, as though to say that it was time to break out of this cramped business. So he stretched, at the same time looking into an out-of-focus distance. The meeting was over, but his thought continued: he seemed to contemplate in his mind's eye the place he had established on the map. Just as we were packing up, helping to move the table back into the house, removing, insofar as possible, at least the physical disruption this mapping business had caused, Joseph turned to me and said, "We'll go to Quarry. I'll show you the cross. Good country. You'll see."

Joseph is an old man. However compelling his words, however ageless his manner, as soon as we had left his encampment-home, some of the magic evaporated. I kept thinking that perhaps he had missed the point. In the course of talking, and prompted by Brian, Joseph had shown his hunting, trapping, and fishing areas on the map; had marked, with coloured felt pens, all the places he had lived during a long life. Yet he had drawn circles and lines in an absent-minded way. As an elder, he had spoken beyond us, addressing the richness of another culture, another spiritual domain, even another time altogether. Perhaps he had not sought to understand the work. He did not question its purpose, still less its technique. When he marked the map he did so with a seeming indifference. At the times he sought precision, it was usually to locate some exact spot in order to digress even further from the job I thought that we had come to do. If he focussed our attention on Quarry, with all its historic meaning to him, this might nonetheless be tangential to present realities. Maybe his concerns were locked in memories, with few links to the importance of the land or its resources for people of today. These thoughts eroded the confidence that Joseph had inspired in me as he talked. A remark by Brian Akattah then added to my unease: "Old man, Joseph. Old-timer." There is ambiguity in the use of these terms. Old-timers are sources of wisdom — but old men? Who knows? Perhaps Brian hoped to explain away Joseph's manner as understandable but senile.

Brian did not, however, seem discouraged. Joseph's welcome and words had given him enough confidence to go directly to another house. And even my pessimistic thoughts lasted only as long as it took to walk from the shelter to the tiny cabin that stands no more than a hundred yards from Joseph's, perched tight on the edge of the bluff. This turned out to be Atsin's place. He had gone home midway through the talk with Joseph and somehow must have known he would be visited next. By the time we came in, he had already cleared the floor space, which is to say the whole space, and had made a surface for the maps — a sheet of old cardboard.

There, in the darkness of a cabin lit only by the bit of light that shone through a tiny frame window, with three people crowded shoulder to shoulder on the floor, Atsin began to explain how he had lived. Stories. And a periodic, almost eruptive reference to the impossibility of such explanation: "Crazy white man. He never understands. Too many, too many." By which Atsin meant that he could never, even in a hundred interviews, mark down all the places he had hunted and travelled. Yet he tried, for he was in fact eager to show how comprehensively he knew his land. He was proud, also, of the immense work and of the achievement such detailed and extensive knowledge represents.

Soon after Atsin had begun his explanation, Joseph and three other men appeared at the cabin doorway. All except Joseph joined Atsin on the floor and watched as he drew his hunting areas. But Joseph just stood at the doorway, listening. Then, taking a few steps inside, and standing just behind Atsin's crouched and kneeling body, Joseph began to speak. This time he did not address the map, or his past, or make reference to specific places. Nor did he speak to any one person. Instead he addressed the room, his people, the issue. In a mixture of Beaver and English, in broken, almost staccato phrases, with all the pauses and gestures that are essential to anyone who speaks in a language not his own, he affirmed the importance of the maps and the mapping. It was political discourse, and had touches of exhortation.

There is no longer time to wait, he said. There is no more room for the white man's intrusions. Now the people have to stand up and defend what has always been theirs. There must be no fooling around, no bullshit. There must be no failure to take advantage of whatever opportunities may now be offered. If Indians are going to continue to be Indians in this place, in these places, in this whole region, then their presence must be made known to everyone, everywhere. This, as he understood it, is the point of messing around with maps; this, he insisted, is the reason for speaking at length and with great truthfulness. Perhaps young people do not understand, perhaps some people of all ages do not want to understand. He knew, however, that the time had come for the Beaver Indians, for all Indians, to insist on the land, a right to its use, and on their right to protect it. The land, using the land in the proper way, is inseparable from the people who live there.

It was clear, finally and unequivocally, from the way that everyone in that dark and ragged cabin listened, from the respectful stillness, from their occasional grunted agreements, that Joseph spoke as an old-timer and elder, not as an old man. He finished what he had to say, once again, by insisting that he would take us to Quarry. A directive seemed to have gone out, at least to the few people there, and perhaps through them to other homes and reserves, that everyone should use the map-making in whatever way he could, to show his own Quarry River. Whatever mapping and researching might be carried out, Joseph Patsah had drawn up his own agenda.

Northeast
British Columbia

All but a very small number of prehistorians are now convinced that the American Indians came from ancient homelands in central or northeastern Asia. Various theories of human history are employed to explain this population spread. Some refer to pressures in Asia which drove marginal groups onto and then beyond the land bridge that became the Bering Strait. Others suggest that peoples of Asia took advantage of new, and possibly excellent, hunting lands left by the receding icecaps of the last ice age. There is less agreement about when these migrations happened than the general fact that they must have happened. Until recently, the experts gave the date as up to ten thousand years ago. New evidence in the form of bone implements suggests that hunting peoples of some kind have been in northwest

Canada for as many as forty thousand years. At least one archaeologist now puts this at one hundred thousand years.

Many Canadian Indians resent the white man's self-styled expertise in these matters. There are Indian beliefs about their origins and the nature of their dispersal over the land. Some British Columbian groups insist that the Indians have been in particular locations since human beings first emerged on the Earth. This insistence is backed by ancient stories and deeply held tradition. They also have their own evidence: there are rivers, mountain tops, and rocks scattered on valley sides that owe their existence to dramatic events that occurred at the time humans were formed. These events are well recorded in oral history. When archaeologists and other "experts" challenge the Indians' own idea of their history, they implicitly undermine the Indians' sense of absolute and eternal belonging to particular places. Whites may be proud of being immigrants but any suggestion that the Indians are also immigrants is increasingly regarded as ignorant and insulting.

Any introduction to the Indians of a region must therefore be careful about the ways in which the narrowly scientific can play a part, albeit unwittingly, in political debate. Archaeologists deepen our appreciation for and understanding of Indian occupancy of North America. But archaeological speculations, even when stripped of spurious certainties, have implications that many Indians consider to be sharply at odds with their own view of themselves and that they fear may even undermine their rights. This is especially so of the Indian peoples whose social and economic systems have entailed a comparatively sedentary way of life. The fishing and whaling people of the North Pacific and Alaskan coastlines, for example, spent most of each year in one large village site. Their links with such sites, and the resources close by, are accordingly precise and intense. Oral histories mark these as places of origin. The Shushwap of central British Columbia say that they became human beings in the Fraser Valley, where they have lived ever since. They do not like this special connection with their ancestral home to be challenged by the suggestion that they immigrated there from somewhere in Asia however many thousands of years ago. Tolerance for such archaeological hypothesizing is not increased by the way the hypotheses seem to keep changing. From an Indian's point of view, only one thing about white opinion is sure: whatever is believed today will be said to be wrong tomorrow. This view may be mistaken when it comes to archaeologists and anthropologists who have in recent years deepened appreciation for both the antiquity and rationality of hunting peoples. Nonetheless, politically articulate Indians are often deeply sensitive to and at odds with scientists.

This problem is less severe in the case of hunting peoples of the North. Their attachment to areas of land has less to do with ideas of their origin, and their mobile life styles mean that they expect to use many different resources and living sites. The Indians of the northern forests, like the Inuit of the Canadian Arctic, have a socioeconomic system that is highly flexible and, generally speaking, without very emphatic ideas of private or even family property. This does not mean that they feel less strongly than other peoples about the land or its resources. However, it does mean that they represent and express these feelings differently. One point of difference is their own belief that they did not necessarily originate in the areas where they now live. Indeed, some groups' oral histories record that in ancient times they immigrated from lands far to the north and west; and other groups say that in quite recent times they came from another part of the North altogether. Such traditions still place the Indians' presence on the land "since time immemorial," and firmly repudiate any idea that anyone else has a right to the lands they have used for generations. But northern hunters are not so averse to archaeologists' notions as are other, less mobile peoples.

The northeast corner of British Columbia has for thousands of years been the homeland of such hunting groups. Archaeologists now say, in fact, that it may be among the most ancient of all such homelands in the New World. Before venturing into uneasy and speculative questions about who came to northeast British Columbia whence and when, something must be said of the region's natural attributes. It has not been widely celebrated for its beauty, though it has long excited the imagination of resource developers and is now thought of in government and business circles as something of an Aladdin's cave. Still the region's magic has not spread far beyond hopeful talk among westward-drifting settlers or geologically minded company directors. There are few evocations that are not local. Northeast British Columbia is not even a name but a geographer's indefinite description, without the established appeal of Siberia, Alaska, Yukon Territory, or Mackenzie Delta. Yet, from the hunter's point of view, it may well be among the best of all possible worlds.

Northeast British Columbia has now become important because of the American need for domestic supplies of energy. One of the possible straight lines between oil and gas fields of north Alaska and the existing pipelines that feed the energy-hungry cities of the midwestern and eastern United States — the hook-up between points of supply and demand — cuts through some four hundred miles of British Columbia. This line roughly bisects a terrain that has geographical limits to the west and to the south (mountains), and political limits to north and east (provincial and territorial boundaries). The homogeneity of the region rests on these boundaries and their related colonial histories. But the region is complex and diverse — and constitutes something far more rich and strange than the word "region" can suggest. It is difficult, yet essential, to establish this physical richness and beauty: difficult simply because neither adventurers nor environmentalists have generated much enthusiasm for the place, and essential because without such enthusiasm any argument on behalf of it and its people is much harder to make. In fact, three landscapes meet, overlap, and moderate one another in northeast British Columbia; and this variety of geographies is the basis for a strong Indian economy.

The southern edge of the region is high in the Rocky Mountains. To reach the Peace River valley from the south, routes must find ways over high passes and down through successions of sharp and deeply gouged hills. These routes quickly descend into a land that pancakes off north and east into the distance. Here, the mountains merge with a northern and western extension of the Great Plains.

From any point in the region, the high peaks of the Rockies are just on or over a horizon that slopes and fractures into foothills.

A hundred miles before the border between British Columbia and the Yukon Territory the flat lands to the east of the mountains include patches of muskeg — where harshness of climate creates a land of tussocks, stunted willows, and swamp — and conceals areas of permafrost, where moisture a few inches beneath the surface is continuously frozen. The scuffed and sparse terrain that characterizes muskeg is drained by the Liard River, a major tributary of the Mackenzie. Here are hints of the Far North. The sub-Arctic lands of the Liard overlap with the more gentle forests of the Peace. Each contains elements of the other, just as the topography and character of both are shaped by the Rockies.

These three worlds — foothills, muskeg, and prairie — are all part of the immense sub-Arctic boreal and shield forests that once covered all of central and northern Canada. In northeast British Columbia, this forest reaches two of its boundaries: tree lines that are caused by either altitude or latitude, by the summer cold of mountain and of Arctic. Yet the microclimates of the area are so intricate that these boundaries do not form clear lines. Within the foothills there are north-facing slopes where the tree line dips so low as to create wide clearings, above which, on other faces, wooded areas continue to rise. Even within the comparatively rich and luxurious forests of these lands, not far from the Peace, there are sudden patches of muskeg. And along the gentlest, most wooded valleys, including that of the Peace itself, there are natural meadows, interruptions in the forest, where grasses, flowers, and berries have the sunlight and space in which to luxuriate. Many, perhaps nearly all such meadows are now incorporated into agricultural land, which has spread along the Peace to the very point where its canyons make a route through the mountains, and along tributary valleys as much as fifty miles to the north. Agriculture has turned prime forest into prairie fields, and has created yet another landscape. But clearing, ploughing, and planting of lands in this mixture of northern habitats is not — or not yet — continuous.

The first Europeans to travel to this area followed the Peace River into the mountains. They were overwhelmed by the beauty of the landscapes, rich in a variety that must always be welcome to those coming from the thousand miles of unbroken prairie and rolling forests to the east. Here they found a changing landscape, teeming, they said, with an unanticipated abundance of wildlife. Alexander Mackenzie, in his 1793 journey via the Peace to the Pacific, was enthusiastic:

From the place which we quitted this morning, the West side of the river displayed a succession of the most beautiful scenery I had ever beheld. The ground rises at intervals to a considerable height, and stretching inwards to a considerable distance: at every interval or pause in the rise, there is a very gently-ascending space or lawn, which is alternate with abrupt precipices to the summit of the whole, or, at least as far as the eye could distinguish. This magnificent theatre of nature has all the decorations which the trees and animals of the country can afford it: groves of poplars in every shape vary the scene; and their intervals are enlivened with vast herds of elks and buffaloes: the former choosing the steeps and uplands, and the latter preferring the plains. At this time the buffaloes were attended with their young ones who were frisking about them; and it appeared that the elks would soon exhibit the same enlivening circumstances. The whole country displayed an exuberant verdure; the trees that bear a blossom were advancing fast to that delightful appearance, and the velvet rind of their branches reflecting the oblique rays of a rising or setting sun, added a splendid gaiety to the scene, which no expressions of mine are qualified to describe. [Note: Mackenzie is probably describing moose, not elk.]

Mackenzie saw only the southern edge of the region. The foothills and forests between the Peace and the Liard support the world's maximum known densities of moose and a strong, if less even, population of mule deer. Much of it is land to which beaver are ideally adapted, where caribou herds move between summer grounds in the mountains and wintering grounds on the lower slopes and flatlands, north of the Halfway River and west of the heights now followed by the Alaska Highway. Large numbers of hoary marmot, locally known as whistler, live high in the foothills; and these terrains, with their creeks, groves, and varieties of flora, are a prime source of food — fish, berries, small mammals — for both black and grizzly bear. This same lush mixture of environments also ensures an abundance of birds.

It is possible that nowhere in northern North America is there a comparable convergence of habitat — where buffalo trails once reached into country still rich in moose, elk, caribou, and deer; where natural lines are so imprecise and the ranges of so many species of wildlife so extensively overlapped. It is not surprising, then, that human occupation of this region is similarly complex. Here, where mountains, forests, and plains all met and the Arctic drainage with its plethora of valleys caused the whole landscape to be accessible, is a region where the hunter must surely have flourished.

As the ice sheets of the last Ice Age receded into the High Arctic, hunting bands moved into the savannah, tundra, and new forests of North America. This change in climate occurred some twelve thousand years ago. Even before this time, hunters hunted and travelled in an ice-free corridor that led along the Yukon River valley and down into interior Alaska, Yukon Territory, and British Columbia. No one is able exactly to locate this corridor; nor is anyone able to say quite when it was first passable. It may turn out to be much longer ago than has been supposed. Perhaps the Indians of the coast will in the end turn out to be right, and they or their ancestors will seem to have been on their lands since the beginning of time!

Even according to shifting and hesitant archaeological estimates, the Indians of northeast British Columbia hold a central and ancient position in the early occupancy of North America. As a result, the region has a focal significance for the florescence of hunting ways of life in the Americas. The earliest appearance of hunters in North

America was almost certainly linked to the Peace and Liard river area. Wherever that ice-free corridor was, it must have given way onto the upper Peace. Plateaux adjacent to its banks have now revealed ten thousand years of continuous occupation. There is no *prima facie* reason why more archaeological investigation will not stretch this back to as much as, or even more than, forty thousand years. Although ties between these early inhabitants and some of the area's present cultures are not demonstrable, artifactual and other evidence does not suggest any discontinuity (as it does, for example, in the case of the successive cultures of the High Arctic). Moreover, archaeologists now believe that the Athapaskan cultures, so widespread in and absolutely integral to the history of the entire northwest of America (with extensions that include the Navaho of the southwest United States), have a northern heartland. This, then, would amount to the cradle of a dominant American hunting culture. Evidence, albeit fragmentary and tentative, suggests that northeast British Columbia is this point of cultural departure.

All this means that in the late eighteenth and early nineteenth centuries, the hunters whom Europeans first encountered in northeast British Columbia may, in their language, tools, economic and religious life, and psychological make-up, have been the direct inheritors of the truly original inhabitants of the Americas. This is by no means to suggest that for thousands of years they led an ossified way of life. We can be sure there was an elaboration and adaptation of techniques and customs with the imagination and purposiveness that guarantee a complex history to all human life. However, a fundamental continuity was the hunting of large mammals. This continuity is the beginning of a distinctive kind of economic interest: an economic, social, even emotional interest and orientation, linking Athapaskans of today with people who travelled and hunted in this region many thousands of years ago. Perhaps nowhere else in the New World can Indians more properly affirm that theirs is a cultural presence and an economic entitlement of a depth and significance beyond our comprehension.

The Athapaskan peoples who make this claim comprise a large

number of language groups, with a northern spread throughout the interior of Alaska, Yukon Territory, much of western and central Northwest Territories, along with northern British Columbia and northern Alberta. Map 2 shows the bands that are now distinguished by their dialects (for the most part mutually unintelligible but clearly related), and by their economic and technological differences. Some of these distinctions are far more important than others. Also, Europeans have often seen differences of tribal grouping where the peoples themselves saw far less fundamental divisions. The Slavey and Kutchin are two Athapaskan groups having different dialects, clothing styles, and clearly separable hunting territories — though in similar kinds of terrain. The Beaver and Sekani, however, are described by early European travellers and in standard anthropological texts as equally dissimilar in custom and location. In fact, the Sekani were a band or group of families whose hunting centred on the eastern foothills, whereas the Beaver were a closely related group with overlapping but more easterly hunting areas. In all other ways the two groups are very closely allied. The similarities and divergences among northern Athapaskans cannot be described here, but in all cases the European presence brought major changes in distribution and organization. The Beaver and Sekani are a striking case in point.

The presence of Europeans in the Americas brought shock waves to northeast British Columbia. By the end of the eighteenth century, the fur trade had already forced a redistribution of Indian populations. The Cree, used by traders as porters, boatmen, middlemen, guides, often sharing the traders' purposes and in possession of firearms, drove the Beaver west, up towards the headwaters of the Peace, into the foothill-plains overlap. The Beaver, eventually also armed, drove the Sekani from the eastern foothills into the heights of the Rockies and across them towards the Pacific drainage. It is said that the Peace River was so named by traders because there the Cree and Beaver ended their conflict. These shifts in patterns of occupancy largely predated any direct encounter between Beaver and European civilization, but they caused a significant westward adjustment in the Beaver Indians' general distribution.

Even before these conflicts, the southernmost Athapaskan hunting group — the Sarcee — had adopted the horse, moving their economic and cultural centres towards the plains and beginning to hunt buffalo on horseback, thus sharing in the most famous and also one of the most recent features of much of North American Indian life. The horse had come by stages as a result of the Spanish presence in Mexico and early colonization north of the Rio Grande and was, therefore, a consequence of the European presence. The Beaver were then centred on the area between the Peace and Sikanni Chief rivers. The horse may have reached them from the Sarcee to their south, or the earliest traders coming from the east. They were in either case the last link in the chain of cultural contacts along which this important contribution to Indian life was gradually passed.

These lines of European influence converged in northeast British Columbia. Only among the Beaver and Slavey peoples was the horse integrated into the northern Athapaskan hunting system; only there did the achievements of the plains, boreal forest, and cordilleran economies converge. The Indians used horses both to travel between camps and to hunt, riding through sub-Arctic forest and over steep foothills. At the same time they developed their own riding styles and specialized tack. This did not entail the loss of ancient Athapaskan skills. Every hunter still had to be able to read tracks, set snares on woodland trails, make snowshoes and walk long distances on them, and use line-hitch dog teams. In the same way, every hunter was using guns by the early years of the nineteenth century, and steel traps were widespread by the 1820s.

Despite this spread of new devices, the region's diversity of landscapes influenced some of the differences between the main cultural groups. The southern edge of the region, being warmer and having more open grassland or forest clearings, is better suited to both the use and maintenance of horses. Also, the distribution of climax evergreen trees (prime habitat for marten, lynx, and other fur

2

THE LAND AND THE PEOPLES

The names of the main cultural groups are marked on the areas they occupy. Athapaskan peoples are shown in darker print. The dark grey areas indicate land of over 1000 m (3,280 feet) above sea level.

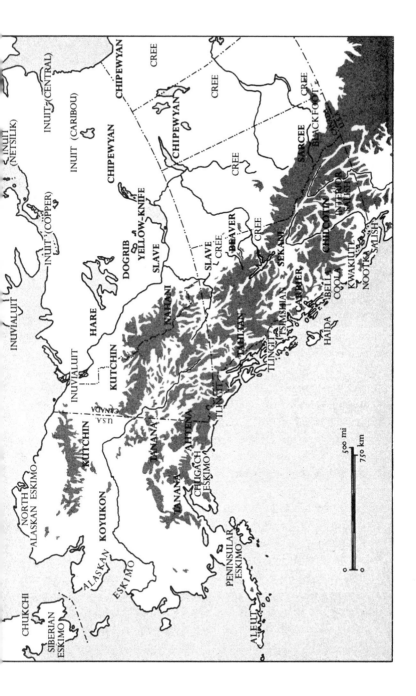

species) varies in different parts of the region: in the north, ever-greens are concentrated along river valleys; between the Peace and Sikanni Chief rivers they are abundant. These details of climate, geography, and habitat affected the region's cultures. The Sekani became expert at the use of mountain resources; the Beaver specialized in the foothills and adjacent forests; the Slavey remained on the muskeg and along the river valleys of the Mackenzie drainage, where they made particularly extensive use of moosehide boats in summer and snowshoes in winter. The people were much influenced by the presence of Europeans and European goods, but in their response to guns, horses, and trade they remained in close touch with their own worlds. Like many other hunting groups, the Athapaskans quickly demonstrated the great flexibility of their cultures — indicat-ing, for the first time, what was to become a continual feature of their dealings with Whites.

European presence in North America, however, very soon brought more than technology and occasional fur traders to northeast British Columbia. In the early 1800s, a trader reported that several Cree Indian families were living in the Fort St. John area. By 1900, there were Cree families in several of the region's communities. At the same time, and for similar reasons, Métis and nonstatus Indians also began to make their contributions to northern British Columbian life.

The Cree, who are members of the Algonkian group of Indian societies of the eastern forests, speak a language that is as different from Beaver as Hungarian is from English. Several Cree groups moved westward to become famous as horsemen and buffalo hunt-ers; others remained — and remain — around James Bay and in the eastern sub-Arctic of the Ungava Peninsula. Cree individuals, and sometimes whole families, travelled with traders who hired them to help in their push westward to the Rockies. In this way the first Cree arrived in northeast British Columbia, and some chose to stay. Today, two of the region's Indian communities — Fort Nelson and Blueberry River — include a significant proportion of Cree. At Moberly Lake, where Sekani and then Beaver people hunted and trapped, there is a separate Cree community. A few individuals in these places speak three languages — Cree, Beaver or Slavey, and English. But all the people's sense of cultural origin and distinctive strengths has persisted.

In the course of the association between Crees and traders, the Métis grew as a separate culture in western Canada. The Métis (often called "Breeds") were for the most part the children of French traders or boatmen and Indian women. Since the women, who did not lose their Indian identity, took the major role in their children's upbringing, these children became a group apart. So much so, indeed, that in the late 1800s the Métis, in alliance with some Cree communities, were in a position to demand and then fight for their own nation. The Riel Rebellion represented the high point and eventual defeat of this hope. But in its aftermath groups of Métis and Cree who had been involved in the rebellion fled westward, some of them eventually arriving and remaining in northeast British Columbia. The Cree amongst them joined those already there.

Almost no one in northeast British Columbia refers to himself or herself as a Métis. But the number of nonstatus Indians in the region probably numbers in the thousands. Since they are not a recognized group for any official purposes (including censuses), one can only make rough estimates. The large number of nonstatus Indians now living there is also a result of political forces. In Canada, a person is an official "status" or "treaty" Indian (to use two of the prevalent terms) because of being on an Indian band's list of members. Indians, or children of Indian parentage, have lost their band membership in several different ways. Before all registered Indians were given the vote (in 1949 for provincial but only in 1960 for federal elections) and were permitted to buy liquor, they were offered these rights in return for agreeing to resign their band memberships. Also, the Department of Indian Affairs offered some Indians money to leave their bands. But most important of all, Indian women who married white men automatically lost their band membership, as did their children. (This did not apply to Indian men who married white women; they, along with their children, were entitled to be band members.)

Between 1955 and 1975, over twelve thousand Canadian Indians, of whom ten thousand were women and their children, thus ceased to be Indians under the law. Several thousand live in northern British Columbia. These nonstatus Indians did not develop the very separate cultural identity of the Métis, but a large proportion felt themselves to be, and still insist that they are, Indians in everything but legal name. Their way of life and interests are a part of the region's heritage: many of them have long depended, and continue to depend, on hunting, trapping, and fishing. Their presence, added to the Cree and Athapaskans, means that northeast British Columbia is a homeland to peoples of six different heritages. Great differences exist among them, just as there are radically different reasons for their having come to live in the region at all. But the main groups I have identified share the feeling that their interests are separate from and often at odds with those of the white man.

An attempt to describe in full detail the substance of such cultural profusion would be endless. In fact, the ethnographic complexity can be rendered somewhat more simple, and the most daring claim can at the same time be made on behalf of the region's importance, by focussing on what all the northern hunting peoples had in common. Their cultural systems varied, they spoke quite different languages, and — in recent times — they have different legal statuses within a large and new political order; but they all have shared a particular kind of economic system.

This system developed around the hunting of comparatively large animals that were either scattered thinly over wide areas or migrated in varying numbers along different routes. Small and mobile bands, with highly flexible social systems, expert at tracking and able to use snares, deadfalls, bows and arrows, and many other hunting techniques were excellently adapted to harvesting such living resources. Their knowledge and techniques grew and changed, as the variety of their cultures testifies. But some of the basic characteristics remained much the same, including the ever-present flexibility that is expressed in virtually every part of the system.

The antiquity of this way of life is not easily grasped, and the Athapaskans of northeast British Columbia might share a socioeconomic development that has unparalleled historical depth. Agricultural man has been on earth for perhaps twelve thousand years; hunters and gatherers, for at least 1.5 million years. In this inaccessible expanse of time, varieties and subtleties of technical form proliferated; and the hunters' first appearance in the Americas, relatively recent when reviewed by the archaeological imagination, may have marked a tremendous extension and burgeoning of hunter-gatherer society. The subsequent spread of cultures in the Americas came to include a broadening of the economic base and the development of agricultural and pastoral economies. But in the North, thanks to great herds of buffalo and caribou or an abundance of moose, deer, and beaver — converters of vegetation into the meat to which humans have become so thoroughly adapted — hunters continued to practise their systems following ancient, though never static, patterns. In this region, with its several overlapping environments and extraordinary variety of game, the system found a setting to which all its skills and attributes were ideally suited.

It is ironic, then, that anthropologists and other social scientists, in the grip of a heady vision of Arctic splendour and space, have passed through (or, more likely, at great speed over) the region in search of the real, supposedly untouched, hunters of the Far North. There are exceptions to this social scientific indifference, but they are few. This tendency moreover has its place within, and makes its particular contribution to, northeast British Columbia's position in the northern colonial and imperialist endeavour: it has been consigned to the status of a corridor, through which one must often go to get to more important and richer areas — be they imagined placer mines in the Yukon or exotic societies at the rim of the Arctic Ocean. This means that few if any social scientists have ever cared to speak up on behalf of the region's real inhabitants, and no lobby before 1979 ever pressed government or industry into a review of possible collisions of interest. The region is now to be crossed by the ultimate corridor — a pipeline that transports energy from Alaska, far to the north, to the cities of the United States. At the same time, the region is more and more a focus of dreams about new sources of energy and unparalleled industrial development. Northeast British Columbia is a route and resource: a place for white men to dream about. The effects of the realization of such dreams upon the peoples for whom this corridor has for thousands of years been an economic and social heartland have long gone unconsidered.

Present-day populations to whom this conflict has become a matter of everyday reality are now centred on nine communities, shown on Map 3. Each of these is small. All are covered by Treaty 8 (to be discussed in Chapter 4). The people have the right to hunt, fish, and trap in "unoccupied Crown land," and can do so without regard to season or other restrictions designed to limit sport and trophy hunting. The treaty, for what it may be worth, grants the region's cultures, at least theoretically, a continued existence. It establishes, in the form of laws and regulations, a minimal continuity between the bands of today and the remarkable heritage that gives the region its primary importance.

Here, then, as a culmination of the region's background, are names and labels. As Table 1 shows, the populations are small. Even if we include an estimate of the considerable number of nonstatus Indians living in the region, they do not add up to more than three thousand. But this population has an interest in the lands and their resources that, from historical, cultural, legal, and moral points of view, transcends any other.

Table 1
Northeast British Columbia Indian reserves

Present bands	Population 1978	Reserves	Date allocated	Terrain	Acreage	Cultures
Salteau	186	East Moberly Lake	1918	high foothills	4490	Cree
West Moberly	62	West Moberly Lake	1916	high foothills	5025	Beaver & Cree
Halfway	136	Halfway River	1925	low foothills	9890	Beaver
Blueberry	115	Blueberry River	1950	boreal forest	2838	Cree & Beaver
Doig	114	Doig River	1950	boreal forest	2473	Beaver
		Beatton River*	1950	boreal forest	883	
Fort Nelson	281	Fort Nelson	1966	muskeg & river valley	444	Slavey & Cree
		Fontas	1966	muskeg & river valley	25	
		Kahntah	1966	muskeg & river valley	26	
		Snake River	1966	muskeg & river valley	28	
Prophet River	112	Prophet River	1966	low foothills & muskeg	924	Beaver

*Held jointly by Blueberry and Doig Bands.
Sources: Indexes and records of the Union of British Columbia Indian Chiefs, Vancouver; Department of Indian Affairs Band Lists and "Black Book Reserve Register"; and Dinah Schooner, 1978 "Notes on Northeast Bands," Union of British Columbia Indian Chiefs, n.p.

3

NORTHEAST BRITISH COLUMBIA

The areas granted as Indian reserves are situated close to the Alaska Highway and towns. The populations, languages spoken, and other details about these reserves are given in Table 1.

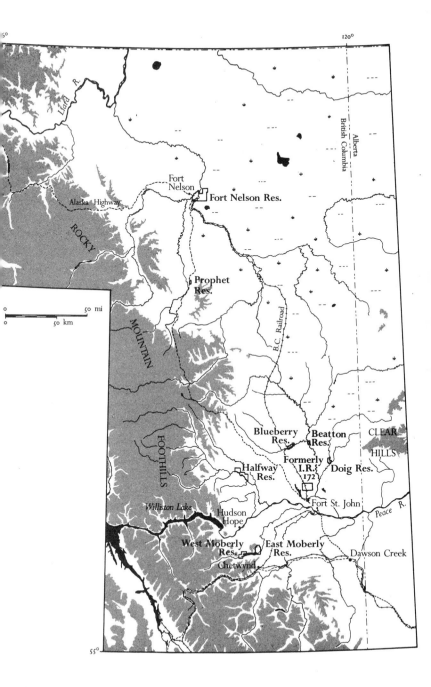

3

Maps of Dreams

The rivers of northeast British Columbia are at their most splendid in the early fall. The northern tributaries of the Peace achieve an extraordinary beauty; they, and their small feeder creeks and streams, are cold yet warm — perfect reflections of autumn. The banks are multicoloured and finely textured; clear water runs in smooth, shallow channels. The low water of late summer reveals gravel and sand beaches, textures and colours that are at other times of the year concealed. Such low water levels mean that all these streams are easily crossed, and so become the throughways along the valleys that have always been at the heart of the Indians' use of the land. In October those who know these creeks can find corners, holes, back eddies where rainbow trout and Dolly Varden abound.

The hunter of moose, deer, caribou (and in historic times, buffalo) does not pursue these large animals without regard to more abundant and predictable, if less satisfying, sources of food. The man who tracks and snares game, and whose success depends on his constant movement, cannot afford to fail for much more than two days running. On the third day of hunger he will find it hard to walk far or fast enough: hunger reduces the efficiency of the hunt. Hunger is inimical to effective hunting on foot; yet continuance of the hunt was, not long ago, the only means to avoid hunger. This potential source of insecurity for a hunter is resolved by his ability to combine two kinds of hunting: he pursues large ungulates in areas and with movements that bring him close to locations where he knows rabbits, grouse, or fish are to be found. These are security, but not staples. Hunting for large animals is the most efficient, the most rational activity for anyone who lives in the boreal forest. But such a hunter would be foolhardy indeed to hunt for the larger animals without a careful and strategic eye on the availability of the smaller ones.

In October, only a month after Joseph Patsah and his family first spoke to us about their lives, they suggested that I go hunting with them — and, of course, fishing. By now the rainbow trout would surely be plentiful and fat. Joseph said that he also hoped we could go far enough to see the cross. One evening, then, he proposed that we should all set out the next day for Bluestone Creek.

Between a proposal to go hunting and actual departure there is a large and perplexing divide. In the white man's world, whether urban or rural, after such a proposal there would be plans and planning; conversation about timing and practical details would also help to build enthusiasm. In Joseph's household, in all the Indian households of northeast British Columbia, and perhaps among hunters generally, planning is so muted as to seem nonexistent. Maybe it is better understood by a very different name, which is still to suppose that planning of some kind does in fact take place.

Protests against the hunting way of life have often paid hostile attention to its seemingly haphazard, irrational, and improvident nature. Before the mind's eye of agricultural or industrial man loom the twin spectres of hunger and homelessness, whose fearsome imminence is escaped only in the bright sunlight of planning. Planners consider many possibilities, weigh methods, review timing, and at least seek to deduce what is best. To this end they advocate reason and temperance, and, most important, they are thrifty and save. These ideas and dispositions, elevated to an ideal in the economics of nineteenth-century and secular puritanism, live on in the reaction of industrial society to hunters — and in the average Canadian's reaction to Indians. And a reaction of this kind means that a person, even if inclined to be sympathetic to hunters and hunting, has immense difficulty in understanding what planning means for hunters of the North.

Joseph and his family float possibilities. "Maybe we should go to Copper Creek. Bet you lots of moose up there." Or, "Could be caribou right now near Black Flats." Or, "I bet you no deer this time down on the Reserve . . ." Somehow a general area is selected from a gossamer of possibilities, and from an accumulation of remarks comes something rather like a consensus. No, that is not really it: rather, a sort of prediction, a combined sense of where we *might* go "tomorrow." Yet the hunt will not have been planned, nor any preparations started, and apparently no one is committed to going. Moreover, the floating conversation will have alighted on several irreconcilable possibilities, or have given rise to quasi-predictions. It is as if the predictions are about other people — or are not quite serious. Although the mood is still one of wait and see, at the end of the day, at the close of much slow and gentle talk about this and that, a strong feeling has arisen about the morning: we shall go to Bluestone, maybe as far as the cross. We shall look for trout as well as moose. A number of individuals agree that they will go. But come morning, nothing is ready. No one has made any practical, formal plans. As often as not — indeed, more often than not — something quite new has drifted into conversations, other predictions have been tentatively reached, a new consensus appears to be forming. As it often seems, everyone has changed his mind.

The way to understand this kind of decision making as also to live by and even share it, is to recognize that some of the most important variables are subtle, elusive, and extremely hard or impossible to assess with finality. The Athapaskan hunter will move in a direction and at a time that are determined by a sense of weather (to indicate a variable that is easily grasped if all too easily oversimplified by the one word) and by a sense of rightness. He will also have ideas about animal movement, his own and others' patterns of land use . . . But already the nature of the hunter's decision making is being misrepresented by this kind of listing. To disconnect the variables, to compartmentalize the thinking, is to fail to acknowledge its sophistication and completeness. He considers variables as a composite, in parallel, and with the help of a blending of the metaphysical and the obviously pragmatic. To make a good, wise, sensible hunting choice is to accept the interconnection of all possible factors, and avoids the mistake of seeking rationally to focus on any one consideration that is held as primary. What is more, the decision is taken in the doing: there is no step or pause between theory and practice. As a consequence, the decision — like the action from which it is inseparable — is always alterable (and therefore may not properly even be termed a decision). The hunter moves in a chosen direction; but, highly sensitive to so many shifting considerations, he is always ready to change his directions.

Planning, as other cultures understand the notion, is at odds with this kind of sensitivity and would confound such flexibility. The hunter, alive to constant movements of nature, spirits, and human moods, maintains a way of doing things that repudiates a firm plan and any precise or specified understanding with others of what he is going to do. His course of action is not, must not be, a matter of predetermination. If a plan constitutes a decision about the right procedure or action, and the decision is congruent with the action, then there is no space left for a "plan," only for a bundle of open-ended and nonrational possibilities. Activity enters so far into this kind of planning as to undermine any so-called plans.

All this is by way of context or background for the seemingly straightforward proposal that we should set out the next morning to hunt moose and fish for trout at Bluestone Creek. Since there are many such apparent decisions in the following chapters, it is important that they be understood for what they are: convenient — but often misleading — reductions to a narrative convention of intimate and unfamiliar patterns of hunters' thought and behaviour.

"The next morning" came several times before we set out in the direction of Bluestone. Several individuals said they would come, but did not; others said they would not come, but did. Eventually, we drove in my rented pickup to a stretch of rolling forests, where hillsides and valley were covered by dense blankets of poplar, aspen, birch, and occasional stands of pine or spruce. After studied consideration of three places, Joseph and Atsin chose a campsite a short walk from a spring that created a narrow pool of good water in a setting of damp and frosted leaves.

There we camped, in a complex of shelters and one tent around a long central fire. It was a place the hunters had often used, and it had probably been an Indian campsite off and on for centuries. It was a clearing among thin-stemmed pine, a woodland tangled and in places made dense by a great number of deadfalls lying at all heights and angles to the ground. Night fell as we completed the camp. The fire was lit and was darkly reflected by these dead trees that crisscrossed against the forest.

Long before dawn (it cannot have been later than five o'clock), the men awoke. The fire rekindled, they sat around it and began the enormous and protracted breakfast that precedes every day's hunting: rabbit stew, boiled eggs, bannock, toasted sliced white bread, barbecued moose meat, whatever happens to be on hand, and cup after cup of strong, sweet tea. A little later, women and children joined the men at the fire and ate no less heartily.

As they ate, the light changed from a slight glimmer, the relief to predawn blackness, to the first brightness that falters without strength at the tops of the trees. As the light grew, the men speculated about where to go, sifting evidence they had accumulated from whatever nearby places they had visited since their arrival. Everyone had walked — to fetch water, cut wood, or simply to stretch the legs a little. Atsin, at the end of a short walk that morning, returned with a rabbit. He had taken it in a snare, evidently set as soon as we arrived the evening before. It was white already, its fur change a dangerously conspicuous anticipation of a winter yet to come. Conversation turned to rabbits. All the men had noticed a proliferation of runs and droppings. It was an excellent year for rabbit, the fifth or sixth in a cycle of seven improving years. It might be a good idea to hunt in some patches of young evergreens, along trails that led towards the river. There could be more rabbits there. Lots of rabbits. Always good to eat lots of rabbit stew. And there could be rainbow trout in that place, below the old cabin, and in other spots. Or maybe it would be good to go high up in the valley . . . This exchange of details and ideas continued off and on throughout the meal. When it had finally ended and everyone had reflected a good deal on the day's possibilities, the men set off. Perhaps it was clear to them where and why, but which possibilities represented a starting point was not easily understood by an outsider.

Atsin's younger brother Sam set off alone, at right angles to a trail that led to the river by way of a place said to be particularly good for rabbits. Two others, Jimmy Wolf and Charlie Fellow — both relations of Joseph's wife Liza — also set off at an angle, but in the opposite direction. I followed Atsin along another, more winding trail: Liza and her oldest child, Tommy, together with two other women and their small children, made their own way behind the men on the main trail; Atsin's son David attached himself to Brian Akattah and his ten-year-old nephew Peter. The choice of partner and trail was, if possible, less obviously planned than direction or hunting objective. Everyone was plainly free to go where and with whom he or she liked. As I became more familiar with this kind of hunt, though, I found that some individuals nearly always hunted alone, whereas others liked a companion, at least at the outset. A sense of great personal freedom was evident from the first. No one gives orders; everyone is, in some fundamental way, responsible to and for himself.

The distance between camp and the particular bend in the river that had been selected as the best possible fishing place was no more than a mile and a half. No time had been appointed for a rendezvous. Indeed clock time is of no significance here. (Only Joseph had a watch and it was never used for hunting purposes.) Everyone nonetheless appeared from the woods and converged on the fishing spot within minutes of one another. This co-ordination of activities is not easily understood, although it testified to the absence of big game, of moose, deer, or bear. If any of the hunters had located fresh tracks, he would have been long gone into the woods. Atsin, who seemed to be an expert at the job, appeared with two rabbits he had shot after glimpsing their helpless whiteness in the dun-coloured undergrowth. But fishing was going to supply the next meal.

The river at this place flows in a short curve around a wooded promontory that juts from the main forest. Both sides are deeply eroded banks, where sandy rubble is given some short-lived firmness by exposed tree roots. On the far side the landscape is barer, with meadowy, more open land for fifty yards before the forested slopes rise towards the mountains. Where the trail meets the creek (sometimes no wider than ten rushing yards), it deepens into a pool. There, the water is held back by a shallow rib of rock over which it quickens and races to the next pool.

The fishing spot itself turned out to be a platform of jumbled logs that must have been carried by the stream in flood, and then piled by currents until they reshaped the banks themselves. The sure-footed can find precarious walkways across this latticework platform. At their ends the logs offer a view down into the deepest part of the hole. Through the sharp clearness of this water rainbow trout could be seen, dark shadows, hovering or moving very slowly among long-sunken logs and roots.

Joseph studied the water and the fish, then produced a nylon line. It was wound tightly around a small piece of shaped wood, a spool that he carried in his pocket, wrapped in cloth. Along with the line were four or five hooks (size 6 or 8) and a chunk of old bacon. On his way along the trail he had broken off a long thin branch, and by the time we had arrived at the creek he had already stripped off its side twigs, peeled away the bark, and broken it to the right length. He tied some line to this homemade rod and handed other lengths to Brian and David. The three of them then clambered along the log platform, found more or less firm places at its edge, and began to fish.

The baited hooks were lowered straight down until they hung just above the stream bed. They did not hover there for long. Almost immediately the fish were being caught. The men could watch a trout swim towards a bait and, with one firm turn of its body, part suck and part grab the hook. The fisherman, with a single upward swing of the rod, would pull it straight out of the water and onto the logs. Then each fish was grabbed at, and missed, fell off the hook among the logs, was grabbed again . . . The fish, and the fishermen, could easily slip between the gaps of the platform. As the trout thrashed and leaped about there were shouts of excitement, advice, and laughter.

The trout were plentiful, as Joseph had said they would be, and fat. One after the other they came flying through the air into someone's hands, then to shore, where Atsin and Liza gutted them. A dozen or more, fish of one or two pounds each, every one of them with a brilliant red patch on its gills and red stripe along its sides — rainbow trout at their most spectacular. Then the fishing slowed down. Enough had been caught. Joseph, Brian, and David climbed back to the bank. We sat around the fires to eat rabbit stew and cook some of the fish.

By this time it was early afternoon, but the meal was unhurried. Perhaps the success of the moose hunt was doubtful, while a good supply of rabbit and fish had already been secured. Conversation turned again to places where it might be worth hunting, directions in which we might go; many possibilities were suggested, and no apparent decision was made. But when the meal ended, the men began to prepare themselves for another hunt. Having eaten and rested and stared into the fire, one by one the hunters, unhurried and apparently indecisive, got up, strolled a little way, and came back. Then each began to fix his clothes, check a gun — began to get ready. By the time the last of the hunters was thus occupied, some had begun to drift away in one direction or another. After a last conversation, the rest of them left, except for Joseph, Brian's wife Mary, Liza, and the children, who stayed by the fire. Perhaps the afternoon was going to be long and hard.

This time a group of men walked in single file, Atsin in front. After a short distance, one went his own way, then others did so, until each of them had taken a separate direction. I again stayed close to Atsin, who made his way, often pushing his way, through dense bushes and small willows, along the river bank. He said once, when we paused to rest and look around, and think, that it was disappointing to find so few signs of moose, but there might be more fishing.

It must have been an hour before the men regrouped, this time on a high and eroded sandbar. The beach here was strewn with well-dried driftwood. Atsin and Robert Fellows began to gather enough of this wood to make a large fire. Brian fetched water for tea. Atsin's brother Sam, together with Jimmy Wolf, cut fishing poles, fixed up lines, went a short way upstream to a spot where the water turned and deepened against the bank, and began to fish. Their lines hung in the water, baits out of sight and judged to be close to the bottom. From time to time they changed the angle of their rods to adjust the depth at which they fished; and by taking advantage of the pole's being longer than the line, they periodically pulled the bait clear of the water, checked that all was well in place, and then dropped it easily back to where the fish should be.

But the fish were not there, or not hungry, or not to be fooled. Sam and Jimmy waited. There were no sudden upward whips of the pole, no bites, no shouts, no laughter. The others sprawled around the fire, watching the two fishermen, drinking tea, limiting themselves to an occasional squinting look towards the river and remarks about the dearth of game. The afternoon was warm and still. There seemed to be no reason for any great activity. Soon Jimmy decided to abandon the river in favour of a rest beside the fire. Sam forded the stream, crossed the sandbar, and tried his luck on the other side. From where we sat and lay we could see his head and shoulders, and the lift and drop of his long rod. It was easy enough to tell whether or not he was catching anything; he was not.

Moments, minutes, even hours of complete stillness: this was not time that could be measured. Hunters at rest, at ease, in wait, are able to discover and enjoy a special form of relaxation. There is a minimum of movement — a hand reaches out for a mug, an adjustment is made to the fire — and whatever is said hardly interrupts the silence, as if words and thoughts can be harmonized without any of the tensions of dialogue. Yet the hunters are a long way from sleep; not even the atmosphere is soporific. They wait, watch, consider. Above all they are still and receptive, prepared for whatever insight or realization may come to them, and ready for whatever stimulus to action might arise. This state of attentive waiting is perhaps as close as people can come to the falcon's suspended flight, when the bird, seemingly motionless, is ready to plummet in decisive action. To the outsider, who has followed along and tried to join in, it looks for all the world as if the hunters have forgotten why they are there. In this restful way hunters can spend many hours, sometimes days, eating, waiting, thinking.

The quality of this resting by the fire can be seen and felt when it is very suddenly changed, just as the nature of the falcon's hover becomes clear when it dives. Among hunters the emergence from repose may be slow or abrupt. But in either case a particular state of mind, a special way of being, has come to an end. One or two individuals move faster and more purposively, someone begins to prepare meat to cook, someone fetches a gun to work on, and conversation resumes its ordinary mode. This transformation took place that afternoon around the fire on the pebbled beach at just the time Sam gave up his fishing and began to walk back towards us. Atsin, Jimmy, and Robert all moved to new positions. Robert stood with his back to us, watching Sam's approach, while Atsin and Jimmy squatted where they could look directly at me.

In retrospect it seems clear that they felt the right time had come for something. Everyone seemed to give the few moments it took for this change to occur some special importance. Plainly the men had something to say and, in their own time, in their own way, they were going to say it. Signs and movements suggested that the flow of events that had begun in Joseph's home and Atsin's cabin, and continued with the fishing at Bluestone Creek, was about to be augmented. Something of significance to the men here was going to happen. I suddenly realized that everyone was watching me. Sam joined the group, but said nothing. Perhaps he, as a younger man, was now leaving events to his elders, to Atsin, Jimmy, and Robert. There was a brief silence made awkward by expectancy, though an awkward pause is a very rare thing among people who accept that there is no need to escape from silence, no need to use words as a way to avoid one another, no need to obscure the real.

Atsin broke this silence. He spoke at first of the research: "I bet some guys make big maps. Lots of work, these maps. Joseph, he sure is happy to see maps."

Silence again. Then Robert continued: "Yeah, lots of maps. All over this country we hunt. Fish too. Trapping places. Nobody knows that. White men don't know that."

Then Jimmy spoke: "Indian guys, old-timers, they make maps too."

With these words, the men introduced their theme. The tone was friendly, but the words were spoken with intensity and firmness. The men seemed apprehensive, as if anxious to be very clearly understood — though nothing said so far required such concern. Once again, it is impossible to render verbatim all that they eventually said. I had no tape recorder and memory is imperfect. But even a verbatim account would fail to do justice to their meaning. Here, then, in summaries and glimpses, is what the men had in mind to say.

Some old-timers, men who became famous for their powers and skills, had been great dreamers. Hunters and dreamers. They did not hunt as most people now do. They did not seek uncertainly for the trails of animals whose movements we can only guess at. No, they located their prey in dreams, found their trails, and made dream-kills. Then, the next day, or a few days later, whenever it seemed auspicious to do so, they could go out, find the trail, re-encounter the animal, and collect the kill.

Maybe, said Atsin, you think this is all nonsense, just so much bullshit. Maybe you don't think this power is possible. Few people understand. The old-timers who were strong dreamers knew many things that are not easy to understand. People — white people, young people — yes, they laugh at such skills. But they do not know. The Indians around this country know a lot about power. In fact, everyone has had some experience of it. The fact that dream-hunting works has been proved many times.

A few years ago a hunter dreamed a cow moose kill. A fine, fat cow. He was so pleased with the animal, so delighted to make this dream-kill, that he marked the animal's hooves. Now he would be sure to recognize it when he went on the coming hunt. The next day, when he went out into the bush, he quickly found the dream-trail. He followed it, and came to a large cow moose. Sure enough, the hooves bore his marks. Everyone saw them. All the men around the fire had been told about the marks, and everyone on the Reserve had come to look at those hooves when the animal was butchered and brought into the people's homes.

And not only that fat cow moose — many such instances are known to the people, whose marks on the animal or other indications show that there was no mistaking, no doubts about the efficacy of such dreams. Do you think this is all lies? No, this is power they had, something they knew how to use. This was their way of doing things, the right way. They understood, those old-timers, just where all the animals came from. The trails converge, and if you were a very strong dreamer you could discover this, and see the source of trails, the origin of game. Dreaming revealed them. Good hunting depended upon such knowledge.

Today it is hard to find men who can dream this way. There are too many problems. Too much drinking. Too little respect. People are not good enough now. Maybe there will again be strong dreamers when these problems are overcome. Then more maps will be made. New maps.

Oh yes, Indians made maps. You would not take any notice of them. You might say such maps are crazy. But maybe the Indians would say that is what your maps are: the same thing. Different maps from different people — different *ways*. Old-timers made maps of trails, ornamented them with lots of fancy. The good people.

None of this is easy to understand. But good men, the really good men, could dream of more than animals. Sometimes they saw heaven and its trails. Those trails are hard to see, and few men have had such dreams. Even if they could see dream-trails to heaven, it is hard to explain them. You draw maps of the land, show everyone where to go. You explain the hills, the rivers, the trails from here to Hudson Hope, the roads. Maybe you make maps of where the hunters go and where the fish can be caught. That is not easy. But easier, for sure, than drawing out the trails to heaven. You may laugh at these maps of the trails to heaven, but they were done by the good men who had the heaven dream, who wanted to tell the truth. They worked hard on their truth.

Atsin had done most of the talking this far. The others interjected a few words and comments, agreeing or elaborating a little. Jimmy told about the cow moose with marked hooves. All of them offered some comparisons between their own and others' maps. And the men's eyes never ceased to remain fixed on me: were they being understood? Disregarded? Thought ridiculous? They had chosen this moment for these explanations, yet no one was entirely secure in it. Several times, Atsin paused and waited, perhaps to give himself a chance to sense or absorb the reaction to his words. These were intense but not tense hiatuses. Everyone was reassuring himself that his seriousness was being recognized. That was all they needed to continue.

The longest of these pauses might have lasted as much as five minutes. During it the fire was rebuilt. It seemed possible, for a few moments, that they had finished, and that their attention was now returning to trout, camp, and the hunt. But the atmosphere hardly altered, and Jimmy quite abruptly took over where Atsin had left off.

The few good men who had the heaven dream were like the Fathers, Catholic priests, men who devoted themselves to helping others with that essential knowledge to which ordinary men and women have limited access. (Roman Catholic priests have drifted in and out of the lives of all the region's Indians, leaving behind fragments of their knowledge and somewhat rarefied and idealized versions of what they had to preach.) Most important of all, a strong dreamer can tell others how to get to heaven. We all have need of the trail, or a complex of trails, but, unlike other important trails, the way to heaven will have been seen in dreams that only a few, special individuals have had. Maps of heaven are thus important. And they must be good, complete maps. Heaven is reached only by careful avoidance of the wrong trails. These must also be shown so that the traveller can recognize and avoid them.

How can we know the general direction we should follow? How can anyone who has not dreamed the whole route begin to locate himself on such a map? When Joseph, or any of the other men, began to draw a hunting map, he had first to find his way. He did this by recognizing features, by fixing points of reference, and then, once he was oriented to the familiar and to the scale or manner in which the familiar was reproduced, he could begin to add his own layers of detailed information. But how can anyone begin to find a way on a map of trails to heaven, across a terrain that ordinary hunters do not experience in everyday activities or even in their dream-hunts?

The route to heaven is not wholly unfamiliar, however. As it happens, heaven is to one side of, and at the same level as, the point where the trails to animals all meet. Many men know where this point is, or at least some of its approach trails, from their own hunting dreams. Hunters can in this way find a basic reference, and once they realize that heaven is in a particular relation to this far more familiar centre, the map as a whole can be read. If this is not enough, a person can take a map with him; some old-timers who made or who were given maps of the trails to heaven choose to have a map buried with them. They can thus remind themselves which ways to travel if the actual experience of the trail proves to be too confusing. Others are given a corner of a map that will help reveal the trail to them. And even those who do not have any powerful dreams are shown the best maps of the route to heaven. The discoveries of the very few most powerful dreamers — and some of the dreamers have been women — are periodically made available to everyone.

The person who wishes to dream must take great care, even if he dreams only of the hunt. He must lie in the correct orientation, with his head towards the rising sun. There should be no ordinary trails, no human pathways, between his pillow and the bush. These would be confusing to the self that travels in dreams towards important and unfamiliar trails which can lead to a kill. Not much of this can be mapped — only the trail to heaven has been drawn up. There has been no equivalent need to make maps to share other important information.

Sometime, said Jimmy Wolf, you will see one of these maps. There are some of them around. Then the competence and strength of the old-timers who drew them will be unquestioned. Different trails can be explained, and heaven can be located on them. Yes, they were pretty smart, the men who drew them. Smarter than any white man in these parts and smarter than Indians of today. Perhaps, said Atsin, in the future there will be men good enough to make new maps of heaven — but not just now. There will be changes, he added, and the people will come once again to understand the things that Atsin's father had tried to teach him. In any case, he said, the older men are now trying to explain the powers and dreams of old-timers to the young, indeed to all those who have not been raised with these spiritual riches. For those who do not understand, hunting and life itself are restricted and difficult. So the people must be told everything, and taught all that they need, in order to withstand the incursions presently being made into their way of life, their land, and into their very dreams.

4

Hunters and Treaties

The New World was the Outer Space of fifteenth- and sixteenth-century Europe. Travellers set off on terrifying journeys into an unknown that was already peopled, in the popular imagination of the day, with all kinds of fantastic monsters. Some of these adventurers returned with wondrous accounts of the lands and savages they had encountered. These accounts entered political and legal arguments of the day, and played their part in the rationalization by European powers of their various claims to new-found lands. If the savages were not really human, or if their ways of life were neither civilized nor Christian, then they had no rights — least of all any right of ownership to the lands they occupied. From the first, then, stereotypes of the aboriginal inhabitants of the Americas have served the interests of Europeans in their claims to and colonization of the land. Such stereotypes have persisted, in many different forms, for over four hundred years.

A formal and public debate in mid-sixteenth-century Spain between two monks — Las Casas and Sepulveda — reflects the intensity and nature of the controversy that had already come to surround questions about the nature of American Indian society. This debate, fully and elegantly described in *Aristotle and the American Indian* by Lewis Hanke, turned on a central and deceptively simple issue: did, or did not, the Indian occupants of Spain's new territories have a way of life that deserved to be respected? In another and later idiom, this becomes a question about whether or not the Indians have a proper social and economic system that European colonists must legally and morally respect. Las Casas, who lived for most of his life in South America and had a wealth of first-hand experience of Indian tribal life, argued that they did have a system, and that it should be respected. Sepulveda, who had never been to the New World, argued from first principles and on the basis of universal laws of reason and religion. He said that they did not have any such system or rights, and therefore could only benefit from Christian control — even if it amounted to enslavement. This debate took place in 1550, and its themes have been at the heart of European intellectual life ever since.

In the course of this debate's long history, advocates on behalf of Indians and other "savages" have included some figures of immense standing, among them Rousseau, Montesquieu, Marx, and Engels. These great men did not always or unambiguously represent the economic interests of the American Indians by whose social systems they were so very impressed. The enthusiasm for the Noble Savage during the Enlightenment had a great deal to do with a vision of simple freedom and a life far removed from the degeneracies and hypocrisy of the European salon. It had very little to do with a resolve that any particular Noble Savages be left their lands and economic system. In 1750, Rousseau wrote: "The American Savages who go naked and live entirely on the products of the chase have always been impossible to subdue. What yoke, indeed, can be imposed on men who stand in need of nothing?" Similarly Marx's and Engels's interest in the primitive communism and city-state form of democracy within the Iroquois Confederacy did not prevent their taking the view, generally, that human freedom could only be achieved when the world's nonindustrial societies had been transformed by thorough-going industrialization. More generally still, the social evolutionist ideas that came to the intellectual fore in the early nineteenth century rendered in the language of science what had for several centuries been ascendant popular and political doctrines: we, being so advanced and wise, have the right if not the duty to give to savage and barbaric societies some share in our spiritual and material achievements. Better that they be labourers in our plantations than remain benighted, heathen, and destitute.

The idea of primitive destitution is expressed in many different ways, and any attempt to encapsulate these in a single formula would be an insult to the sophistication of several centuries of the history of ideas. Between the Puritan revolution of the 1600s and the rapid industrialization of the 1800s, however, all the prejudices and ideological preoccupations of a society struggling to establish the social and economic orders of trade, of businessman and industrial labourer, contributed to the way man-the-hunter was perceived. Agriculture was thought to represent the basis, the very starting point, of civilization; the disciplines and routines of the factory were among its greatest achievements. Seen from this point of view, hunters were beyond the pale. The ideals of Puritanism, and the habits of both work and mind that it vehemently enjoined, were entirely at odds with the hunter's way of life.

Marshall Sahlins, in his remarkable essay, "The Original Affluent Society," neatly identifies those characteristics of hunting and gathering economies that appalled traders, missionaries, and other representatives of European civilization. Hunters were seemingly haphazard, wasteful, greedy, impoverished, and yet indifferent to material goods. Sahlins, noting that hunters "have the kind of nonchalance that would be appropriate to a people who have mastered the problems of production," quotes one European's particularly opposite account of the Yahgan Indians:

> The Indian does not even exercise care when he could conveniently do so. A European is likely to shake his head at the boundless indifference of these people who drag brand-new objects, precious clothing, fresh provisions, and valuable items through thick mud, or abandon them to their swift destruction by children and dogs. . . .

Accounts of hunting societies were read, and dealings with hunters were administered, by people who believed, perhaps more passionately than any people ever had, in the importance of careful, rational planning, saving, and above all in the accumulation of material goods. Theirs was the economic order that had begun to celebrate a vivid and highly moralistic ideal of economic man. Nothing appeared to oppose this ideal more completely than man-the-hunter who, as Sahlins observes, one is tempted to call "uneconomic man."

It is not surprising, then, that hunters were overwhelmingly stereotyped in the most negative ways. This was reflected until the 1940s and '50s in the writing of mainstream archaeologists and anthropologists. Even in the 1960s, a monograph characterizes the hunter's existence as "some half a million years of savagery" and his economy as a "catch as catch can existence." The academic voice added to a prejudice that made it impossible for Europeans to see hunting societies as real economic systems. Since the work of Marshall Sahlins, Richard Lee, and others, social scientists have discovered and explained the economic and social strengths of the hunting way of life. But this new appreciation is at odds with a long-lived, self-serving, and popular point of view. Despite the careful and excellently argued work of scientists who demonstrate the hunters' rationality and sophistication, most hunting groups still have to endure the consequences of an intellectual myopia which has had its practical counterpart in the endless succession of well-meaning Europeans who were dismayed, and then indignant, to find that the improvident and impoverished savages appeared to be indifferent to many of the benefits that were brought to them. Noneconomic man was infuriatingly unresponsive to benevolent attempts to change him. This unresponsiveness, in turn, fuelled the negative stereotype. Not only was the hunter poor, but he was too ignorant even to appreciate the fact!

When it came to the Arctic and sub-Arctic, the European view of the hunter was reinforced and exaggerated by popular notions about the harshness of the North. Hunters up there were marginal human societies in a marginal environment: the stereotype was sure to achieve its own extremes.

In the eighteenth century, scurvy, the disease that horrifyingly decimated many shiploads of explorers and whalers, came to be associated with the Far North. The first symptoms of scurvy are despondency and increasing lethargy. According to medical authorities of the day, these were brought on by the bleakness of northern terrain and the long, gloomy darkness of an Arctic winter. According to such theories, bleakness of surroundings precipitated a bleakness of spirits, and hence the onset of the disease. As it progressed, scurvy led to drastic deterioration of the gums, loss of all teeth, increasing weakness, and — after weeks of despondency and great pain — a slow death. If the horrors of scurvy reflected the harshness of the North, it was a terrible place indeed.

Eighteenth-century medical men prescribed entertainments and exercise for its prevention — to alleviate the gloom brought on by the environment. And they prescribed a diet of gruel and soups for its cure: fresh meat was thought to be a contributory cause. In the 1800s the connection between scurvy and vitamin C was at last discovered; fresh fruit then became the standard prevention and cure. But only in the early 1900s, thanks to the work of Vilhjalmiur Stefansson, especially his *Not By Bread Alone,* did Europeans realize that fresh meat also prevents the disease. Even now, many popular ideas about diet suggest that anyone who eats only meat would be seriously malnourished. The hunters of the North, with their meat diets and evident good health, somehow failed to impress early European explorers with the obvious: here were human beings alive and well and living exclusively in a place that Europeans said of itself caused a potentially, indeed frequently fatal, malady.

Theories about the causes of scurvy are an excellent little window onto European ideas of the North. The great imperial powers of the past five hundred years have been northern. But these same nations viewed lands yet farther north as wild and forbidding. The European imagination was chilled by the prospect of polar seas and *terrae incognitae* whipped by icy winds. Coastlines on old maps petered out in vague uncertainties, in a blurred suggestion of icecapped inaccessibility. There may have been whales, as the Basques had discovered by the sixteenth century, and there might have been routes to the Orient, as tenacious seekers for the Northwest Passage insisted. But even if there were land beyond the charted margins of the North, there could not be civilization — even in rudimentary form — in regions that were dark, frozen, impassable. The North was thought a priori to be poor because it was nature unrelieved by even the possibility of culture.

Discovery, however, led to a more realistic (though still marvellous) representation of new-found creatures. And in time, with European penetration of the boreal forests and the Arctic coasts, maps even began to acknowledge a human presence. The uninhabitable turned out to be inhabited, by hunters, gatherers, and fishermen. Discovering these peoples in one of the world's most extreme climates made it even easier for Europeans to represent the hopelessness of such ways of life than in the cases of hunters, gatherers, and fishermen encountered in the tropics and the African savannah. For those who tried to imagine the conditions of existence for northern hunting people, and who sought to picture to others what might be the needs of such outposts of human endeavour, it was scarcely necessary to do more than render in the language of culture the death sentence issued by nature. The poor Indians and Inuit of North America roamed through wild forest and over barren tundra, enduring relentless storms and crossing ice-infested seas, eking out a precarious living in pitiful defiance of seven- or even nine-month winters. Then there were the unfortunate Aleuts, on their storm-swept islets on the very rim of the North Pacific; and the ragged, wild bands of Chukchi, Evenki, Khanti, Yuit, and the many other inhabitants of the dreaded Siberian wastes. These peoples appealed to the European imagination because of their apparent destitution and their fingertip hold on existence. They were children of nature at her worst, and therefore unqualifiably childlike and unbelievably poor. They could never find time to rest, create art, still less develop proper institutions and a sound economy.

Hunters of the North were judged to have no real or viable economy of their own. This self-serving opinion removed, at an ideological stroke, any prospect for legal or moral opposition to European economic expansion into places where hunters lived. The possibility of a conflict of economic interest between frontiersmen and hunters was hypothesized into irrelevancy. Stereotypes of the savage accompanied the push west, the advance of the northern frontier, and all the excited expansion, first of European and then American interests, which constituted the progressive expropriation or destruction of the hunters' terrain.

Yet this general statement does not do justice to the way different frontiers were promoted by different economic interests. This is apparent in the way both stereotypes of the North and of hunters went through important changes, and this is well illustrated by a look at early accounts of the lands and people of northern British Columbia.

In the late eighteenth and early nineteenth centuries, fur traders reached the area. Alexander Mackenzie, as a representative of the North West Company, travelled along the Peace River and into northern British Columbia in 1793. George Simpson, governor of the Hudson's Bay Company, followed much the same route in 1828. The earliest descriptions of the region's Indians can be found in the two men's journals. Both were impressed by the landscape and both observed that the Indians were well supplied with game. Mackenzie goes into some detail about the different cultural groups. Although his tone is superior and patronizing, he is not deprecating of the Sekani or Beaver peoples. Although Simpson gives less detail, he too is not hostile to the Indians. In some comments on the Beaver, he remarks that they are affected with pulmonary ailments and "excessively addicted to spiritous liquors"; but he also notes that they are good hunters and could be good trappers. Mackenzie and Simpson viewed the region and its people with the eyes of the fur trade: they saw game and they saw potential trappers.

The interests of the trade were best served by fostering in the Indians a dependence on trade goods, so that they would trap and sell furs in order to obtain them. This was done, in part, by providing liquor to Indian trappers, whose societies had never made or used any such drugs. The drunkenness and violence that ensued were at times lamented (as by Simpson), and at times restrained (as by traders who watered the rum). But enthusiasm for drinking parties was fostered by traders who wanted Indians to develop the habit of visiting and trading at the posts, and so acquire the needs that would force them to return to the bush for ever more intensive and productive trapping of the fine furs from which the traders hoped to make large profits. The fur trade needed Indians who needed the fur trade. By this process traders encouraged the Indians to continue to spend much of their time in the bush.

There are, therefore, important points of contact between the fur trade and Indian economies. The European idea of hunters helped traders to feel superior, and to have few if any doubts about their right to change Indian life and take Indian lands as and when they so desired. But many Indian skills and patterns of land use were essential to the fur trade. This placed certain limits on the use traders might make of the negative stereotype of the hunter. When Indians attacked the newcomers, this did not lead to extreme reprisals. In 1824, four traders had been killed by Beaver Indians at the Fort St. John post, but Simpson — who refers several times to the events — chooses to conclude that the Indians "could not strictly be charged with any share in the massacre," although those thought to have had a part in the attack were denied the right to trade at Fort St. John for ten years. This was bound to cause hardship to people dependent on trade goods, but was not, in the traders' eyes, a punishment that fitted the crime. Simpson's conclusion is the wisdom of a fur trader speaking on his company's behalf: nothing could be gained, and much lost, by ongoing hostilities.

The fur trade in northern British Columbia thus moderated in practice the hostile picture of Indians that was conveyed by the stereotype of northern hunters. In addition, the fur traders' penetration of this country resulted in a moderation of the picture of the North itself. Lands that in the early 1800s were said to be part of the inhospitable and terrible North were described fifty years later as part of a wonderfully rich agricultural frontier. In this way, places once depicted as unutterably inhospitable become celebrated as veritable Gardens of Eden where any young man with a wish to do well for himself could profitably settle. The North, then, is the other side of a conveniently sliding divide. The "real" North keeps moving north, though it never ceases to exist. After all, the Arctic is in its way a polar appeal by which the push north is romanticized and celebrated as a special human achievement. The early accounts of northeast British Columbia and the Indians there are coloured by the way the region, which was a wild outpost of the northern fur trade in 1820, was by 1872 being heralded as one of the most exciting of mining and agricultural frontiers.

I give 1872 as the date because it was then that Simpson's 1828 journal was republished in an abridged and popular edition that reveals the change. The original text remained unalterably moderate in its treatment of the Indians, but Malcolm McLeod, its new editor, transformed the thrust and quality of the original in his many notes. In his preface he made his purpose abundantly clear:

> The object of the present *brochure*, at this juncture, is to direct attention . . . to the fact that *beyond* that *"Belt"* of *supposed limited* fertility . . . there is, in our North West, an area, continuous in every direction and easily accessible to its utmost limits,

containing *over three hundred millions* of acres of wheat and
pasture lands, with forests of finest timber, and the largest
known coal and bitumen, and also probably richest gold areas
in the world. . . . Much of Northern British Columbia, is not
too high, nor too cold, nor objectionable on any score of
settlement, especially to Canadians accustomed to contend
with frost and snow in the measure to be there found.

These sanguine sentiments of the preface are echoed in later passages
also written by McLeod. In one of his notes, he refers to the large
numbers of gold diggers pouring into the area, and says that they "are
entitled to that protection of law and order, which I fear is not to be
found there at present." He goes on to say, though observing that his
remark "may not be strictly in place," "The first difficulty to cope
with — and it is a most formidable one — in those parts of British
Columbia, is the Indian one. The Indian must be bought or killed, else
he will kill." This may be compared with statements made by
Americans at about the same time, for instance, the statement in 1870
by a U.S. Commissioner of Indian Affairs, quoted by J. E. Chamberlin in his excellent discussion of the issue, *The Harrowing of Eden:* "The
Westward course of population is neither to be denied nor delayed
for the sake of all the Indians who ever called this country their home.
They must yield or perish."

Throughout the 1890s, the Canadian Department of Indian Affairs' annual reports recorded that an unknown number of "nomads"
were living on the western side of the Rockies. On the eastern side
the Beaver and Slavey were only slightly better known. All the
northern Indians were feared and, increasingly, openly despised. "A
wild band" of 500 Beaver Indians was reported to have attacked "the
innocent gold-seekers." This story, implausible if only for its wildly
exaggerated numbers (Athapaskan bands never numbered more than
a tenth of this), became both local folklore and an open-ended
justification for any form of "pacification."

Vivid accounts of the Indians' destitution matched the hostile
picture of their belligerence. To the reports of Mackenzie and

Simpson in the early 1800s can be added other later and much more disparaging reports. In 1897, Inspector Moodie of the Royal Canadian Mounted Police reported on the condition of the people along the trail that was expected to become a gold rush route via the Peace River to the Yukon, and observed that the Indians were "a miserable lot, half starved most of the winter, and utterly unreliable. . . . their morals are of the lowest. . . . the murder of the aged and helpless is no uncommon occurrence. . . . [and they] were often starving from their inability to procure game." In 1912, Philip Godsell, popular author and adventurer, described the Indians of the Fort St. John region as "barbarous . . . primitive . . . unwhipped . . . insolent . . . unfriendly . . . untamed . . . pagan . . . impudent . . . fierce . . . cruel . . . insulting." In 1913, the annual report to the Department of Indian Affairs observed that the Indians of Fort St. John are "impoverished . . . make no progress . . . lie completely outside civilization . . . suffer extremely from drunkenness and tuberculosis." Game officers rivaled one another in their belittling descriptions of the Indians of the region.

At the time of the letters and reports from which these comments are excerpted, the Indians were still living a highly nomadic existence. They had already experienced, however, a century of White presence on or near their lands. I have referred to Simpson's note of 1828 that the Beaver Indians were suffering from tuberculosis and the effects of heavy alcohol use — the two most notorious afflictions brought by Europeans. Joseph Patsah, during his mapping session, mentioned a shortage of game in his father's traditional hunting area. Perhaps this was a widespread problem; many of the region's older Indians tell stories of hardship and some starvation, possibly as a result of depletion of game by white hunters, or disruption to traditional seasonal hunting patterns by repeated visits to trading posts. In 1918-19 the worldwide flu epidemic reached the area, causing some deaths and hardship among the Indians there. It was not the only such epidemic. It is possible, then, that the commentators I have quoted were accurate rather than, or as well as, bigoted. Perhaps the stereotype of the northern hunter was something of a truth when applied to northeast British Columbia in the early years of this century.

However, the old people of today do not say that their way of life was in special difficulties at that time. There is no evidence to suggest that their system had somehow failed. And we can fairly assume that many administrators, or others in official positions, made much of any sign of Indian weakness and poverty. There was hardship, of course, and some hunger. The Indian system was never infallible. But the actual state of health or sickness among the Indians was seldom the basis for the Whites' opinions.

White observers normally saw poverty, destitution, and savagery because of the absence of all that, in their world view, made human life worth living. Hatred, suspicion, and fear were aroused by the Athapaskans' forthright manner, indifference to material goods, and lack of permanent dwellings. A corresponding want of religion, morality, and honesty were easily added to what the eye could see by a troubled, perhaps even a challenged imagination. Moreover, as white observers noted again and again, these scantily clad, homeless, and improvident Indians were living in a climate where five-month winters seized every creek, lake, and hillside in terrifying extremes of cold. Europeans, with the very best knowledge, understanding, and equipment, triumphantly managed (but only just) to overcome the natural odds, while out there, the Indians scraped together a basic and uncertain livelihood without so much as a decent tent. Here was savagery indeed!

All these stereotypes and partial realities converge in present-day perceptions of Indian peoples and the Indian economic interest. The image of drunken bums who hang about on street corners and outside bars, waiting for handouts: this is perhaps the most wide-spread impression of, or belief about, the modern Indian. The community of Indians where there is no material basis for life, no real economy, and a desperate need for access to the employment and social benefits available to everyone else: this portrayal is the most persistent influence on social agencies and economic planners who concern themselves with the Indians' well-being. These images and stereotypes consign the Indian interest to the past; and give the future to white dreamers. The implication is that without the dreamers' plans and projects, the Indian will remain in a state of modern savagery, the result either of an original but enduring simplicity or an accumulation of intrusions onto what might once have been a functioning way of life. In either case, any use we may make of their lands can only be to the Indians' long-term benefit. Stereotypes of Indian life now conveniently obscure any possible conflict of interest between the worldwide importance of hydrocarbons or hydroelectricity and a few communities of Indians who have, supposedly, ceased to need even the little they once may have had.

In the first decades of this century, however, events and discussions show very clearly that the Indians of northeast British Columbia had great confidence in their way of life. The history of the drafting and signing of Treaty 8 uncovers the purposes and misconceptions of the Whites. Indeed, it bears upon every question that has been raised in this chapter and is an episode that continues to influence life in the region.

History books, old maps, western movies tell of the existence of an "Indian nation," though its boundary, beyond which the white man's law did not run, was pushed steadily westward to the Mississippi, the western plains, the Rockies . . . Such a division of the New World into two kinds of society may, in fact, never have penetrated very far into the expansionists' consciousness. By freezing slices of history, maps and movies mystify or obscure events and processes. Nevertheless, Indian reservations in the United States and reserves in Canada cement nineteenth-century ideas of the separateness of Indians. These ideas lie behind the terms of most treaties that assimilationists of today seem unable to comprehend.

What Europeans at first regarded as a single Indian nation west of the colonies on the Atlantic seaboard was gradually settled and incorporated into the western frontier. Indian bands, tribes, or nations, in the wake of military and other defeats, were often crammed into enclaves on their former lands. The treaties legally established and entrenched these enclaves. While this involved a terrible reduction of the possibilities of tribal strength, the signing of each one of them reconfirmed a commitment to Indian life and economy. This commitment is in its way very famous, if only for the reiterated assurance to Indian leaders that they would live as they always lived on lands now granted to them by treaty "as long as the sun shall rise and the rivers shall run."

The Indians who signed these treaties were often exhausted and decimated by encounters with westward-expanding colonists, settlers, and their military protectors. Moreover, the struggle against colonists, or the activities of settlers, or relocation as a result of war, or confinement to reserves had often damaged and disrupted the Indians' ability to maintain their economic systems. But the treaties they signed acknowledged the Indian claim to distinctive ways of life. The Indians were not simply consigned to the national melting pots. There were many, including those most ignorant of Indian needs and experience, who hoped that the restriction of roaming bands of hunters to reservations would facilitate their rapid progress towards a civilized form of economy. But the men who negotiated directly with the Indians, along with those who wished them well and were their advisers, saw the reserve as a way of isolating and even protecting, rather than changing, the Indian way of life. This was so especially in the case of the Indians of the northern forests, where a seeming infinity of land made everything appear possible.

Dealings between successive federal governments of the United States and the Plains Indians are well known, at least in broad outline, as a struggle between two stereotypes: the worthy settler and the murderous savage. Far less well known is the history of similar events and negotiations in Canada, and it was in northern Canada that treaties were made with hunters who had not been overrun and destroyed by settlement or war.

In the seventeenth and eighteenth centuries, British interest in good relations with the Iroquois Confederacy was inseparable from the wars against the French: the Iroquois eventually were allies. After the Cession of Canada in 1763, the British wished to preserve this alliance, but also hoped to maintain the good relations that the

French had developed in their extensive fur trade with northern Indians. The Royal Proclamation of 1763, the so-called Magna Carta of Indian rights in British North America, reserved as a hunting territory for Indians all lands west of the Allegheny Mountains. Here was British or Canadian recognition of the idea of an Indian nation, although it was never so named. The Royal Proclamation also established procedures for white settlement and development of these lands, procedures that only the Crown could negotiate with the Indians. This provided the legal basis for the signing, during the nineteenth and twentieth centuries, of the eleven numbered treaties with Canadian Indians.

Seven of these treaties, signed between 1870 and 1877, were negotiated for the explicit purpose of opening western Canada for settlement and for the new nation's first transcontinental railway. Instructions in 1871 to the government of the North-West Territories were clear enough:

> You will turn your attention promptly to the condition of the [Hudson's Bay] company outside the province of Manitoba on the north and west and while assuring the Indians of your desire to establish friendly relations with them, you will ascertain and report to his Excellency the course you may think the most advisable to pursue whether by treaty or otherwise *for the removal of any obstructions that might be presented* to the flow of population into the fertile lands that lie between Manitoba and the Rocky Mountains. [*Canada Sessional Papers*, 1871, No. 20, p. 8, my italics.]

Indians constituted such an "obstruction," and the treaties provided a means for their "removal." If unimpeded settlement of the West was to proceed, some limitation of Indian presence was required. This was secured with the help of Treaties 1 to 7. Treaty 8 was different in purpose, though identical in principle: it was deemed necessary to permit the unchallenged extraction of oil, gas, and minerals, which were believed to be abundant in the Athabasca and

Mackenzie basins, including northeast British Columbia. Prospective oil reserves were an important, if at times fanciful, aspect of dreams about the frontier as early as the 1890s.

The negotiation of all these treaties aimed at overcoming any hostility or resistance by the Indian inhabitants of frontier areas to the advance of the several sectors of the frontier economy. Treaties sought to deal with Indian opposition by offering various guarantees, promising federal protection, and making annual payments. Although Treaties 1 to 8 aimed to protect the economic interests of the white man's frontiers, nothing in them indicates that the Indian economy, as such, was understood to be an obstacle. This was partly because few officials in Ottawa believed that the Indians had a coherent economy, partly because the negotiators supposed that the Indians' marginal and haphazard existence could muddle along within or at the edge of whatever reserve lands a treaty might grant them, and partly because Indian participation in a continuing fur trade gave them at least one activity that overlapped with White interests. Even when a treaty secured lands for agricultural settlement, the comforting vastness of the still unsettled area seemed to allow the Indians unlimited possibilities for carrying on their own ways of life. These northern treaties do not suggest a direct contradiction or antagonism between different economic forms or different means of production. Their terms do not principally spring from an immediate conflict of economic interest (as they had in the case of the American plains twenty years earlier), but from a wish to protect the white man's frontier (whenever or wherever it might need to be) against possible limitation in the future. The Indians were to be restrained, reassured legally, and neatly conquered. The niceties of this process are open to significantly different interpretations, but its general character is not hard to grasp.

Treaty 8 was signed in 1899. By it, the Beaver, Cree, Chipewyan, and Slavey Indians ceded the greater part of northern Alberta and northeast British Columbia to the Federal Government. (In 1921, the Indians of the Mackenzie River basin, who included the Slavey living beyond northern British Columbia, adhered to Treaty 11. In this way, northern Slavey were administratively split from their southern families, though Treaties 8 and 11 provide similar hunting rights and vulnerabilities to developers. Map 4 shows the dates and areas of the numbered treaties.) The Privy Council Report of 1891 had indicated a need to remove the legal basis for Indian title to the Peace, Athabasca, and Mackenzie regions. At about the same time, North West Mounted Police detachments had reported that the Indians of these regions were outraged by white trappers' use of poisons and by white gold seekers' disregard for or wasteful use of land and animals. An 1897 police report noted: "The Indians felt it unjust that people who are not owners of the country are allowed to rob them of their living."

Charles Mair, who was on the commission that eventually negotiated Treaty 8, was dismayed by the situation. In his *Through the Mackenzie Basin: A Narrative of the Athabasca Peace River Expedition of 1899,* he observed:

> The gold seekers plunged into the wilderness of Athabaska without hesitation and without as much as by your leave to the natives. Some of these marauders, as was to be expected, exhibited a congenital contempt for Indians' rights. At various places, his horses killed, his dogs shot, his bear traps broken up.

Both Indians and Whites believed that a treaty was the way to resolve such conflicts. In June 1898, a group of Indians from the Fort St. John band refused to allow police and miners to pass through the area until a treaty was signed. This was the group that Whites claimed to have been wild, dangerous killers, and to have numbered no fewer than five hundred, a panicky report which further nourished the Indians' demand. That same year the Cabinet gave its approval to the negotiation of a treaty, and in 1899 it was signed.

Thus did the Indians "hereby cede, release, surrender and yield up to the Government, all their rights, titles and privileges whatsoever in the area covered by Treaty 8." In return for this surrender of rights and land, they received an annual payment of $5 a person, with an

4

AREAS AND DATES OF CANADA'S NUMBERED TREATIES WITH INDIANS

Lands around the Great Lakes and in southern Quebec were ceded by treaties that are not numbered. The earliest of these (Quebec) was signed in 1765; the most recent, with Chippewas between Lake Ontario and Georgian Bay, in 1923. The dotted lines between Treaties 7 and 4 mark a boundary that is undecided.

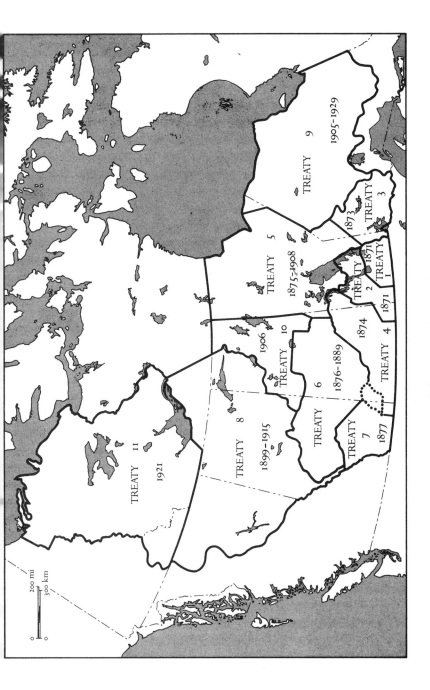

TREATY 9
1905-1929

TREATY 3
1873

TREATY 5
1875-1908

TREATY 1
1871

TREATY 2
1871

TREATY 10
1906

TREATY 4
1874

TREATY 6
1876-1889

TREATY 8
1899-1915

TREATY 11
1921

TREATY 7
1877

0 ___ 200 mi
0 ___ 300 km

additional payment to the chief or head man; reserves allocated on a formula of one square mile of land for each family of five; certain agricultural implements and other supplies; and the offer of educational assistance.

Treaty 8 also provided that the Indians should have the right to pursue their "usual vocation" of hunting, trapping, and fishing anywhere and at any time they chose over the tracts of land they had surrendered, "subject to such regulations as may be made by the Government of the country, and saving and excepting such tracts as may be required or taken up from time to time for settlement, mining, lumbering, trading or other purposes."

This Treaty is the basis both for Indian life on reserves and for their use of Crown land. It is also the basis for all agricultural settlement and industrial development of Crown land, up to the very perimeters and sometimes even to the virtual encirclement of the reserves. On the one hand, the Treaty granted a basis for the continued existence of traditional Indian life; on the other, it facilitated the process whereby Indians in so many places have come increasingly to endure in distressed enclaves, on diminishing islands of Indian life.

The Indians' legal position bears directly on the question of their economic interests. The relationship between Treaty 8 and Indian economic life is made ambiguous by virtue of different and perhaps conflicting contemporary purposes. Above all, there is a world of difference between the terms of Treaty 8 and the understanding the Indian signatories had of it. In evidence to the Alaska Highway Pipeline hearings in December 1979, Michael Jackson, Professor of Law at the University of British Columbia, described the misunderstanding. He noted that the evidence of those who participated in negotiations or were present at the signing of the Treaty and the oral history of the Indians themselves make it clear that the Indians did not understand Treaty 8 to be a surrender of rights. "They understood it as a treaty of peace and friendship. The condition precedent to their friendship was the affirmation or recognition of their rights to the land." In particular, Jackson points out that some Indians refused to sign the treaty until they had received hunting, trapping, and fishing guarantees and an assurance that "their freedoms to engage in those activities, throughout the region, would not be affected, would not be restricted." (Transcript of Hearings, Vol. 17, 1936-37.) Jackson quotes the report of one of the Treaty commissioners, which clearly shows what the Indians' central negotiating position really was:

> Our chief difficulty was the apprehension that the hunting and fishing privileges were to be curtailed. We had to solemnly assure them that only such laws as to hunting and fishing as were in the interests of the Indians or were found necessary to protect the fish and fur-bearing animals will be made, and that they would be as free to hunt and fish after the treaty as they would be, if they never entered into it.
>
> We assured them that the treaty would not lead to any forced interference. The Indians were generally adverse to being placed on reserves. It would have been impossible to make a treaty if we had not assured them that there was no intention of confining them to reserves. [Treaty No. 8, B.I.M.D., Publication No. QS-0576-000-EE-A-16, 1966, p. 12.]

The Beaver, Slavey, and Cree hunting peoples who were granted reserves under Treaty 8 were not, thereby, accepting a loss, or even a change, in their economic system. On the contrary, they were sure — had indeed been reassured — that "to take treaty" (the expression used at the time and itself a clouding of the real issues: were the Indians making a deal or accepting a predetermined formula?) would protect their mode of life. In fact, they were not reassured quickly or easily. Reports in 1907 from commissioners for Treaty 8 state that only about half of the Indians in the Fort St. John area "had been given sufficient assurances to justify their signing the Treaty." The Slaveys at Fort Nelson signed the Treaty in 1911; some of the Beaver Indians from the Halfway River area did not sign until 1915. Tardiness in signing represented a reluctance to believe in the Treaty's value, and a persistent independence that entailed a profound antipathy towards any prospect of reserve-based life. Such signs indicate a vigour in the hunting economy that the Treaty did not overtly seek to undermine.

However the treaties were perceived at the time, whether by sympathetic bureaucrats, concerned missionaries, or by the Indian signatories themselves, they nevertheless prepared the way for whatever use white newcomers would care to make of the land. This was, in the first place, quite direct: Indians were quickly deprived of large areas wanted for agricultural settlement. It was also indirect: the treaty-created reserves came under the administrative control of Whites, a control which created possibilities (not all of them legal) for successive further appropriations of Indian resources. The treaties established white bureaucrats as the defenders of Indian interests. In the United States this is indicated by the existence and functions of the Bureau of Indian Affairs; in Canada the Department of Indian Affairs and Northern Development, under various guises and with a network of local offices, supposedly acts on behalf of all the country's Indians.

These bureaucracies and offices, officials and persons "in the field" (an expression that so neatly reveals that the location of paramount interest is somewhere else, *not* in the field) constituted a dominance of Indian life that reached into every home. Moreover, the bureaucrats repeatedly sought to ensure that white men's dreams of freedom, wealth, and unlimited expansion should not be disturbed by Indians. They could often do their work in good conscience: bureaucrats, by and large, believed that Indians would prosper if their lands and resources were under the developmental aegis of the white man and his economic devices. The stereotype of the Indian as a person without a viable way of life was helpful, as usual.

The treaties, and the bureaucracies to which they gave rise, are in need of a detailed history — a history that would be a succession of dismal and corrosive episodes in North American life. Behind the treaties, or alongside them, stands the great vision of the New World, a vision that startled, excited, and inspired generation after generation of Europeans. The discovery of America is often represented as a sudden and revelatory moment, a historic event much like the 1969 moon landing (with which it has been compared). In fact, realization of the momentous importance of the discovery of the Americas came only with a whole series of later discoveries — and these may not yet have come to an end. The northern treaties continue to serve their purposes. They, and stereotypic ideas about hunters, make it possible for settlers and developers to pay no heed to the Indians' economic and cultural systems. If the Indians objected to or obstructed the frontiersman's dream of untold resources, then the Indians either did not appreciate their own need for the benefits of civilization, or they had not understood the terms of a treaty. Old ideas bore their ugly fruits, and the stage was set for the continuing advance of the frontier.

5

A Funeral

Many northern reserves appear to be grim and even hateful little places, clusters of houses crowded together by planners in order to achieve economies of administration and service. The Reserve where Joseph Patsah lives is no exception although his house is one of five that stand on their own, out of sight and well located. The other fifteen homes crowd up to one another, clustered to ease the supply of municipal services; yet none has running water, drains, or electricity. There is no garbage collection nor are there any other amenities or services on the Reserve. Such compression of a people distinctive for their free roamings through unbounded forest is bizarre and painful. They pay the price for modernity, yet receive few of its benefits.

There is a school. It stands a little to one side of the Indians' houses and is surrounded by a neat and brightly painted picket fence. Behind the school is a clinic, to which a federal nurse comes twice a week, and where there are facilities that can be used in emergencies. These buildings have electricity, supplied by a generator which also stands inside the fence. The teachers at the school, who spend the weekdays living on the Reserve, have a residence in the same complex. The high quality of services there is a small measure of the social chasm that prevents any everyday contact or understanding between the personnel who maintain and use the facilities within the fenced compound and the Indians whom they seek to help. There is virtually no visiting, except by nurses who periodically make checks on people in their homes. Many Whites are unashamedly afraid of visiting Indians — there might be parties and the danger of drunkenness. Indians very rarely have either much wish or reason to visit the teachers.

Life in the Reserve's houses, then, is not directly intruded upon by the administration. There is, however, a Band hall, and most formal encounters between Indians and Whites take place in it. The hall is large and well equipped. A meeting room opens on to two other areas — a kitchen and a church. These two rooms are used only on very special occasions, though the meeting hall is a centre for community activities and is the place where meetings with government officials occur. The community washing machine was also kept there until the Department of Indian Affairs in 1979 provided a trailer equipped as a laundromat.

I first saw the inside of the hall one morning shortly after our fishing trip to Quarry. Brian Akattah took me there with Stan, a young man of about his own age who wanted to draw a hunting map. Brian said that we should use the hall, because Stan's house was too crowded for mapping and we needed plenty of space. In fact, Stan suggested that we make use of a large table which he had seen in the hall. He was enthusiastic about drawing a map and anxious to do it under the best possible circumstances. The table in the hall seemed like a very good idea.

Brian, loaded down with his huge folder of base maps and boxes of coloured pens, led us into the meeting room area. At the doorway we passed a group of women who had taken the washing machine outside. With the help of a long extension cable and a large fire, they had established a sort of public wash camp. Stan paused to talk with them; Brian and I went ahead to find the table.

The table was the church altar. Large, with collapsible legs, it clearly would serve our purpose. So we carried it from the church into the main hall and laid out the base maps. Stan joined us at the table and began to search the maps for creeks and trails that he knew. At Brian's prompting, he then began to mark his fishing places. Once this was done, Stan offered to identify his moose-hunting area. Very slowly, and with repeated correction and redrafting, he drew a wide circle. From time to time Brian queried an area, and once reminded Stan that he had failed to include a valley which Brian knew he had hunted. Finally Stan stood back from the table, satisfied that he had finished.

When I looked at the moose-hunting circle, it struck me that it was very like the one drawn by Atsin. I asked the two men about this. Did Stan, a hunter no more than thirty years old, have more or less the same land use as Atsin, a man of nearly sixty? Brian looked at me in surprise. "Atsin is pretty old now," he said. "Can't get around so good. We boys have to hunt hard to get the meat." But Atsin had been travelling and hunting twenty years before they were born, and surely would have used areas that Stan and Brian had never seen. Perhaps Atsin had not marked some of these, or had forgotten. Or had Stan exaggerated? When I made these suggestions, Brian looked puzzled. He and Stan, and other young men, had travelled with Atsin when they were children. They had hunted everywhere together and had made use of the same areas. They had begun to hunt properly when they were twelve or thirteen, many years before there were any houses on the Reserve. Stan, who is a shy person, followed this conversation but continued to glance at the map. He left it to Brian to explain and, if necessary, to defend the truth of what he had drawn. His silence was a little unnerving. I was wondering if he was angry with my questions when he suddenly said, pointing to the map, "Look here, right here. Right here, Quarry. We lived up there. Everywhere there. Atsin, Brian, and me. That right?" Brian said, "That's right."

Stan said no more about the maps. He had made his point. Once again Quarry had been used to affirm the people's claim to the land. But now it was young men who made such points and, describing Quarry in much the same way as did Atsin and Joseph, they also insisted that the similarities between all the men's hunting was obvious if you remembered that they all had lived up there. As small boys they had gone on winter and spring hunts and to summer camps. They may not have used each place as often, but they had certainly used the same areas as their elders. So how could there be a great difference between their and their fathers' maps? Stan and Brian regarded my questions as silly. Did I suppose the young men were not Indians? Did I not understand what it meant to have been brought up at Quarry? I wanted to talk about this more with them, but Brian made a joke about the altar. We'd better put it back in the church, he said, because there was a funeral that afternoon and the Father would miss it. Perhaps we should get him to make a map, too! So the table was returned. I asked if Brian was going to do more maps, but he said he was not. We should go to the graveyard instead and help with the work up there.

The graveyard is a little way beyond the houses, on the edge of a small ridge. Several trails lead to this ridge and up to the graves. Brian led the way along one of them, past five houses and into a small patch of woodland that had been left standing between two fields. Then we climbed a steep and muddy slope directly below the graves. It was one of those days when the light is unbelievably clear. Where the trail led out onto the height of the ridge, we could see far into the distance. The foothills between the Reserve and the first sharp ridges of the Rockies appeared to rise not so very far away, and behind them the peaks of the mountains, now capped in new snow, were jaggedly outlined against the sky. The Reserve's "downtown," regular and neat, smoke rising from chimneys and outdoor fires, was below us. We could see the group of women near the hall, beside the washing machine and the large fire. Viewed from the graveyard on a fine autumn day, the Reserve looked peaceful and appealing.

The graveyard itself consists of two short rows of graves and is surrounded by a single-rail corral. A shallow wooden structure, creating the impression of a narrow cabin, sits on top of each grave. These structures are evocative of above-ground burials, and are built — I later discovered — over all Beaver Indian graves. Cars can reach the graveyard along a track that forks off the road leading to the Reserve. This track had become overgrown and some men were clearing it. Others were mending and extending the corral around the graves. A thick-set young man, Buddy Wolf, appeared to be in charge. He worked with a chain saw, cutting out small poplars and old tree stumps in an attempt to widen the road. The other men worked with axes, cutting poles or stripping bark off corral rails as these were nailed into place. The chain saw's hoarse whine and the insistent thuds of falling axes disturbed and enlivened the graveyard's potential solemnity.

The atmosphere was not at all that of a funeral. Men were jovial. As some worked, others watched, sat and chatted, and occasionally lent a steady, unhurried, and unintrusive hand. People came and went, a few on horseback, others on foot. Towards midday some women appeared carrying a tray of sandwiches — looking rather formal, a bit incongruous, but very welcome. A few minutes later Atsin rode up to the corral on a powerful-looking brown horse. His wrinkled face, his stiff upright posture, and the horse's quick and strong walk were impressive. He rode to the corral, dismounted, dropped the reins to the ground — no need to tether a good horse — and produced a thermos of coffee. Joseph, who had been watching and giving occasional advice to the men working with axes, welcomed the arrival of the sandwiches and coffee by lighting a fire in the shelter of trees behind the graves. He and a few other men brewed cans of tea. The unhurried but persistent noise, the men's and women's voices, and the hills rolling off into the distance, a flickering of yellow leaves in the wind, clouds and sun . . . it was a morning of great beauty.

My own thoughts slowed and began to centre contentedly on the lengths of wood whose bark had to be removed, or on branches that from time to time someone asked me to pull to one side. Thoughts of maps or research of any kind disappeared. When thirsty or hungry, I felt free to help myself to tea or coffee from the flask, or to a sandwich. When tired, I felt equally free to stop, lean on the new rails around the graves, or sit and stare over the Reserve farmland towards the mountains. I noticed several times when I stopped and leaned or sat and stared that someone would also stop, a dozen or more yards away, and join me. The others were not perceptibly aware of me, unless they silently acknowledged a collaboration in which I was now included. I may well have been stopping because of work rhythms that had occurred generally. Repose and activity seemed to be collective in the most subtle ways. Contact between people, each in a seemingly individual and private domain, was free of any discernible strain or anxiety. All were busy, in their own way, without instructions. Yet the contact was as compelling as it was unspoken. In spite of my immense self-consciousness among men and women I had not met before, on an occasion full of disturbing significance, I was somehow lulled into or infected by the others' way of doing things.

Perhaps some of what I sensed and noticed was a consequence of the nature of the work, and connected somehow to the proximity of death. And this may also have affected the way the men joked and teased one another. Buddy warned me against going to the Valley Creek Reserve: should I go there my genitals would be put in a noose and cut off. It had not happened to him, he said, but he had been lucky. It's what they do over there. He should know. His wife came from Valley Creek. There were other raucous jokes. And Stan was teased mercilessly about an unsuccessful hunt on the previous evening. Did Stan shoot at a moose last night? Knowing Stan, it was probably a buffalo. He could never tell the difference! Or was it a steer, Stan? Didn't anyone else see it and tell him it was a buffalo?

The work's pace, the mood, and the joking continued until about 2:00 P.M. Then someone came up from the houses to announce that Father had arrived, and there was to be a funeral service in the church after which the body was to be brought up the hill and buried. The men had only just begun to dig the new grave. This work now became quite urgent. Joseph cut and measured a six-foot pole, which he rather solemnly stood upright in the grave. At least four feet of it rose above ground. This demonstration of the work to be done caused the diggers to dig somewhat feverishly.

At about two-thirty, Buddy asked me to go with him in the Band pickup to help carry the coffin from the church. All the other men stayed at the graveyard and continued to dig, chop, chat, or sit around the fire in the trees. Two teen-age boys and Buddy's wife Mary went with us. Buddy sat in the front but asked Mary to drive, and she went quite fast over the rutted trail and down the steep hillside. Buddy laughed as the three of us who rode in the back rocked and swayed and clung on more desperately at each unanticipated lurch. He shouted to his wife to drive faster, so that he could see if we were any good as cowboys!

Windswept and laughing, we arrived at the hall. Outside some children were playing, and a small group of men and women stood talking. Buddy and I went in and found the service under way. A young priest, robed and looking hopelessly uncomfortable, stood in front of two batches of chairs. He was reading a passage about Jesus being love. He showed signs of great nervousness. His voice was urgent and exaggeratedly mellifluous, as if he were trying to force his way through much tangible resistance. Yet there were very few people in the seats: three visitors from town, the Reserve's teachers, the Chief (a young woman at that time occupied this elected position) with three or four elders, and two women. The elders and women were very upset and crying loudly, murmuring words I could not understand, and leaning on, almost clutching the Chief who was sitting between them. A man lay on the floor at the back of the church, behind the chairs. He was unconscious, presumably from drink. The elders and the two crying women kept getting up from their seats. Twice they walked to the coffin, leaned against it, and called out loudly in a painful show of unhappiness. At the same time, children were coming and going from the hall to the entrance of the church, talking noisily to one another.

Buddy and I stood at the doorway to the church for a while. The priest persisted, acknowledging all the disturbance only in the tone of his voice. When he had said some prayers, one of the schoolteachers began to read a long passage from the Bible. The shouts and footfalls of children now playing tag in the main part of the hall added to the noise. The man lying at the back did not stir. The service just carried on, the priest and teachers doing it their way, while the Indians did it theirs. Perhaps the priest felt indignant; the people probably felt criticized. Suddenly the incongruity and hidden tension of this encounter reminded me of an episode in a P. G. Wodehouse story. I began to laugh and had to leave. Buddy had left a moment before and it was easy enough to follow him.

The group outside had grown larger. Buddy joined it and began talking to a stranger, a local white rancher who needed to use the Reserve radiotelephone. His own was not working and he wanted to order spare parts for a tractor. Buddy led him away to the clinic to show him the phone, saying they would only be a few minutes. As they walked off, Buddy murmured to me that it would be O.K. if the service finished before he got back: "Father will be able to wait a bit."

I returned to the church to find the service just ending. The priest took and offered Communion, gave a final blessing, and then rather abruptly left. The women, along with an old man and the Chief, went over to the coffin. It was partially uncovered. A woman's head and shoulders were visible. The two women stroked and held the head, then leaned over and kissed it many times. The Chief slowly and firmly laid her hand flat over the dead woman's face. The old man walked shakily around behind the coffin, tears on his cheekbones, confusion and pain in his expression. The voices of the priest and teacher no longer intruded upon the people's feelings. The atmosphere in the church had changed to that of a funeral. At the end of the incomprehensible service, beside the coffin, in sight of the dead woman's countenance and the texture of her skin, I felt frightened and intolerably sad; then ashamed and confused. The priest had struck me as a fatuous intruder, but I had thought of a P. G. Wodehouse story — hardly less of an insult. I hurried outside again.

For a while nothing happened. The children continued to play; men and women stood around uneasily in knots. Until Buddy came back with his pickup, there would be no way of getting the coffin up the hill. So everyone waited. After a time some people began to walk up the trail anyway. Then Mary drove up in the pickup. Buddy was still helping the rancher with his phone call, so she suggested we go on ahead of him. A group of young men loaded the coffin onto the back, fifteen of us climbing on with it. Mary drove away as we gripped the sides, trying to keep our balance in the crush of passengers. Several young boys jumped on and clung precariously to the back. Along the way, just below the point where the trail turns sharply up towards the ridge, Mary stopped for Buddy. He had left the rancher and begun to walk back to the graveyard. Laughing and joking loudly he squeezed in the front seat — he is a large man and four people were already crowded in there. With shouts of alarm and excitement, as the pickup rolled over ruts and into potholes, we finally arrived at the freshly cleared access road. Mary parked alongside the corral, which was still not finished. A large crowd was already there, and several horses were tethered back in the trees. Joseph stood beside his fire with some of the older men. Atsin was working with Brian and Stan, finishing off the grave. Brian measured it with Joseph's pole: it was now at least the required six feet.

The priest and teachers arrived a few minutes later, driving up in the priest's camper. The visitors from town followed behind in a car, bringing some of the Reserve residents who had not walked on earlier. At last, with everyone gathered around the grave, two young men climbed onto the pickup to help unload the coffin. Suddenly, two young women, who had been talking loudly a few minutes earlier, began to shout. They were standing to one side of the pickup and now they climbed on with the boys. The priest, who had also situated himself beside the pickup in order to accompany the coffin to the grave, was only a few yards from the dispute. He stood very still, as if these moments were not in fact occurring, and pointedly ignored the trouble. It must have been hard for him, because the combatants wished to have a last look at the dead woman and proceeded to force the head end of the coffin open again. This done, the argument became fiercer. No one else in the crowd said anything. It was up to the two women to sort out their differences. Interference would no doubt have been deemed improper. The dispute soon petered out. A few obscenities were given a certain importance by virtue of being shouted a couple of yards from the frozen priest's ears, but the significance of the argument was obscure. Judging by appearances, I thought that the funeral was being further complicated by drunkenness. There had no doubt been some sort of wake during the previous night and this morning. In any case, the women soon climbed off the pickup; the priest came back to life; the coffin was re-covered and carried to the grave.

The burial itself took place with surprising speed. The coffin was lowered, the priest said a very few quick words, threw a handful of earth into the grave, and scurried away. The other visitors hurried after him. As the camper and car drove off, their wheels spinning on the trail, the men began to shovel the sandy earth back into the grave. Everyone took a turn and it was soon filled, but the people did not leave the graveyard. Instead, they lit another fire in the trees and sat or stood around. Then Mary drove away, taking two other women with her. They soon came back and began to unload pots of soup and boxes of food. A feast had been prepared in advance. Soon everyone gathered around piles of sandwiches, cheeses, hot dogs, pickles, and biscuits. Mary passed out bowls of soup. Some women filled them for their husbands and themselves. Some men took their own. Everyone, including the two women who a few minutes before had been arguing, was calm and friendly. The service, the priest, along with the crying and shouting, seemed to fade into an irrelevant distance.

When everyone had eaten enough and had sat for a time drinking tea, Buddy said that the work might as well continue; it wouldn't take long to get the job finished. The men who had been there all day picked up their axes and returned to fencing the grave area and removing bark from new rails. Joseph, Atsin, Mary, Annie Patsah, and a few others continued to sit around the fire. Within half an hour the peaceful rhythms that had been ascendant for most of the day were firmly re-established. The work, moods, the place itself had been invaded, interrupted by a funeral. But that felt long gone. Buddy made more jokes. Stan was once again teased about the moose he had missed. After a while, Mary drove off, taking the pots and dishes back to the homes from which they had been borrowed. Most of the women went with her. Soon some of the younger boys and girls left, several of them on one horse and one girl on a tiny pony. Then I noticed that Stan was about to set off down the hill with one of his young sons. Buddy and four or five others lingered to put the finishing touches on the work but also, I thought, to enjoy the peace and beauty of the place. Buddy confirmed this when he went and sat at the very edge of the ridge, ten yards or so below the corral. Perched there on a steep slope, he stared out towards the mountains. After a few minutes the others joined him. I was the last. It must have been four or five o'clock. We sat there, looking into the afternoon sun, warm, comfortable, and relaxed. Buddy and most of the others had been at the grave site since nine in the morning.

I wondered, as we sat there, what the priest was doing and thinking just then. Perhaps he was telling his colleagues in town about the way the Indians had behaved. Perhaps he felt dismay and indignation, or was simply puzzled as to how such a people could be changed. It probably never could have occurred to him that the men and women at the graveyard might enjoy such a sense of peace and good will after he left. He had missed the feast and perhaps had not even noticed Joseph's fire. In any case, the sun shone on us, and the wind was cool and gentle from the southwest. No one said much until Buddy remarked that it was good to have got all the work done on the corral fence. As we chatted it suddenly struck me that I did not know whose funeral it had been. The woman had been away from the Reserve for some time before she died, and I had never met her. To my astonishment, Buddy told me that she was his sister. "Too bad that she died," he said; then after a short and, for me, discomforting silence, "We could do more work up here tomorrow. Always lots of work here and too few men wanting to do it." And he laughed.

One by one the men left. Mary appeared with the pickup again and

Buddy drove off. I declined the offer of a lift and walked down the trail that Brian had led me along in the morning. As he drove away, Buddy shouted to watch out for bears, though, he added, perhaps I need not worry since maybe a white man wouldn't taste too good anyway! As I walked down the ridge, the trees beautiful in their autumn bareness, I wondered if Buddy had been joking or not and kept an eye open for bears. The funeral now seemed a very long way away. On the trail I met Brian, his wife Mary, and his nephew Peter. They were waiting for me and suggested that we all go fishing until dark. Good evening to try, said Brian, especially at the place where two rivers meet, only a few miles away. There would be another two hours of daylight, they assured me. So the day ended on a long stony beach, where the confluence of two rivers had cut a deep pool into a nearby bank. We caught one rainbow trout immediately, then no more. After an hour we returned to the Reserve. Perhaps Mary and Brian had needed to put some distance between themselves and the events of the day. As we drove back in the twilight, Brian spotted three mule deer on the roadside. We stopped and watched them for a second, but they were nervous and soon dashed out of sight. Brian then talked about the possibility of deer hunting in the coming days. No one spoke of the funeral, yet it did not seem that they were avoiding the topic.

A few days later, however, Atsin raised the subject with me. Something must have reminded him of the funeral, for he broke a silence with a chuckle and said, "We boys sure did lots of good work the other day. Digging the grave." This led us into talking about the event. Atsin brought up the argument at the graveside. He told me that it arose when one of the women accused the other of having caused the death. The accused had then accused back. I expressed surprise at this: didn't the death occur in hospital? Hadn't it been a death in labour? Surely no one should feel responsible. Atsin gave me a quick look. White men don't understand how things happen, he said. Beaver Indians know that they can cause good and bad with medicine. Some pretty strong medicine, he said. "Pretty soon you find that out." He went on to explain that behind every event, and beyond its immediate causes, are the activities of people. There is no such thing as luck, no merely natural happenings. The women wanted to say whose medicine had caused the death. "But crazy women," Atsin went on, "they don't know whose medicine did that. I can tell you, though, they got it all wrong. The medicine against that woman was done by — ." He went on to give me his version of the causes, laying his blame, and left me trying to recall all the events of the funeral, trying to re-experience them from the point of view implied by an understanding of medicine-power.

But the events had slipped away or become fixed by my understanding, and lack of understanding, at the time. Only a single detail suddenly assumed a new significance. At one point, as we stood side by side at the grave, and while the medicine fight was beginning, Brian Akattah had whispered to me, "Let's go home. No good if white men hear this. They think all the people are just drinking guys." We had stayed, in fact, but I once again realized just how easy it is to fall back on simple, blinding stereotypes. Every white person there, including me, went away believing that the funeral had been marred by drunkenness. Then I remembered that morning, doing Stan's map on the altar table in the Band hall, and pressing Stan and Brian with questions about the similarities between Stan's and Atsin's hunting areas. Atsin was right: I, along with the other white visitors, understood very little.

6

Traplines and Traps

The aboriginal inhabitants of what is now northeast British Columbia are the inheritors of one of the purest forms of hunting economy; purest in the sense that they are peoples who are flexible in the face of every changing circumstance, to whom material possessions are more of a hindrance than a help, and whose skills and mobility secured (as long as their hunts were successful) a life of relative affluence and good health. Everything about the Indian of northeast British Columbia points towards a readiness to change and to move: hunting techniques, clothing, spiritual and religious systems that govern relations among people and between the people and their land, reliance upon knowledge and skill (which of course are carried in the head), and a resolute indifference to any accumulation of wealth.

There are many differences among the northern Athapaskan groups — the Kutchin, Hare, Dogrib, Slavey, Beaver and Sekani, Tahltan, Carrier, Kaska, and others — a great aggregate of language groups that came to populate northwestern North America. These differences attest to a multitude of local responses to change and an immensely complex history. A readiness to adapt to new environments, to use different resources, and to seize new technological advantages has always been at the heart of Athapaskan culture.

Such anthropological and historical observations are not matters of remote theoretical concern. In historic times these peoples have been able to use their flexibility to escape restrictions imposed by treaties, and to defy any stereotypic suggestion that their way of life is dead. No one should be surprised when the Indians of today insist that their ways of looking at the world and harvesting its resources will outlive any other. It is not nostalgia, or sentimentality, when the Indians affirm their own identity and special interests; they are not paying their respects to an idealized or fossilized past. They do not say that they have not changed, but — a little paradoxically — they insist, sometimes with remarkable conviction, that their way of changing is what will guarantee survival. And indeed, at every point in their dealings with European newcomers to the continent, this way has revealed itself. The flexibility, adaptability, and mobility of the Athapaskan people is the background and the context for every social and economic innovation that Whites and their institutions have introduced in the North. If this background is kept firmly in mind, several problematical issues become much clearer. This is particularly so in the case of traplines and their consequences for the Indian life and economy.

In the 1920s and '30s, white trappers came in large numbers and with high hopes to the fur-rich country of northern British Columbia. This invasion was in part a result of the Depression, and trappers were but one stream in the flood of footloose, hungry, and eternally hopeful vagrants, whose prospects of both urban and agricultural success had been so sharply and severely curtailed by the economic conditions of the late 1920s. At the same time, the postwar fur market was buoyant. High prices for fine furs persisted throughout the Depression and remained high afterwards, despite yearly fluctuations and some gradual decline. Until the late 1930s, white trappers set out from their homes with dreams of great riches, taking up trapping as others had earlier joined the gold rushes. Once again, world economic circumstances had caused a movement of population that affected lands and lives far away from the centres of power.

White trappers spread through the area between the Peace and Liard rivers and deep into Beaver, Cree, and Slavey country. This was country where Indian bands used all of the land, travelling from camp to camp in a seasonal round. This round varied from year to year, and some territories were left fallow for several seasons — depending on the hunters' and trappers' assessments of a resource. The Indians' system was not easy to discern but, as I shall show, it was patterned and thoughtful. The Indians certainly did not think that they were surrounded by limitless and underused resources, nor did they ever accept that their hunting practices were wasteful. But their way of life was hidden from newcomers' eyes, and even if Whites had wished to respect its customs and needs, few would have had an opportunity to come to terms with it.

Instead, many white trappers found themselves repeatedly at odds with an altogether unfamiliar, even incomprehensible, way of harvesting the land's resources. White and Indian trappers depended on many of the same animals: fox, lynx, bear, marten, wolverine, mink, beaver, muskrat, otter — an abundance of valuable pelts for trade; and on moose and deer to supply meat with which to provision their winter cabins. But there the similarities ended. White settlers and trappers had clear notions of orderly land use that were based on well-tried patterns of frontier homesteading. They imagined that a trapping area they had claimed would be theirs alone, an area where they would have an exclusive right to harvest furs. The Indians' system was based on freedom of access, flexible use, and rotational conservation, which meant that some areas went untrapped for seasons on end. There were bound to be confrontations and disagreements.

Most confrontations were minor, but were nonetheless so numerous and troubling as to cause all manner of negotiation among those who deemed themselves to be responsible for Indians or wildlife and the peaceful opening up and settlement of the North. As these collisions and attendant discussions proliferated, they gave rise to vehement and venomous statements about Indians. Racial stereotypes, which had long been nurtured by conflicts on the North American frontiers and had served white interests well, once more played a loud and ugly part in the history of this region. The need for Treaty 8 had been expressed in some of these terms, but the conflict over trapping institutionalized White-Indian discord and made real changes in every Indian's life. Interracial conflict became more overt and more precisely focussed. Moreover, the trapline issue took over where the Treaty left off, raising questions that the Treaty had not clearly answered: the new disputes consolidated many of the limitations on Indian land use that the Treaty had implied would never take place. These limitations were widely thought by white settlers to be necessary for the proper pacification and restriction of the Indians, but the Indians had understood that in return for signing the Treaty, their economic system was to be guaranteed and protected.

During the 1920s, government officials began to map trapping areas. These were then given to individuals or to families who, in return for the purchase of an annual trapping licence, acquired an exclusive right to trap their "registered lines." This system was first introduced in British Columbia, but spread to all parts of northern Canada excluding the High Arctic, which still lay beyond the reach of all but the most adventurous of white trappers. These registered traplines were an attempt to introduce an orderly White presence in the wilderness, and were also held to be the only way of protecting limited wildlife resources from excessive harvesting. They were equally an attempt to bring what were considered the Indians' unusual economic practices into line with ideas of ownership and exclusivity in the interests of rational production for a market economy. Registration was not designed with Indian land use or

Indian interests in mind, but Indians everywhere were urged to register lines and accept the rules of the newest colonial game. This was the first direct attack upon and restriction of Indian life in the region.

Some details of how this took place emerge from correspondence among Indian agents (men in the field whose task it was to administer and protect Indian interests on behalf of the Federal Government), regional game officers, and officers of the Royal Canadian Mounted Police who periodically had to deal with trapline registration and its attendant problems. This correspondence clearly shows how the Indians were perceived by those whose business it was to administer and control the North; and it also explains much about Indian-White conflict.

Virtually all white officials shared the view that the Indians of northeast British Columbia were ignorant and destitute. In 1933, M. Christianson, Inspector of Indian Agencies, Alberta, described one of the reserves close to Fort St. John, probably the old Montnay lands:

> This reserve is situated about 14 or 15 miles from the village of Fort St. John and as I stated in my report last fall, there is some excellent land at this place. There is not even a shack built on this reserve, as the Indians only remain there for a month or so in the summer, after which they go back to the bush. There are 170 Indians in the band, belonging to the Beaver tribe, and they are certainly a very poor type of Indian. They have become diseased, inbred and through poverty they are simply on their last legs. They have absolutely nothing. I have never seen a band of Indians that had less. During the two days I spent with these Indians, the first day paying treaty and the second day at a meeting with the band, it rained continually, and [I] noticed that these people did not even have tents. There were only two good tepees in the whole outfit and the only shelter they had was a piece of canvas hung over willows, under which I saw the old people huddled. They were very poorly clad and some of

the children had practically no clothing on. They seem to have become [so] poverty stricken that they haven't even any cooking utensils. As the department is aware, these Indians are the talk of the country.

Other parts of the correspondence describe the Indians' use of the land and include many intriguing references to the trapline problem. Here, for example, are extracts from a report by G. M. Kerkhoff of the Fort St. John detachment, British Columbia Game Department, also written in 1933:

In the Fort St. John district, the White men hold big areas for traplines and between these areas the Indians are registered.

The Indians are roving and have no permanent place of abode; they have been allotted their reservations, but do not live on them except during a short time in the summer to receive their treaty money, which I believe is Five Dollars for a Male and One Dollar for Females and Children. . . . They are a poor tribe and left to shift for themselves. Their whole existence is the killing of game. . . .

The correspondents also observed that many Indian trappers do not use the same land year after year, but move in family-size units now into one area, now into another, covering what seemed to these white officials incomprehensibly and extravagantly large expanses of territory.

Regarded as poor and ignorant, these roving Indians were a problem to everyone. They repeatedly were accused of killing game far beyond their needs, and their rovings brought them into hostile contact with white trappers. The policy of the day was to divide the whole region into traplines, the hunting equivalent to individual farms. It is not surprising that Kerkhoff's 1933 description of the Fort St. John band concludes, "At a meeting with the band they laid the complaint about their trapping lines. That all their old hunting grounds were taken up by White men."

The clash between Indian and white trappers embodied a clash of economic interests; and condemnation of Indians by Whites had all the vigour that rivalry over valuable resources engenders. The government's protection, even direct encouragement, of white trappers resulted in bitter disputes. Between 1925 and 1933 there were many reports of intrusions, conflicts, and difficulties with Indians whose way of life just did not fit in with the arrangement of land to serve the interests of white trappers. Officials most sympathetic to Indian people detailed their difficulties while trying to secure lines for Indians who wished to be trappers. Less sympathetic officials merely detailed difficulties. In 1925 the RCMP constable in charge of the Fort St. John detachment, C. G. Barber, reported on a dispute in which Indians had complained that some of their dogs had been poisoned by a white trapper, who in turn said Indians had been trespassing on his trapline. Both the substance and idiom of his report give a vivid impression of how Whites saw such conflicts:

> . . . there are numerous instances where I have issued licences for a certain district and then white man got established, in comes a bunch of Indians and start to trap right beside him, only yesterday, Nov. 19th a trapper complained that he had got his line cut and cabins built, a bunch of Indians come along and start preparations to trap on the same line, now I know positively that . . . an Indian has not trapped that territory for the past five years.

Also in 1925, Constable Barber discussed a case against Chief Joseph Apsassin:

> Mr. Laird's [the Indian Agent] hard feeling towards the Police Department was caused by the conviction on March 17th 1925 of Joseph Apsassin (Indian) for killing five moose, same being in excess of requirements for himself and family, for this Laird gave me a great calling down before the Indians on Treaty day July 23rd 1924, I gave Mr Laird to understand, that I would

prosecute an Indian everytime an occasion warranted.

There is bitter controversy all through this district between the Indian and white trapper, the Indians claiming the white man is encroaching too much on their hunting grounds. I do think they have cause for complaint, but it is quite a problem to overcome.

Between 1925 and 1935 the government's attempts to limit and control the Indians led to much tension. Some Indian agents, especially Harper Reed, who struggled for years on behalf of the Tahltan of the Telegraph Creek area, insisted again and again on the Indians' need for rights to an extensive undivided area of land. These agents also reiterated, albeit to hostile and deaf superiors, their first-hand experience and genuine understanding of how the Indians protect and conserve the land and its animals.

The government's Game Department in the 1930s worked hard to limit Indian hunting, while the Department of Indian Affairs at times tried to make sure the Indians were left with at least a minimum of land. Game Department officials welcomed white trappers: they were easy to control and contributed dollars, through purchase of trapping and firearms licences, to a cash-poor bureaucracy. Indian Affairs officials wanted to be sure that some traplines went to Indians; otherwise they feared that the problem of Indian poverty (as they saw it) was likely to worsen. This difference in points of view about land use led to various exchanges between the two departments. In one of them, between Indian Agent H. A. Brown and Game Department Inspector T. Van Dyk, there arose the matter of a trapline that was being sold to a White who was not thought to be a decent and law-abiding citizen. Indeed, both the Game Department and the Department of Indian Affairs regarded him as a dangerous man who would encourage Indian opposition to the government. As so often happens, white officials were quick to see evidence of outside interference, and they readily imagined that agitators were urging the Indians to continue their profligate hunting and to disregard the new law and order. Any failure on the part of Indians to follow the new rules was promptly seen as a result of alien interference. After all, the new laws and regulations were so eminently sensible, so wise, that no reasonable person would thinkingly choose to disregard them.

In November of 1934, Brown wrote to Van Dyk that he had "mentioned to Ottawa the necessity of trying to undo a deal which was completed not long ago in which Wm Fraser's line was sold to a Communist (Red) by the name of Tucker who is or rather exercises a sinister influence amongst one band of Indians to the north of here. . . ." Unfortunately, Van Dyk went on to say, the deal could not be prevented. "Of course, in confidence, both Tucker and Fraser are being watched very closely and just as soon as the slightest break is made they will be apprehended."

In this particular exchange of letters, Van Dyk raised the most enduring of White objections to the way the Indians used their land. In a reply to Brown, written at the very end of 1934, he tried to use the "red" menace to calm a more dangerous storm:

> In the matter of the Indians killing wholesale game, it has been my experience that the Indians are amenable to reason, and, if shown that it is detrimental to their interest to kill more than what they can actually take care of, the wholesale slaughter is discontinued. It may require a few years to educate your Indians, but if a continuous campaigning of education is resorted to, I am positive that good results will be obtained. There is always the odd individual, especially if you have red agitators in the country, who will disregard all laws, regulations, and advice, but, we will have to deal with such cases as they are brought to our attention, and make an example.

Repeatedly in the correspondence and reports of the day, the Indians' hunting is said to be wasteful and destructive. These accusations contributed to the belief that registration of traplines would only improve conditions for everyone. This improvement, however, seemed to be argued in disregard for the terms of Treaty 8 — at least as the Indians understood them — which some of the bands had signed, it is to be recalled, only a decade before trapline registration began. The Treaty had granted them the right to hunt, to trap, and to fish throughout Crown lands, according to their traditional system. How startling it is, then, that one official reported the country to be "over-run by Indians," and G. M. Kerkhoff wrote,

> All those Indians are of a very ignorant type and have not the slightest idea, what it means to register a trapline; they have no knowledge of maps and are satisfied as long as they have visited the office; that no doubt is the reason why the traplines of any Indians are just little scratches on the map. . . .
>
> A great improvement would be to place the Indians between some rivers and to make them understand that they were not to trap or hunt outside of these areas; this would also mean during hunting time, for an Indian with his pack of dogs going over or hunting on an area does not leave much for the white trapper in the trapping season.
>
> If no such measures are taken, for the protection of the white trapper and for the preservation of Game, it will be necessary to bring in all the Indians and their Bands, who are found hunting or trapping on any other area but their trapline.

The attack on Indian people was firmly under way. Whatever self-righteous and well-meaning protestations have been made to the contrary, the attempt to extend the registration of traplines to Indian people constituted a violation of Indian rights; its explanation to Indians amounted to an outright lie. To try to confine Indians to their own registered traplines and, by the same token, to consider their use of other traplines as a trespass is to disregard the one unlimited right that the Treaty does guarantee. Whether or not and to what extent white officials admitted this to themselves is not always clear. In justifying their actions to the public, however, they followed two lines of argument.

Both justifications for the registration of Indian trapping areas started from, or accompanied, an insistence that harsh realities could not be avoided. White trappers, along with white farmers and other settlers, were moving into the country. Their social and economic order depended upon private ownership of land and resources, cash flows, and production for cash. White officials like Kerkhoff saw as their primary duty the protection of these new settlers and their economic base; in fact, the protection of their own culture and economy. Indians who could not be settled, who had unlimited rights to use Crown land, whose movements could not be predicted, who might turn up anywhere, any time, doing anything, were an obvious threat. Registration gave to the white trappers a legal right of ownership and thus security within the white economic system. And it nailed Indian trappers down to particular places nearly as well as Kerkhoff's desire to "place the Indians between some rivers" would have done.

Paradoxically, those who were sympathetic to the Indians began with the same fact, the white invasion of Indian lands, and ended with the same solution to the problem, registration of traplines. Their arguments, however, followed a different path. They had observed that in the face of white encroachment, the Indians — poor and ignorant, as they thought — retreated. White officials took this as proof that without help — their help in fact — the Indian system would not be able to compete. The Indians, to avoid losing their resource base entirely and sinking into even worse poverty, would have to fight the Whites on their own terms. They would have to establish their own rights to land; in short, they would have to register traplines. So Indians were urged, even by those they trusted most, and for their own well-being, to participate in trapline registration. Otherwise, they were told, all the good land would fall into the hands of Whites. In addition to this persuasive and seemingly beneficent urging, Indians were encouraged to believe that the guarantees promised in Treaty 8 would be secured by a registered trapline. In truth, registration amounted to a severe limitation on Indian land use, and was a limitation that had no legal basis whatever.

The marvellous intricacy of the deception practised by these officials is revealed in a report filed in 1932 by C. C. Perry, who at the time was Assistant Indian Commissioner for British Columbia. Perry addressed the trapline problem and its resolution. He argued that thanks to a recent conference at Prince George, all problems were resolved and there could no longer be any basis for Indian complaints against the machinery for establishing registered traplines. It was necessary, he said, to press for the establishment of extensive trapping and hunting territories — a tacit recognition of the fact that the Indians were being misled into the belief that traplines were hunting territories. Perry went on to say that because all conflicts had now been resolved, there was no need to give the Indians any more hunting lands "until such time as the settlement of that country makes it necessary for the Indians, who have no estate right in their traplines, to move on." Here Perry revealed that senior members of the bureaucracy did not for a moment suppose that Indians were acquiring, still less maintaining, entrenched rights to part of the land. These officials took the position that the Indians would, sooner or later, move on, wherever and whenever the settlement frontier advanced — for nothing, certainly not a few registered traplines, was going to hold back the frontier.

In fact, the confining and destroying forces of the colonial frontier advanced without too much opposition; that the Indians could and did "move on" is a testament to their adaptability and flexibility. They could avoid the White presence, to the extent that it was destructive, by moving deeper into the woods and hills, beyond the intruders' reach. When hunters wanted to trade with, or get help from, or simply visit the Whites, they could travel to the trading posts and settlements. Thus did the aboriginal peoples of northern Canada facilitate and accommodate frontier settlement.

There were occasional confrontations and, gradually, these merged into a local tradition of Indian resistance and discord. But when one remembers that this history was spread over more than a century, and was in essence the gradual expropriation by Whites of Indian territory, including centres of Indian economic life, then this history is far more remarkable for its peacefulness and quiescence than for conflict and violence.

With the reserve system, the limitation or obfuscation of hunters' rights, the registration of traplines, and any and every form of administration of Indian life by government agencies, the Indians were progressively restricted to the edges, and even to pockets at the edges, of the territory that had always been theirs. In a general and insidious manner, the frontier took advantage of the Indians' ability to move on. After all, there was no single place for which the Indians would make a stand and, with the spread of white trappers into the country, even the Indians' usefulness as suppliers of pelts was superceded. The Indians could and would move on — until there was nowhere else for them to move on to.

Trapline registration may seem remote from present-day problems. Not so, however. It is impossible to make sense of the issues that now preoccupy the Indians unless their progressive loss of land and gradual confinement are well understood. The effects of new frontiers, in particular of the energy frontier, must be seen against the background of Indian withdrawal. People are not passive or static in the face of intrusions onto their lands. Moreover, their reactions are much influenced by how far they are from their economic and cultural limits. Many different tensions and strains are created between the Indians' cultural and psychological preparedness to accommodate, adapt to, and withdraw before the frontier and the impossibility of continuing to withdraw and still retain enough land to serve as an economic base.

One of these tensions is paradoxical. It is a paradox that arises in many colonial contexts, and is a political difficulty that many anti-colonialist movements face. In a colonial situation, the colonized may find that any challenge or resistance to the new order is acutely difficult. In a culture where the wisest and most competent members regard outspokenness and adamance as foolhardy, childish, and profoundly self-defeating, how can a way of life protect itself, when its protection requires outspoken and adamant protest? Can peace be won by warfare? Can Athapaskan Indians defend a social and economic system based on flexibility, accommodation, and avoidance of conflict by making an absolute demand for a definite territory? Can persons who have become dependent upon intruders, while keeping their real selves hidden from prying and moralistic eyes, come out into the open and demand that the invasion go no further? The answers to such questions are anything but simple. The people must make demands. Yet they must not. There must be some middle ground.

So long as the people of northeast British Columbia continued to slip away from confrontation into the sanctuaries of their own domains, into themselves and the privacy of their own lives, the Indian system remained strong. But this, their own form of resistance to restriction and dispossession, can continue only so long as there are places, domains, and selves that are large and secure, and into which they can still retreat. Many older men and women of the reserves in northeast British Columbia now feel themselves to be surrounded and encroached upon in ways they have never before known. They are pressed up against the mountains to the west; there are new limitations within their society; failures among the young . . . The younger generations say much the same. Every Indian knows that countless accommodations have been made; most of them feel that there is no space and no time to withdraw any further.

All this is made plain by the way Indians now talk about their traplines — the present distribution of the Indians' registered trapping areas is shown on Map 5. When respect is not shown for the trapline, when other uses of trapping areas proceed without any consultation, without the least regard for Indian interest in the land, there is widespread confusion and dismay.

"How can they be doing that on my line? That is my land, those are my animals!"

"The white men came and stole my trapline. They stole my animals from my line."

"They come in and log on my trapline, taking my timber."

"All this country is Indian land. It has belonged to my family a long time. I registered this line in 1935."

Even if a family is not using it, their trapline's existence through fallow years is a source of real security: it is important because it is there. Registered traplines are far more than areas in which an Indian can make money from furs; they are a stake in the land and its future. Moreover, the traplines taken together constitute a land base away from the reserve and, for nearly all reserves, traplines represent a large proportion of a hunting territory. Later chapters will refer to Indian acceptance of ranchers, loggers, roads, pipelines, oil and gas rigs, and other developments. Such acceptance has been facilitated by the Indians' belief that whatever happened, whoever came into the country, they would always have their traplines. Indignation over intrusion upon and damage to a trapline, whether or not it has been trapped lately, is therefore not at all surprising. Trapping is only a specific use of that land. For some individuals the fight in defence of a trapline is a fight for the possibility of making money from furs. For everyone, active trapper or not, it has become a struggle for the right to be an Indian. By twists of history and confusion over realities, the trapline has come to mean to the Indians something tantamount to the terms of the Treaty. Although they continue to insist upon and to exercise their right to hunt on Crown land wherever they can, it is registered traplines that they hold to be especially and irreversibly theirs. For a long time, the government had led them to believe this. The Indians are perplexed and angry now that, once again, the truth appears to be changing.

The registered traplines represent land that remains to Indian people; the land to which, in spite of previous and great losses, they feel they have clear title. Here, in a circle drawn on a map in some white game official's office, and in circles that are drawn on maps in the people's own minds, there still is room for the Beaver, Cree, or Slavey way of life. For them it is the bitterest of ironies, therefore, to be told that in Canadian law, registered traplines grant no hunting rights and no protection against other activities that would destroy the wildlife on them. Only if the term "trapline" is fortified by the meanings that the Indians give the word can the importance of their traplines be grasped. The Indians' dismay and fury when new intrusions threaten their traplines are a measure of the importance they attach to them.

In November 1979, at a public meeting in his reserve, Chief Yahey

5

TRAPLINES REGISTERED TO INDIANS, 1979

The traplines shown here include only those registered to Indians living on reserves in northeast British Columbia. A small number of Albertan and Yukon Indians have lines within the region. These are not included. Virtually the entire area not marked is taken up by lines registered to white trappers.

Source: Department of Fish and Wildlife, Government of British Columbia.

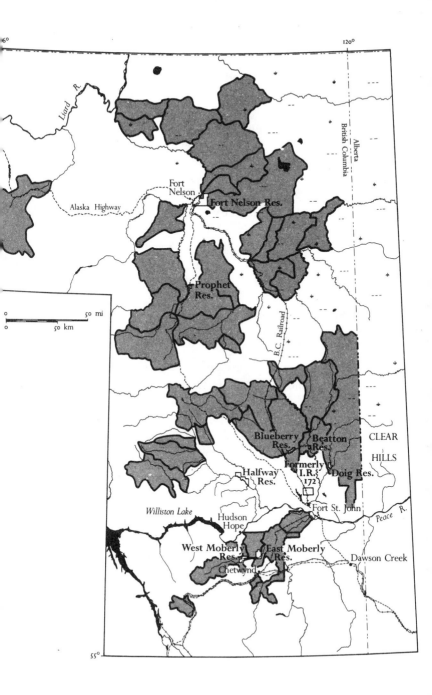

of the Blueberry Reserve expressed his people's feelings about their traplines.

> The first time they sign Treaty 8, I guess the Government tell the Indians no white man will go to your trapline and no one is going to touch it for years, for another hundred years and now they turn around and they go and put the pipeline right through the Indians' trapline and most of it will go right through the Indians' trapline, because they promised not to let the white man go hunt on their trapline or they said it's all yours. That's why they have signed the Treaty 8 and that's only eighty years ago they signed there, and they turn around again and they just pick on Indians' land and it doesn't matter what they say.

And Chief Metecheah of the Halfway Reserve expressed, in a personal way, the depth of her concern:

> I just want to speak about that I got oldest son. He is only ten year old and he got twenty-two squirrels and one beaver and he really was enjoying the trapping and we showed him how to set a trap, how to set a snare. Now he really was happy, I don't know why they were talking about build a pipeline through. If they build a pipeline through some of the people will lose their trapline.

These chiefs' words are a cry of protest against the persistent and ruthless disregard of the Indians' right to maintain the economic life guaranteed in Treaty 8 and then seemingly confirmed by registration of traplines. The people's preparedness to believe in the negotiators' or officials' good intentions appears to have led the Indians into a trap.

7

Return from Bluestone

Moose rut in the autumn. You can hear the bulls: their bellowing is a hoarse and frantic gurgle. It is the one time of year that they can be dangerous. They lower their heavily antlered heads to the ground and charge any creature large enough to appear to be a sexual rival. These charges are wild and blind: once a rival is located, the bull moose rushes unseeing towards it. Some hunters take advantage of this blind haste by imitating a bull's call, luring a maddened animal to attack. A funnel of bark or cardboard or a loosely clenched fist can be used as a resonator. Joseph Patsah, however, has always used the cleaned scapula of a moose or deer. He scrapes its hard, smooth edge against the rough bark of a small pine to produce, with startling exactness, the bellow of a bull moose in rut. The real bull, angered by the sound of a rival, may charge in its direction — to be met at very close range by a carefully timed shot in the head or neck.

Joseph says he has often used this technique to good effect, but it did not work for him or any of the other men last year. Atsin tried calling through his fists, but the sound went unheeded by the bulls whose bellows earlier in the day had echoed back and forth through the woods. In fact, the rut was nearly over by the time Joseph and his family camped at Bluestone Creek, where they hoped to prepare a supply of dry meat for the coming winter. By this time — late October — after weeks of sexual battle, bulls are exhausted and skinny — and they stink. They are not enthusiastically hunted. The hunters now concentrate their hopes on cows, which are fat from the good browsing of late summer and, with their last year's calves, are skulking among willow or poplar thickets to keep away from the excessive and violent attentions of the bulls.

In late October or early November, autumn gives way to winter. The camp at Bluestone was the last before the people moved either to their homes on the Reserve or to trapping cabins. It was at this camp that everyone felt the first bite, startling and invigorating, of the coming winter. The air has teeth and the ground a strange firmness. Each morning the ice has spread farther and thicker over the creeks. There is a new silence, yet the earth, or its covering of crusted leaves and frost-spiked grasses, crackles under every footstep. The noise can be a disadvantage: moose might well hear a hunter's approach. But the hunter can easily see and understand tracks and droppings, dark and clear against the frost.

Despite the cold, Atsin and the younger men set up an open camp. They stretched a tarpaulin over two long poles that sloped from a high ridge pole at the front to a low ridge pole at the back. A second tarpaulin was then stretched over poles leaning in the opposite direction. The result was two open-sided tents — only roofs, really, which were held in place and at a slope by pegs and thongs along each side. If there are more than two or three hunters at one campsite, open camps are made in pairs so that everyone can sit and sleep near a central fire. Our camp at Bluestone was like that: a fire beneath the central poles burned between two symmetrical open camps. The fire was large; logs were over five feet long and threw up a wall of flames between the two shelters. The sides, open to prevailing winds, were covered with spruce boughs, pieces of canvas, scraps of plastic — anything at hand. Overlapping spruce boughs covered the ground; blankets and sleeping bags were laid on top of them. The men slept parallel to the fire, two on one side, three on the other; Atsin and Thomas Fellow were nearest, the younger men farthest away.

Beside our double open camp, Joseph pitched a tent in which he and Liza and their son Tommy slept, though they shared the warmth and use of the large fire between the open shelters. Brian Akattah pitched a tent about fifteen yards away, where he, his wife Mary, and son Peter slept and ate near their own fire.

On the first morning of the hunt, the men woke long before dawn. They quickly relit the fires, brewed tea, and we ate an enormous breakfast. Soon after first light, when Liza, Mary, Tommy, and Peter were only just stirring, we set out. In calm weather the coldest hour of the day is just after dawn, and for a while everyone walked fast and energetically, until we had warmed up. It was then possible to enjoy the intense well-being that sweeps through you as you begin to feel warm, then hot, in very cold weather. Within an hour, the sun was bright, and frost gleamed on the grasses and low bushes of the hillsides. The hunters had high hopes of making a kill.

We walked far into the hills, following tracks that were many and fresh, that twisted and turned where the moose had browsed among the willows. Small heaps of round faeces here and there testified to the animals' presence. Sometimes the hunters felt them: a slight warmth shows that the moose have been there no more than an hour before; a glaze of frost means that a longer time has elapsed. All the droppings were hard and cold. The hunt was likely to be a long one.

Near the top of the first slope, willow thickets merged into a more densely forested area. At this point the four men who had left camp together split up, each taking his own direction. The moose we had been following had evidently moved soon after dawn from the open hillside, where willow browse was plentiful, to the cover of the forest.

Here they might continue to feed, or lie down to rest in hiding through the middle part of the day. It was going to be difficult to find them; the hunters were disappointed. Still, each selected a direction he thought was hopeful, and everyone fanned out, quickly to disappear among the trees. I followed Brian, who chose a steep climb high into a stand of large firs and then followed the hillsides several miles to the west. We saw old tracks, but no sign of any moose that Brian thought would be worth tracking. At about midday we and the others converged — as usual, and by mysterious means, within minutes of one another — and we all returned to camp. The morning's hunt had lasted a little over five hours, but no one had even had a chance of making a kill.

After some lunch and a rest sprawled beside the fire, Joseph declared that it was a good afternoon to have a look at the cross. No, it was not far, hardly more than a quick walk. This reassurance was welcome, for the morning's walk through thickets, up steep slopes, and in dense woodland had been tiring. So we set out again, first across the ice-rimmed Bluestone Creek, and then along a trail that headed roughly north, parallel to the hills. The group included two of Joseph's nephews, Dan Fellow and David Crown, Joseph's nine-year-old son Tommy, and eleven-year-old Peter.

"Hardly more than a quick walk" turned out to be a round trip of fourteen miles that took four hours. The pace never altered. There is a short-stepped rhythm to Beaver walking that is fast but unhurried, and remorselessly unvaried. Sometimes Tommy had trouble keeping up with us. When he fell behind, he would run to catch up, and for spells he would jog-trot alongside David or Peter.

For the first half mile or so the trail followed a valley bottom and passed across the edge of a rancher's fields. Then it entered woodland and roamed along the side of a high bank, from which we could glimpse a succession of beaver dams. It was to this area, said Dan Fellow, that Joseph liked to come in spring. A mile or two beyond the dams David spotted a group of ruffed grouse perched in a high bush a short distance from our trail. He, Dan, and Peter delayed to take some shots at them — grouse are singularly unwary of hunters or even of the noise of rifle fire. As he scrambled through the dense undergrowth around the bush, David noticed another, larger group of grouse. We all hunted them for a while, but eventually cached only four birds in the grass. We would collect them on our way back to camp. A mile beyond the grouse David then spotted a rabbit, and we made a short but difficult detour in the hope of coming across more. One was killed, and it too was cached beside the trail. Except for these few shots at grouse and rabbits, we took no time to hunt. This walk was to see the cross. The walk seemed to be something of a pilgrimage, a journey made necessary by Joseph's concern that our mapping be properly understood. We should see with our own eyes the emblem, or even the magic, that he had so often talked about. The importance of the cross permeated everything that he and others had been trying to explain about their feeling for and use of this land.

Yet when we finally arrived, Dan almost immediately turned around and began to head back to camp. It was enough, he indicated, just to see the cross. Nothing actually to look at, ponder over, or make any fuss about. If Peter and Tommy had not wanted to rest awhile, we should not have had even the five minutes we did spend looking at the cross itself.

In fact, the cross had rotted at its base and fallen back to lean, precarious and dilapidated, into the pines that surrounded it. The clothing and bundles its arms had supported were long gone. The panel near its base, once ornamented with "all kinds of fancy," the dream inscriptions of animals that the people would hunt, had fallen. Split in two pieces, it lay beside the cross's broken stump. The panel was pitted and decayed, the colour of its peeled wood now hardly different from so many other deadfalls. It would be quite easy to pass the cross, unnoticing, so nearly did it merge with the woodland around.

Once noticed, however, its presence could be felt. Was it because so much had been explained, and so much, therefore, anticipated? Or because in a landscape so devoid of monuments or cultural structures of any permanence, the cross had a special and remarkable significance? Though it inspired feelings of awe in me, they were subtly undermined by a dispiriting poignancy. I knew that a logging road was scheduled to be pushed along Bluestone Creek towards Quarry River. It would probably follow the trail that led us from the camp to the cross. The cross itself, so inconspicuous, blending into the trees from which the Indians had built it, would all too easily be bulldozed into the ragged brush piles that lie alongside new roads on the frontier.

For a few minutes we sat there, resting, and staring. No one said much. Perhaps we all felt emanations from that dilapidated symbol, or shared in some faint way the memories of it that are so central to Joseph's view of life. No doubt the others had heard him speak many times of the cross and of the dream prophesies that surround its construction. No doubt they also felt the new winter cold that stings the cheeks and thought it was time to hurry back to camp. Just as we were leaving, though, David remarked, "Sometime we better put up a new cross. That one's getting pretty old now."

By the time we returned it was dusk. Wood for the night had to be cut and hauled. The next day the men would try again for a moose. Should they fail, said Joseph, we might as well return to the Reserve. It was getting too cold. There was little talk of the cross. Joseph, Atsin, and the others all appeared to be satisfied that we had seen it. A monument in the minds of the people. But its very lack of grandeur and limited physical life signify, in ways that Joseph and Atsin would never feel needed to be stated, both the vitality of the hunter's mind and the irrelevance to it of grandiose material encumbrances. To share in this understanding is to share in the real presence of the people on the land.

The next day was colder still. Grey clouds were thick in the northwest sky. As the men set out on the hunt, Joseph said he would be ready to leave for the Reserve as soon as the hunters were back. The weather was changing; they should be prepared for a snowstorm. While the men were away, Joseph broke camp. He piled tarpaulins, gear, everything in readiness for the move. But late in the day Sam Crown returned with the news that he had killed a large cow moose high in the hills. He had only had time to do the butchering. We would have to stay another night. In the morning everyone would move to a trail below the kill and help pack out the meat. Camp was remade, more wood cut.

Joseph, Liza, Mary, and the children went to sleep early, but the younger men, delighted by success, sat by the fire for a long time, talking and laughing. Late into the night we were all conscious of the coldness of the wind. Bit by bit the men began to protect the campsite against the weather. They cut new spruce boughs and piled them on the branches already set along the sides of the sloping tarpaulins. By the time we were ready to sleep the camp seemed to have sunk into the ground and become a part of the woods.

It was only 3 A.M. when Brian Akattah came from his tent and woke everyone up. He lit the fire and urged the others to get up. It was snowing. The camp was already covered. The woods were heavy with an inch of soft snow. In fresh snow, then, and with much tripping over hidden stumps and logs, we broke camp and moved to the kill. Joseph said that we should not set up a new camp but make do with a fire in the shelter of trees beside the trail leading up to the kill. He and Liza gathered wood, lit a fire, and brewed tea while the rest of us followed Sam to the dead moose.

The butchered carcass had to be hauled, sled-like, down the hillside. Brian roped two quarters into the hide and, single-handed, dragged this huge slithering bag over deadfalls and between tree trunks the whole distance from kill to fire. It was hard enough to pack a single quarter, and at the end of a second load everyone was hot and exhausted. By the time all the meat had been hauled and packed and everyone was ready to set off for home, it was late afternoon. Along the dirt road the snow was driving towards us in hard, dry clouds, reducing the world to a small bowl of whiteness. Four months of winter had begun.

Back at the Reserve, the next weeks were not easy. At the onset of winter, while Joseph and his family had been camped at Bluestone, the men who had been working in the mountains as guides to trophy hunters were returning to their families. They came with a lot of money. After their hard work and isolation, it was party time. Early winter is the holiday season for many Indians of northeast British Columbia. Holidays mean parties and parties mean heavy drinking.

Everyone gets caught up in the festivity, and in a series of community-wide sprees. When Indians of northeast British Columbia are drinking, they do so with an abandon that may astonish and frighten a stranger. This is not the drinking of the real alcoholic, for it is almost never solitary. Their drinking is a group, family, and community affair — and it stops as suddenly and completely as it begins. After a week of partying comes a sickening and community-wide hangover. But after a day of sleep and some food, the spree is over. The drinkers now stay sober longer than they have been drunk, but with no determined resolution, no personal struggle against the demons of compulsion and habit. This kind of drinking is not alcoholism as larger, urban, and psychologically very different societies usually understand the term.

Not surprisingly, when Atsin, Sam, Brian, or any of the other Reserve people drink, they change. They change in every aspect of their behaviour, in their facial expressions, in everything that they say. The changes are far more drastic than those in white drinkers. Possibly this is something that has to be seen to be believed. These Indian men and women when sober are reserved and shy. Many of them are superb exponents of the skills upon which their culture depends: quick and graceful on foot, poised and comfortable on a horse, cautious and accurate in all their physical movements. They are people whose daily lives require excellent co-ordination of eye and hand. They make judgements only after quiet deliberation. The drunken loss of all these achievements, displaced by the wildness and chaos of uninhibited spree drinking, is both dismaying and terrifying. Suddenly there is deep trouble, often rage. There is wreckage. Perhaps it is accumulated bitterness, the ghosts of generations of Indians frustrated by the apparently inescapable advance of the white man's frontiers who lurch, and stagger, inchoate and seemingly imponderable, into the present.

Soon after our return from Bluestone, the memory of the first harsh mornings of winter still fresh in our minds, we were regaled with accounts of recent chaos. Gossip was made up of a casualty list which grew during the following weeks. Taxis came and went between the Reserve and the closest sources of liquor — the scrappy cluster of trailers, gas stations, and the single bar that constitute a service and stopping place thirty miles away on the Alaska Highway. A bootlegger timed his visits to the Reserve to coincide with the return home of guides or other workers with pay in their pockets, making his way from house to house selling cheap rye whiskey at grotesquely inflated prices to anyone drunk enough to be impervious to the profit margin but sober enough to hand over money. The bootlegger even sold drink to children who had picked up enough dollar bills to buy it.

There were accidents and crises. Brian fell against a stove and severely burned his back and side. After two days of great pain, he was rushed to the Fort St. John hospital. A man, badly hurt in a fight, had to take a taxi for emergency treatment in the same hospital. A teen-age boy, in drunken confusion, slashed a woman across the face with the edge of a pan. Taxis were called; more liquor was bought; the bootlegger drove back and forth in his pickup. Some young men sold their saddles, horses, and whatever else they could find to keep the party going. House after house ran out of food and firewood.

It was not all a horror show, of course. Many parties were joyous. Self-destruction and chaos were not the only outcome. But those who did not drink, who sat at home at the side of the spree's clamour, could only anticipate more accidents, another crisis. So it was at Joseph's house. He does not drink and has not for several years. He likes to tell people, with a firmness that in Beaver society comes as close as a wise man will get to proselytizing, "I quit everything. Beer, tobacco, whiskey, wine — everything! Too much. Now quit." (And sometimes, perhaps to make a joke and surely avoid sounding moralistic, he includes in his list of abstentions, with a wry grin and the same form of words, "I quit women. Too much, too many.") So his house is an escape from troubles elsewhere in the community. There one can sit and avoid the worst.

The spree lasted a little under three weeks, then stopped. After a few days it revived. Then stopped again. By Christmas time the money was spent. One afternoon, only a few days after the partying seemed to have abated, though not for certain, Joseph's nearest neighbour sent him a message. Alan Itsak, a middle-aged man and the head of a household, was desperately ill. A throng of people crowded the doorway and main room of Alan's house. In a small bedroom Alan lay on an iron-frame bed, partly covered by an old blanket. Sodden with sweat, his hair drenched, he was groaning softly. His expression described intolerable pain. The pain came in spasms. Cramps in his legs and arms forced him to gasp rather than breathe. At times, his spasms were so acute that he doubled up, flailed wildly, shrieked, and gasped out his breath in long, frightening moans that were more like the hooting of a night bird than any human sound. He clutched at an arm, at a leg, at his stomach. He turned over and back again. He begged to have his hands held. When the worst of each spasm had passed, he lay back exhausted. Most of the time his wife sat on the bed, near the wall, holding his right hand. Neighbours and relatives hesitated at the door or lingered just inside the tiny room, watching and waiting.

No one seemed to know what to do. One of Alan's brothers sat closest to him, touching his head from time to time, and feeling — trying to soothe — the muscles of Alan's arms and legs, which were like taut ropes. Periodically he had to pull the blanket back over his brother. Alan's wife thought he should be taken to the hospital. Someone, she said, should phone Derek who lives on the Highway and drives an ambulance. (Earlier in the day Alan had refused to travel in a taxi.) I was sent off to use the nearest working telephone, a drive ten miles down the road to a schoolteacher's house. The radio telephone on the Reserve was out of order.

I came back from telephoning with the news that Derek would drive his ambulance over as soon as he could. Alan's suffering continued. The people in the house had become more and more fearful for him. Robert Fellow asked for a cup of cold water, with which he then moistened Alan's shins and lower arms, concluding as

he did so that the trouble lay in Alan's heart. After an hour or more
the ambulance at last arrived. With great difficulty and movements
that caused Alan to shriek with pain, he was carried from his house
and driven to town. One of his young relatives accompanied him on
the ride to hospital.

At about this time, three teen-aged boys injured two older women
and a young man. Dismayed and indignant, some of the elders of the
Reserve asked the police to deal with the offenders. If the boys did
not respect their elders, there was no way of exercising control: in the
old days, before everyone was settled on reserves, people would have
moved away from troublemakers. Hopes were now expressed that
the boys would be taken away to prison or maybe to a reform school.
Every day they were the subject of discussion and the centrepiece of
virulent criticism.

When the police came, a group of men was five miles from the
Reserve houses, butchering and packing a moose that Sam Crown
had killed the day before. Sam and Atsin had lit a fire as the
butchering was finished. Several hunters were brewing tea and
barbecuing fresh meat. Suddenly, one of the boys appeared on
horseback through the trees. He had followed the hunters' tracks to
the kill. He was, someone murmured, running away from the police.
However, when he joined the group no one made any such remarks
to him. He was treated as if he were just another hunter. Atsin urged
him to eat some meat. Robert handed him a cup and pointed to a
fresh kettle of tea. He helped load the pack horse for the trip back;
and during the return journey he rode in line with the others, talking
and being talked to easily and amicably. The group included the very
men who had been most outspokenly critical of him during the
previous days. Some of them had agreed that it would be an excellent
thing for the Reserve, and for the boys themselves, if he and his two
comrades were taken by the police, or soundly thrashed, or both. But
in the bush it appeared that he could be trusted, and was treated
accordingly.

Ideas about social control implicit in this episode were recognized
directly: some of the men decided that the three boys should be taken

out trapping, to Robert Fellow's cabin on Highland Creek. Once in the bush, they argued, the boys would be away from trouble and — far more important than the experience of isolation — they would be educated in ways that would serve everyone's interest. There, the boys would lack the opportunity and lose the inclination to cause trouble. Sure enough, three months later, at the end of winter — when everyone concluded that the police either could not or would not take any steps against the Reserve's young offenders — Robert took the three of them with him to the cabin, where they all hunted and trapped.

At the end of winter, Alan Itsak also left the Reserve. He had come back from hospital after a few days, and remained at home for a while. Then he went with his wife and children to work as a horse minder and general hand for one of the local outfitters. But he continued to drink, and his convulsive fits returned. In early spring he shot himself.

8

This New West

Treaties and traplines encircle the Indians with legal and territorial limits. At the same time, potential settlement and resources have become the subjects of a new northern mythology. Harsh as its climate may be, the North begins to be characterized as a place of limitless material possibilities. Gold for the panning, land for the clearing, vistas of infinite economic expansion — these were and are the prospects held out to northern adventurers. New visions of this kind represent a shift towards domestic or internal expansion. Mercantile colonialism gives way to a more comprehensive occupany of the North. But the white man's dreams and maps are the omens and portents of a future in which Indians are expected to play no part. The "North" conveniently moves north.

The Americans in Alaska, the Russians in Siberia, and the British and French in Canada have all pushed back the North and have proclaimed their new frontiers. The economic histories of these countries are dissimilar, but in each case the northern frontier has been established by an integration of activities. Each sector — from administrative development to pipeline construction — has its own needs and objectives, but a gradual coincidence of purpose turns their combined activities into a frontier. This fact is well illustrated by the economic history of Canada, where the North has shifted, finally, into the endlessly rotating pack ice of the polar seas. In northeast British Columbia, the old North became the new West.

The change in images, and the frontier process in western and northern Canada, follows the course taken by the fur trade, which in the early 1800s looked towards the Athabasca and Mackenzie rivers and to the Pacific coast for new and rich potential. Everyone interested in the early economic history of North America recognizes the importance of fur — an easily portable, highly valuable, renewable resource. Prime furs, such as marten, otter, and fox, could be sold for fabulous prices in Chinese and European markets. Other pelts were less valuable but more numerous: buffalo, beaver, muskrat, and squirrel. The fur trade held prospects of great profits. The Hudson's Bay Company struggled, at times violently, with its several rivals for supremacy in extension of the trade.

From their bases in the east, the fur traders followed North America's river systems westward and northward, eventually linking much of the continent with canoe routes that began at Hudson Bay or Montreal. The Peace River was a route along which the trade was pushed westward. By 1805, the North West Company — helped by Alexander Mackenzie's 1792 journey to the Pacific — had set up posts on both the Peace and Liard rivers, and in 1806 had established the first of a succession of posts at or near present-day Fort St. John. At this time the Hudson's Bay Company was also pursuing a policy of expansion which took them into the same northwestern territory. Head offices in London and Montreal waited breathlessly for news of struggles and gains from this high adventure in western Canada, and the two companies came close to destroying themselves before their prudent amalgamation in 1821. It was George Simpson, governor of the Northern Department of the Hudson's Bay Company after the amalgamation, whose 1824 and 1828 journeys through the region marked the establishment of new fur-trading posts on the upper reaches of the Peace. Simpson also sent traders to explore the tributaries of the Liard River, thus taking the trade through northeast British Columbia and into the Mackenzie River system, towards the High Arctic.

This trade along the Peace and Liard never produced the wealth that had been realized by the purchase of sea otter pelts along the coast. However, an important pattern was established as company factors in their tiny posts deep in the wilderness waited for instructions and supplies from their bosses far away in the east; while those very bosses looked towards that wilderness, which they began to term "this new west," for untold riches. The development of northern British Columbia followed the course well worn by other shifting last frontiers that the East had progressively dominated.

To this familiar form of development was added another. In 1871, British Columbia became a province of Canada. Because the headwaters of both the Peace and Liard rivers lay within its boundaries, the new provincial government seized upon this new west. Like individuals and corporations in the east, the government, based in the very southwestern corner of the country, dreamed of the region's incalculable resources, and added a vision of inexhaustible revenues. The interplay between provincial and other dreamers rapidly came to determine a century of northern British Columbian history. Increasingly this was a history that disregarded the presence of Indians. As one follows the accumulation of events and the grandeur of the dreams that underpinned them, it becomes harder and harder to imagine that Indians could find any room on the white man's crowded maps.

One of British Columbia's conditions for joining Canadian Confederation was the completion, within a decade, of a railroad from eastern Canada to the Pacific coast. Provincial developers, surveyors, and politicans campaigned energetically for the trans-Canadian railway route to cut across the northern part of the province, and for a time they duly dreamed of the region's rapid settlement — and of economic expansion that would be independent of the fur trade. Dreams of the northern route were not realized, but hopes for a new pace and scale to settlement of the northeast region were not entirely frustrated.

The Dominion government paid for railway construction. But it did so by grants and sales of land. The "railway belt," a strip of land up to twenty miles wide on either side of the track, served both as a communication and a settlement corridor. In British Columbia, the path of the railway ran from the heights of the Rocky Mountains to the Pacific coast through land that was too wild and mountainous to have much agricultural value. The government of British Columbia was persuaded that it should give the federal government lands that were of real value to compensate for the lack of good land along the actual route of the railway. The negotiations for this grant took fourteen years. Only in 1884, with the passing of the Settlement Act, did the Dominion receive the compensatory lands: 10.9 million acres on Vancouver Island and 3.5 million acres in the Peace River area. Some of this grant was in lieu of valuable railway lands; the balance (and perhaps the larger part) was for primary developments in British Columbia that the federal government claimed to have subsidized.

The 3.5 million acres in northern British Columbia became known as the Peace River Block. Valued in 1912 at $17.5 million, this was the best agricultural land in the whole region — though the actual cost of the railway construction for which it had been granted in compensation was less than $3 million. The first wave of agricultural settlement into this land occurred in the early 1900s, by which time the reports of fur traders, missionaries, and other travellers had spread the news that the land was rich and its climate favourable to agriculture.

A Special Committee of the Canadian Senate looked into the economic prospects for northeast British Columbia and, in 1907, reported that "there is in the Peace River section of this country as much good agricultural land fit for settlement and yet unsettled as there is settled in Manitoba, Saskatchewan and Alberta today. . . ." Rail speculators and other advertisers of the new frontier added their endorsements. A. M. Bezanson, a land prospector, distributed 5,000 copies of a pamphlet containing his encouragement:

> Great as has been the influx of settlers into all Western Canada in recent years, the supply of land within easy reach from the railroads has, to date, been equal to the demand; but the time is now at hand when the landseeker must leave the railroads behind in the push out into the more remote regions.

In 1911, the white population of the region was less than 2,000. Only ten years later, it had risen to 20,000. The attraction was cheap land, but this was made all the more appealing by postwar social and economic problems. For $10 a family could apply for a quarter section (160 acres) of land. Local officials had authority to dispose of rights to land, timber, and mineral resources on the spot. Rail links were being established between regional centres and new towns in northern Alberta, in central British Columbia, and eventually with Vancouver.

The area's agricultural potential was now of real interest to farmers whose clearing and ploughing of the newly available lands represented a continuation of their westward push. The experience of these farmers, combined with their preparedness to be innovative, made them good colonizers of new land. Local officials of the federal government encouraged their work by research, an experimental farm, and a succession of surveys.

Despite uncertainties and hesitations in population growth (brought about mainly by the disappointment of the region's grander dreams of rail links), prospects continued to be encouraging. Between 1923 and 1927, farmers of the Peace River region won prizes for their wheat, oats, and timothy. At the 1926 International Live Stock and Grain and Hay Show in Chicago, Peace River farmers ranked at the top. The area's potential was proven. Between 1926 and 1929, grain harvests ranged from good to bumper-sized. Such recognition and results spurred further settlement.

By 1931, the population of the town of Peace River alone had risen to 6,300, by 1945, to 7,600. The rate of increase had slowed down, largely because of a glut of wheat on the market in the early 1930s and because of the dampening effects of the Depression, although history of trapping shows that the Depression also had some reverse effects on areas that appealed to transient, land-hungry poor. At the outbreak of World War II, the population of Fort St. John and its hinterland had grown to about 2,000. By that date the whole region was interconnected by trails and small roads, and linked to the east and north by railways. This new west had been subdued. The Alaska Highway, built with all the urgency and haste inspired by fears of a new battlefront in the North Pacific, was completed in 1945. In British Columbia it passed through a region that had already witnessed the fur trade, the Cariboo and Klondike gold rushes, and comprehensive agricultural settlement. The Highway certainly facilitated the spread of white settlement from the Peace River region to the Liard basin, and thence to the Yukon. But Whites had been in the southern parts of the region for some fifty years before the Highway was built, brought there by land sales and frontierism underwritten by both the provincial and federal governments.

The changes I have been describing represent the advance of the agricultural frontier from southern Alberta into northern Alberta and northeastern British Columbia. There were surges of settlement into the region after World War I, during the Depression, after World War II, and then again in the 1960s, when the British Columbia Railway reached Dawson Creek and Fort St. John. Economists now consider the region's agricultural potential to have been very nearly reached. This is reflected in the decline in the rate at which land was cleared between 1971 and 1977, and by a decline, during the same years, in the population of the farming towns. The loss of population from these historic centres appears even more significant when it is compared with the rapid increase in population in the region as a whole and in Fort St. John in particular.

Another important trend in the agriculture of British Columbia's northeast frontier is in average farm size. In 1941, half of the region's farms were less than 300 acres; by 1976, over 65 per cent of them were more than 400 acres, and average size had quadrupled to about 1,120 acres. Farmers had been encouraged to enlarge their holdings, and capitalization had leapt from $4,000 in 1941 to $150,000 in 1976. Tenant farming had tripled during the same period, reaching 20 per cent of total farm acreage. As James Harper and Richard Overstall point out in their studies of white and industrial land use in northeastern British Columbia (and from whose work I have taken much valuable information), the day of the small homesteader, who made a living with family labour and a heavy reliance on production for subsistence, has given way to large-scale farming operations, much like agriculture in adjacent Alberta and the prairie provinces beyond.

Agriculture is still celebrated in northern British Columbia with the help of some of the old imagery and dreams. Cowboy clothes, rodeos, homespun and populist conservatism — these all express with an anachronistic quaintness the customs and values that flourish on a small farm frontier. Everyone continues to boast that agriculture has a great future. But small-scale farming, the extension of European peasant life into the North American frontier, is now a thing of the past, and survives mainly in a convenient mythology that seems to make the area distinctive and important. Ironically, the Peace River region is one of the few parts of British Columbia where Crown land is still available for agriculture: more than a million acres of it are not yet farmed, although most of this land is of marginal agricultural value. From time to time the provincial government gives impetus to the farming frontier by selling Crown land at public auction. Between 1965 and 1971, the province released 12,000 acres of Crown land in the Fort Nelson area in just this way, but only about 15 per cent is said to be of value. The reality is expressed in a simple statistic: in 1941, farmers constituted 69.8 per cent of the region's total population; by

1976, this proportion had shrunk to under 12 per cent. For all the rhetorical insistence that land for homes and farms is a first priority, farming is near its maximum extent and of rapidly declining economic importance. Stetsons and riding boots may be common in the bars and on the streets of Fort St. John, and the annual rodeos may be enjoyed with a feverish enthusiasm, but the challenges of today's frontier have little to do with the romanticized world of cowboys and ranches. That world is not irrelevant, but it has been overshadowed by the grim-looking clouds of nonrenewable resource development.

Distinctions between renewable and nonrenewable resources are more difficult to define than is sometimes supposed. Fish or tree populations, to take two examples, recuperate naturally, whereas coal and oil deposits do not. The latter represent resources that are exhaustible; are, in the jargon, nonrenewable. But does this imply that renewable resources are not exhaustible?

The lifetime of a resource is dependent upon its care and management. Greedy and destructive harvesting can quickly exhaust a fishery, and in extreme cases a fish population can be reduced below its capacity for renewal. A timber resource can easily be logged out where a marginal climate and poor soils retard growth, and if rates of harvest are not carefully adjusted to rates of reforestation. If these rates of regrowth and harvest are not reconciled, forestry becomes a form of mining. The interactions between the exploitation of more than one of a region's resources can also lead to failure of renewal. Logging around the headwaters of a salmon-spawning river can, for example, destroy the fish population's natural ability to regenerate. Such problems are likely to occur in areas that have extremes of climate or that permit an uncontrolled and poorly planned exploitation of resources. Northeast British Columbia has suffered from both.

It is with alarm, therefore, that observers of the region's forest industry have noted that, at present rates of cutting and clearing, all the accessible timber in the entire region — which is to say, the prime spruce stands — will have been harvested within 20 years.

Sub-Arctic spruce forest requires up to 150 years for regrowth to its previous level — if all measures are taken to ensure its recovery. But the forest products industry plans to harvest on an 80-year renewal basis, with inevitable shortfalls to be made up by harvesting secondary growth of poplar and pine. In any case, only 20 per cent of felled spruce forest returns to its original state; the balance becomes aspen and similar noncommercial bush. Timber in northeast British Columbia may thus be turned into a nonrenewable resource.

Forestry was, at first, an extension of agricultural settlement in the region. Smallholders, with the help of portable sawmills, used conifers they had felled in the course of clearing land to build their own houses and barns. They then sold the surplus to neighbouring farms and nearby villages. As early as the 1930s, timber from some of the larger spruce stands went beyond local markets to the United States, shipped from the terminus of the Northern Alberta Railway at Dawson Creek. However, forestry only became a major exporting industry with the extension of the Pacific Great Eastern Railway, now called British Columbia Railway, to Fort St. John in 1958 and to Fort Nelson in 1971. Sawmills followed the railway and made use of the Alaska Highway. Winter roads and ice bridges gave seasonal access to areas of prime timber.

Five companies came to dominate production in the southern part of the region. Two of them are located at Chetwynd, and there is one each in Taylor, Fort St. John, and Dawson Creek. Only the smallest of the five is locally owned; three of them have headquarters in the United States, and one is based in Vancouver. In the northern area, three more companies operate from Fort Nelson. Only one of them is locally owned. The forestry industry has outgrown its agricultural parentage, and has little to do with local needs. The major companies exert intense political pressure to have released for logging critical wildlife habitats, areas of unstable soils, sites with poor regeneration potential, and parks. The logic is alarming: the more capital invested in marginal areas, the greater the risk; the greater the risk, the greater the pressure for development upon areas that might, viewed dispassionately, be judged best suited for other purposes.

Deforestation is the most obvious consequence of logging, but it is not the worst of the industry's effects. Logging is followed by a chain of other developments. Pulp mills demand large amounts of energy. Indeed, the primary raw material needed to make pulp and paper may be said to be not wood fibre, but heat and motion. Northeast British Columbia has become a supplier of this energy of oil, natural gas, and hydroelectricity. The dramatic growth of British Columbia's pulp, mining, and smelting industries would not have been possible without the availability of these cheap supplies of energy.

In 1968, the Peace River canyon was dammed and Williston Lake created to provide energy for the development of the resources of interior British Columbia. The 1968 Bennett Dam (named after the British Columbian premier of the day, W. A. C. Bennett) provides 2,100 megawatts capacity — about 30 per cent of the provincial total. Site 1, a new generating system fourteen miles downstream from the Bennett Dam, near Hudson Hope, will provide an additional 700 megawatts. In accordance with its policy of developing completely the potential of one river before moving on to the next, the British Columbia Hydro-Power Authority has decided, if the necessary permissions can be obtained, to construct a 240-foot earth-filled dam yet further downstream on the Peace River at Site C, below the confluence with Moberly River, near Taylor and Fort St. John. This dam would flood the Peace River valley for fifty miles back to the dam at Site 1. The Site C reservoir would flood 18,260 acres of land, an area that includes 19 per cent of all Class I and Class II agricultural land in the Peace Valley. Further down the river, Site E, close to the Alberta border, has also already been marked on planning maps as a possible dam site.

The hydroelectric development of the Peace during the 1960s was made possible by new technology that permits high-voltage power to be economically transmitted over long distances. Recent technological advances will permit line voltages to be raised from the present 500 kV to 750 kV or even to 1,000 kV. The rivers in northernmost British Columbia are now within economic reach of B.C. Hydro's

electrical grid, and a series of dams on the Liard River, northwest of
Fort Nelson, is a real possibility.

Many critics of B.C. Hydro contend that these dams are being
built to export power. In December 1979, B.C. Hydro applied to the
National Energy Board for a licence to export to the United States
10,000 million kilowatt-hours of electricity per year, more than a
sixfold increase over the 1975-80 average annual export of 1,600
million kilowatt-hours. Only a few critics have noted that these
exports have been, and will continue to be, made possible only by the
massive flooding of Indian lands. Indeed, it is land — not power —
that is being sold cheap.

But Indian lands were viewed with an eye for their potential
sources of energy long before the Bennett Dam was planned. In 1792,
Alexander Mackenzie had noted that "Along the face of some of
these precipices [in the Peach River Canyon], there appears a
stratum of a bituminous substances which resembles coal. . . ."
Many later travellers have commented on the appearances of coal in
the region, and mining has been contemplated since about 1900.
Enthusiasm for the development of coal has grown in recent years.
Indeed, mining has repeatedly been proclaimed as imminent.
Throughout the 1970s a statement that next year would see the
beginning of the coal industry in northeast British Columbia was an
annual ritual. These statements were based on the knowledge that
there are some 7.7 billion tons of metallurgical coal embedded in
rock formations on the eastern flank of the Rockies.

Let us echo the ritual. At present, four mines are scheduled for
development. The provincial government has promised to contribute
more than $700 million to infrastructures for the mines, including a
new town site for an anticipated population of 10,000, extensive
construction and upgrading of highways, and a new rail connection to
facilitate the freighting of coal to a deep-water port at Prince Rupert.
Negotiations with potential long-term buyers in Asia have secured
the necessary markets and prices. By 1982-83, the region may see the
preliminary stages of large-scale coal-mining operations. In May

1981, the *Christian Science Monitor* headlined an article about this coal: "British Columbia Moves to Populate Its Nearly Empty Northeast" and continued, "For decades Canada has had a dream; a vision of its immense northern areas populated with thriving communities." Coal mining in the Peace River country is expected to make the breakthrough.

Ever hopeful as promoters of coal developments may be, the wildest dreams about that frontier are of oil and gas. For thirty years, northeast British Columbia has off and on been in the grip of drilling fever. The future of the region is now inseparable from the world's demand for energy, and all the attendant apprehensions and crisis. External dominance of the region's economy began with the fur trade; it culminated in an oil and gas frontier.

Northeast British Columbia was known to be a possible source of oil long before energy became a matter of global politics. Alexander Mackenzie concluded his account of his 1789 and 1793 journeys with a brief geographical overview of the immense territory he had explored, mentioning that coal and bitumen (as he called oil) occurred "at the commencement of the rocky mountains in 56 North latitude, and 120 West longitude" — that is, in present-day northeast British Columbia. Later travellers reported oil slicks that oozed from the ground. Just before World War I and up to 1916, Lord Rhondda, the British coal magnate, invested a quarter million dollars in prospecting for both coal and oil in the Peace River country. In 1915, he drilled for oil, but was unsuccessful. Nonetheless, Rhondda applied for a charter to build a railway from his imagined oil fields to a Pacific port. He got his charter, but he never built the railway.

It would be many years before these early hopes for an energy frontier in northern British Columbia were realized. The burgeoning of oil and gas activities far to the south, however, intensified the hopes. The early oil booms in Texas and Oklahoma reached towards, and then into, the Canadian west, feeding hopes of striking the northern hydrocarbon basin whose existence geologists had been predicting since the early 1900s. In 1923, a mining engineer reported that the area north of Hudson Hope was "even more favourable than it was previously known to be." By that time, Imperial Oil had spent half a million dollars on exploration in the Peace River area, and Albertan lands adjacent to northeast British Columbia had "proved up" a potential yield of 10.5 trillion cubic feet of natural gas. The presence of both oil and gas in the region was ever more firmly established through the 1920s and into the 1930s. But no producing well was drilled. Even at the peak of this northward spread, neither natural gas nor northeast British Columbia were of much importance. Gas had almost no value; if found it was flared off. And British Columbia was still beyond the margin of private enterprise activity. Later it was to become forbidden territory.

In November 1933, T. D. Pattullo became premier of British Columbia. A man with populist and liberal leanings, Pattullo did not like big oil companies. At the same time, the coal revenues on which British Columbia had long depended were declining at an alarming rate: demand for coal was being undercut by the growing use of oil. Pattullo's actions were based as much on his conviction that northern British Columbia was going to be a major supplier of oil in the future as on his populism (though the two ideas inflamed one another), and he was soon in collision with the oil interests. Pattullo's first term saw a major commission of inquiry into oil, gas, and coal, and a series of skirmishes with the major American companies. But he fought his 1937 re-election campaign on the strengths of his northern vision. As Margaret Ormsby put it in her rather sanguine history of British Columbia, he "now turned to the great northland whose treasures, he felt, were quite unexploited." Pattullo's victory of thirty-one to seventeen over all opposition parties reflected the way a combination of populism and hopes for northern development were integral to British Columbian life. But the government was soon fiercely at odds with the corporations that had their own plans for the North. This conflict took its course through injunctions, a Supreme Court ruling (in the premier's favour), and new legislation. In the end, the provincial government was the winner: in 1938 it established its own trading company and outlets and, most important of all, closed the northeast region of the province to private oil and gas companies.

From the point of view of corporate capitalism, the Peace River Aladdin's cave was shut.

This closure of the region could only add to fantasies about its riches. Pattullo himself nurtured belief in the oil dream, if only to give credence to his government. In November 1939, he told the B.C. Legislature: "I have not the slightest doubt that we will strike oil, and when we strike it our financial difficulties will be over."

The big companies, led by Imperial, Gulf, and Shell, tried to gain access but repeatedly failed; meanwhile, the government's own exploration and development programme continued in a very limited way. Pattullo announced a $200,000 exploration programme in the Peace River country. In 1942, a 6,900-foot well was drilled at the junction of Commotion Creek and Pine River, but yielded nothing. In an attempt to keep hopes high, the government insisted the oil was just another 2,000 feet away. On the world stage, the demand for oil was rising faster than ever before. The prewar economic revival, followed by wartime concern over secure supplies, followed in turn by the immediate postwar boom, meant that energy had unprecedented economic and political importance. In northeast British Columbia itself the construction of the Alaska Highway during the war opened up hundreds of thousands of square miles that had hitherto been accessible only along winter trails and rough wagon roads.

Yet the early dreams of oil bonanzas in the foothills of the Rockies still came to very little. Cheap supplies from either the southern United States or the Middle East made the northward progress of the energy frontier — ever farther from major markets and ever deeper into difficult terrain — hopelessly uneconomic. The existence of vast reserves was touted, yet in 1945 there was still no producing oil well in British Columbia. All this changed, however, in February 1947, when the oil field now known as Leduc Number 1 was discovered by Imperial Oil. This field, a little to the south of Edmonton, Alberta, was hailed as one of the most massive discoveries in the world. It ended three decades of unrealized hopes: before this strike, western Canada had imported 90 per cent of its oil; since then it has imported none. The Leduc discovery was followed by others in 1948, 1950, 1951, and, bringing this series to a climax, by the Drayton Valley strike in 1953. A potential of 3 billion barrels of crude oil and 18 trillion cubic feet of natural gas were thus proved in Canada's west. John Richard and Larry Pratt, in their *Prairie Capitalism: Power and Influence in the New West,* describe the way the American "Big Six" — Exxon-Imperial, Mobil, Shell-Canada, Gulf-Canada, Texaco, and Standard of Indiana — dominated these developments. Not surprisingly, then, within months of the Leduc discovery a new coalition government in British Columbia reversed the 1938 restriction on the Peace River country and unleashed a spate of intensive activity.

This activity is bound up with the name of Frank McMahon, who eventually created both Pacific Petroleum and Westcoast Transmission — two of British Columbia's most powerful energy corporations. It is also bound up with the new importance of natural gas. The first productive wells in the region were sunk in 1951, and with the help of wildcatters the area began to see a plethora of successful drillings. It was soon realized that the natural gas potential was greater even than had been imagined, and by the end of the decade dreams of northern British Columbia energy grew to new dimensions.

The resources of the old northwest now figured in dreams of mid-Canadian riches. The North was now pushed firmly away into the economic distance but was not left there for long. In 1956, Canada's premier John Diefenbaker proclaimed his northern vision: a prospect of endless frontiers reaching to the Arctic Ocean. In northeast British Columbia this prospect was at least a partial reality in the 1950s, and had been hastened along by the exploitation of gas rather than oil.

In fact, natural gas became economically significant because of the rapid growth of industrial centres in California, Oregon, and Washington State. Cheap energy was needed for many processes, including the refining of oil. McMahon seized the initiative and, with the help of Canada's National Energy Board's approval, was the first to export cheap gas to the United States. By this time — the mid-1950s — McMahon's corporate ventures were intertwined with Phillips Petroleum of Bartlesville, Oklahoma, and El Paso (Texas) Pipeline, a combination of producer and deliverer of energy. The importance of the United States market for gas is tokened not only by this kind of co-operation. The price paid in America was 30 per cent less than that paid by British Columbian consumers. The first developments of northeast gas, therefore, saw the subsidization of exports by differential domestic prices. American capital was working in the interests of American profits.

The 1950s rush to northeast British Columbia bore fruit. By 1960, 68 oil wells and 200 gas wells were in production, between them generating $13 million in royalties for the provincial government. It finally did seem as though British Columbia was going to join the hydrocarbon major league. In the same year, the *Vancouver Province* declared that there was more gas in British Columbia than in the whole United States. In 1960, the new Social Credit government led by W. A. C. Bennett announced its plan to build an oil pipeline from the Peace River to supply interior British Columbia. New revenues, an oil pipeline, and the economics of natural gas caused the dreams to become even more optimistic. The Bennett government predicted that in the coming decade, 1960-70, oil and gas revenues would total $100 million. The kind of importance this estimate gave to British Columbian energy can be grasped by comparing Bennett's estimates with the forecast, for the same period, of a combined total of $1 billion in revenue to all the oil-producing countries of the Middle East.

Once again, however, the dreams faltered on reality. The boom was followed by a slump. Middle East energy was cheap; so were oil and gas produced in the United States. Northern reserves of gas had proved economic to a fairly high level; first strikes of oil had also been worth developing. But the ceiling was soon reached. And this was more than a British Columbian problem. Expenditure on oil and gas by United States companies rose by only 6.4 per cent between 1960 and 1971, whereas capital spending on other industries rose during the same period by over 65 per cent. The 1960s boom in western economies did not benefit the energy developers, and the door to Aladdin's cave seemed yet again to have begun to close. It took the United States' insistence on a worldwide energy shortfall — the 1971-73 so-called crisis — and the Arab world's sudden and drastic price initiatives to start the drills spinning as fast as fantasy required.

Since 1974, provincial hopes for a glorious economic future have again been dominated by northeast energy. Between 1974 and 1979 the province collected in excess of $1.5 billion in rents from the gas industry. Over and above this sum it also took royalties on oil production of some forty thousand barrels per day. At the same time, a provincially created British Columbia Resource Investment Corporation was set up in 1977 to function in the free enterprise market place, beginning with a gift of five free shares to every *bona fide* British Columbian resident, and with permits to explore for oil and gas on 23 million acres of Crown lands in the northeast region.

The province has again insisted that its economic prospects are now bound up with the future of the hydrocarbon industry. According to *British Columbia Government News,* April 1980, over 10 per cent of the 1979-80 provincial budget was to come from oil and gas revenues, and this proportion was expected to increase to more than 30 per cent of the 1980-81 budget. As it turned out, the 1970s boom in energy production was accompanied by increased costs of British Columbian gas to the United States, and a consequent fall in exports. High hopes of great revenues were not being realized. But any suggestion that, in the interests of the Indians, of the land, or of a more balanced economy, the provincial government should slow down or modify the rate and scale of the development of this newest of the new frontiers is not welcome. The oil and gas play has confirmed the region's status as a hinterland of the great American urban centres. A network of major and minor pipelines leads south and east, and on over the United States border.

Land use by the oil and gas industry has its own patterns. Seismic exploration and other techniques generate the knowledge required to justify test drilling. Normally four years are needed to ensure sufficient production to warrant the installation of field-gathering lines for carrying gas through trunk systems to regional centres. Finally, major processing facilities are set up to separate petroleum by-products and transmit oil southward. In the field, the drilling of wells advances into more and more marginal areas to gather more information, to justify more drilling . . . The limits of geological knowledge continue to be pressed outward at a speed determined by rates of investment and risk, not by any consideration of the balance between long-term resources and short-term economic returns.

The dream that we are all encouraged to share is one of limitless expansion, or, conversely, we are offered the possible nightmare of not extending the energy frontier: an end to light, heat, cars, to the civilization we know and depend upon. In northern Canada this is nurtured by provincial governments and large corporations. And behind their activities is an industrial system that feels endangered by even remote threats to its ever-growing need for oil and gas.

The large area west of the Alaska Highway, including all of the eastern foothills between Fort St. John and Fort Nelson, is to become the centre of yet more exploration and drilling. Cutlines, wellside access roads, and pipeline rights-of-way now run everywhere across the country — and can only be expected to proliferate. But the ravening American demand for energy has another consequence for northeast British Columbia: the Alaska Highway pipeline.

The United States, threatened by shortages of energy because of shifts in world politics, has embarked upon a series of projects to achieve continental self-sufficiency in oil and gas. The largest of these projects — at a 1981 estimated cost of $35 billion, possibly the most expensive single project in history — involves the shipment of gas from northern Alaska to the central and eastern United States by means of an overland energy corridor. This will carry the 2,300-mile-long Alaska Highway gas pipeline and, later, an oil pipeline that may branch off from the main corridor to join existing lines. Four hundred miles of this corridor will pass through northeast British Columbia.

It may seem curious that this particular development has not been described earlier. After all, what could be more indicative of the subordination of local interests to distant — and even foreign — interests than a pipeline that slices through British Columbia on its way from one part of the United States to another? And what better illustrates the utter disregard for the Indian interest than the haste and lack of concern over environmental effects with which the Alaska Highway pipeline has been planned? The word "corridor" is almost a metaphor in itself for what this particular project shows about the nature of frontier activity: a corridor is a convenient means of getting from one room to another.

The prospect of the Alaska Highway pipeline was the direct cause of the research upon which much of this book is based. More than any of the many ventures that have preceded it in the economic history of the region, the pipeline has catalyzed and galvanized the Indian people's insistence on their rights. So why is it mentioned only in the wake of descriptions of so many other projects and developments? The answer to this is that the Alaska Highway pipeline will add its effects to a succession of previous frontiers. However much its vehement opponents and its evangelistic supporters are obsessed and perhaps blinded by its overwhelming scale, its apparently transcendent importance and uniqueness, the pipeline will not be a scar on virgin lands. It takes its place in the long series of agricultural and industrial developments that have advanced upon the region, some on brief foray, some to settle in permanently. The Alaska Highway pipeline in particular and the boom in exploitation of the region's energy resources in general must be seen in the larger scheme of things.

The hunting peoples of the North occupy all of the North. The comprehensive extension of frontier interests entails potential for conflict that is no less widespread. Yet such a conflict is conceivable only to those who admit to the efficacy of these northern hunting economies. Europeans have discovered that there have been people in the North for thousands of years. Modern anthropologists have explained that all hunting societies have their own rationality and have secured relative prosperity with minimum of effort — the very

essence of sound economic practice. But the critical change in point
of view has not automatically followed: be they monsters, quasi-
humans, or true societies, the present and living economic interests
of the northern Indians are still rarely reckoned with. The stereotypes
are tenacious and expedient: there may have once been successful
hunters, but policy makers and a poorly informed public both tend to
insist that Indians either never had, or sadly have lost, a real way of
economic life. This conveniently implies that dwellers beyond or at
the frontier need a new, a real, an industrial economy.

The W. A. C. Bennett Hydroelectric Dam illustrates the kind of
disregard for the Indian interest that has accompanied northern
development. The Bennett Dam created Williston Lake, is the largest
body of fresh water in British Columbia — over 250 miles in length, it
covers a total of 640 square miles. The lake has flooded the valleys of
the Parsnip and its several tributaries. This flooding was completed
by 1970.

White homesteaders, whose farms were flooded, were relocated
in valleys said to be of equal agricultural value. There were white
trappers whose registered lines lay in the flooded area. Some thought
was given to ways of compensating them. The upper Peace River and
Parsnip River valleys were also critical land for the wintering of a
large moose population in that area of the eastern foothills, and a
scheme was devised for provision of substitute habitat. But the
flooded valleys were the principal hunting, trapping, and fishing
territories of several Sekani Indian bands. Their reserves were
destroyed; they were dispossessed of the entire area of their traditional homeland, expected to move along, make do, or somehow
disappear. And silently they did, withdrawing to higher ground,
where they have lived ever since at the edge of other bands, in dire
poverty and some social distress.

In 1962, C. B. Cunningham reported to B.C. Hydro on what was
going to happen to the people who lived in the area to be flooded, and
quoted an Indian as saying, "By the time the water comes, I find some
other place." There is no other reference in Cunningham's report to
the Indian point of view, though it gives some insight into how

developments would serve the region's interest: "We lose one tourist attraction which few have taken advantage of to get another which will be in reach of so many." Unfortunately the Indians who lived in the valley did not have the status of tourists.

Until the hunters' and trappers' economic system — with all its needs and rights — is recognized, conflict may be unpleasant and unfortunate but is unlikely to raise significant moral or political questions. Such questions might be raised in retrospect. But in the North, where aboriginal occupants are scattered and deemed impoverished, extreme forms of conflict scarcely arise. Only if the Indians are seen as having an economic system does conflict of interest become even a theoretical problem. The vital questions still remain: Is there an Indian system on these lands? Is this system a practical reality of today? And there is the even starker question: Can an Indian economy possibly endure alongside, or in spite of, the energy frontier by which this new west is now so dominated?

9

Round-Trip
to Fort St. John

One morning, a few weeks after our return from the Bluestone Creek hunting camp, I visited Atsin's cabin. The light of an overcast and wintery dawn left the cabin's interior in darkness. Atsin was eating breakfast by candlelight; David was still asleep. I accepted the offer of some tea and sipped it, while Atsin split wood to blaze up the stove and shouted to David that unless he got up soon he would not be able to come to town with us, and would miss his dental appointment. In this way Atsin suggested that I drive the pickup on a round trip to Fort St. John.

In the next hour or two (David in fact had plenty of time to sleep in), we gradually got ready to go. Liza and Shirley prepared two large bags of washing to take the Fort St. John laundromat. Sam Crown said he would come with us for the ride but wanted to make sure that Stan's wife Clara knew we were going — she had washing to do, and badly needed to buy groceries. As word of our trip spread from home to home, others asked for a ride, or gave us lists of things they needed from town. By the time we left, it was midmorning and no fewer than eight of us were packed into the two bench seats in the front of the pickup. Three hardy passengers, along with several bags of washing, rode in the back.

As we turned out of the Reserve onto the dirt road that twists and turns for twenty miles to the Alaska Highway, I asked Atsin how long he thought we should stay in town. "All day," he said. "Lots of things to do and no need to hurry. David got to see the dentist." This mention of the dentist led Atsin to tell me the story of his lost nephew.

In the summer of 1960, Atsin's brother had to go to the Fort St. John hospital. He was, he told Atsin, pretty sick and might never return home. Should he die, it was to be Atsin's job to take care of his children. That was Atsin's brother's last message. He went to town, got drunk instead of going to the hospital, and was killed as he wandered out onto the Alaska Highway.

Telling this story, Atsin expressed pride in his success as foster father to his brother's children. He managed to kill enough moose, deer, whatever was necessary, and to trap well enough to buy groceries. He looked after all the children, his own and his brother's. It is not easy, he said, for a man to provide for one family; how much harder, then, to be a good and reliable provider for two!

Then, in 1963, one of Atsin's nephews had to go to the dentist in Fort St. John. They arrived at the wrong time, or the dentist was running behind schedule, or the appointment had been rearranged, or it was the lunch break — no one seemed to know what was the matter. But the boy was told to wait for a while. He was left there, alone in the waiting room, until the dentist was ready to see him. Atsin said he would come and collect the boy later.

But when the dentist appeared, the boy was nowhere to be seen. The waiting room was empty. For three hours Atsin and others looked for him, and then reported his disappearance to the police. For the rest of the day, Atsin and his friends searched the town. They looked in all the bars, went to every cafe, and roamed the streets. The police searched, too. But the boy was never found. Not a sign of him anywhere — no one had seen him. And they never heard anything about him again.

The boy disappeared in January. At first, said Atsin, many of them were convinced that he had been murdered. But a body would not easily have been disposed of — frozen rivers, hard snow: there would be nowhere to hide a corpse. So what had happened? There are several theories. Maybe the dentist killed him by mistake and then hid the body out of fear and shame. Maybe he was taken by a Bushman, a wild man-creature that roams the woods and sometimes disturbs Indian camps in that country. Maybe he ran away someplace. Who knows? Who can say? It is a mystery. Maybe he is alive somewhere today. He was a nine-year-old at the time, a healthy, sharp-witted kid. If he were around now, he would be in his twenties and might be a great help to Atsin and to the others in his family. Every household needs strong young people. The boy, now a young man, would indeed be a real asset to any white family that might have kidnapped him. But he should be here, on the Reserve, with Atsin, hunting, cutting wood, looking after Indian people. Yes, Fort St. John was a rough place then. And it's a rough place now.

The dirt road to Fort St. John was snow-packed and, in places, made treacherous by newly frozen meltwater. We drove slowly. Atsin finished his story before we had reached the Highway. Then Shirley told David to turn on the radio and tune in to the Fort St. John station. We mustn't miss midday message time, she said. But it was not yet midday, and for the next few miles we drove along to the exuberant voice of a disc jockey, frequent advertisements, and the rhythm of hard rock and country-and-western music.

The voices, commercials, and music of this radio station are a background, literally and ideologically, to the region as a frontier. The commercials boast of food stores, auto sales, real estate, farm supplies, oil rig equipment, and all manner of other goods for sale in a boom town. With naive and strident optimism, the radio announces what is going to happen in the world around Fort St. John in a style that somehow puts its words beyond all question or doubt. A favourite with the disc jockeys who dish up the weather — which they do many times each hour — goes like this: ". . . and now here in Fort St. John, the pride and pearl of the Peace, we have overcast skies and. . . ." The voices bounce along, proclaiming a future that is as inevitable as it should be gladdening to any normal person's heart. As one listens it is difficult to remember that Fort St. John is a tough, bustling frontier town. Instant radio glorifications sustain an ideology and mythology that rest on real people, events, and activities in much the same way that the frontier rests on the land. Looked at in the right way, through the right eyes, it is possible to see only progress.

Driving along the last miles of the winding dirt road that connects the Midden River valley with the Alaska Highway, we passed a succession of ranches, with their cattle ranges and bunches of roaming horses. Farmhouses and farm buildings could be glimpsed among the trees, or were partly hidden by the slope of the land. The road here climbs through the broken edge of the foothills and then levels off at the point where it meets the Highway. A short distance along the Highway, a few miles to the south of the turnoff that leads from the Reserve, stands a gas rig whose sulphurous stench prompted the obvious joke: "Why do you always fart when you go to Fort St. John?"

North of Fort St. John, the forest on both sides of the Highway is being or has already been cleared. Bare ground freshly cleared of trees may appeal to the agriculturalist who sees it as new farmland; but to other eyes it has neither the established beauty of the mixed forest that has been felled, nor of the meadows, crops, and herds of cattle that will eventually be there. These clearings express the process but not the achievements of the farming frontier. For most of its length the road to Fort St. John runs through a similarly scarred landscape.

As we drove through this landscape, the Fort St. John disc jockey announced message time. In an attempt to be a community radio the local station broadcasts a swap-and-shop programme, occasional community news and views, but — most important of all — four message times each day. Anyone can use this free radio time: you phone the station and send news, encouragement, or requests. Message time is important; and everyone now listened to it with great attention.

"To Joe at the Dew's Ranch: the pickup rear axle is broken. Please borrow Sam's car."

"To anyone at the Horse Range: I shall be arriving on the afternoon plane, Friday. Please meet me then. That's from Mary Anne."

"To the chiefs and managers of all the Fort St. John Indian bands: there will be a meeting at the Friendship Centre on Tuesday afternoon. That's from the Department of Indian Affairs."

"To Karen Belisle at the North Pine Reserve: please let us know if the moose hide has been fixed. That's from Annie."

"To Mary: your mum is in hospital. She says, please go visit her. That's from your mother."

Message time is a constant feature of life in the region, and it reaches into most Indian homes. Hunters take transistor radios into the bush, to trapping cabins, and listen to them beside campfires. These radios are often a mere crackle in the background, but when message time comes, everyone is silent. The volume is turned up and the people listen. When the batteries become weak and reception is poor, someone fiddles with tuning adjustments, lines up the aerial, and turns the radio to face the best possible direction. Then, heads bowed to the speaker, everyone strains to catch the messages. They listen to the voices of developers, settlers, and ranchers as well as to messages from Indian to Indian, and from administration to reserve. Perhaps nothing is more expressive of the dominant society's ability to build, celebrate, and then perpetuate the myths and culture that serve the interests of an effective development frontier. With the local radio stations, town is never very far away.

As soon as message time was over, everyone stopped paying

attention to the radio. David turned down the volume and we began to talk about the day ahead. Within half an hour we were approaching the outskirts of the town. Atsin and the others observed developments: a newly opened cafe, a store that had been moved, another storey added to a new hotel. They no more than noted these changes. They were reading the information. No one exclaimed in delight or dismay, nor did anyone offer anything beyond the occasional and general prediction, "I bet you pretty soon lots more people here in Fort St. John."

Nor did anyone make any comment on the town sign that welcomes all drivers into Fort St. John. They are all too familiar with it and with others in the same spirit. The sign shows a cluster of oil and gas rigs, brightly painted, over which is written: WELCOME TO FORT ST. JOHN — LAND OF THE NEW TOTEMS. Behind the sign, as we approached from the north, we could see a sprawl of single-storey buildings amidst a tangle of poles and cables. Winter snow and ice concealed much of the dust and litter that is fully exposed at other times of the year. But the town centre was an undisguisedly shabby mess from rapid and proliferating construction, unattractive evidence of urban boom and its sprawl. (I had already learned from the radio that more hotel rooms were under construction than in use.)

When the pickup had turned off the Alaska Highway onto the town's main avenue, the others asked to be dropped here and there. David and Shirley wanted to be left at the Northern Taxi stand, from which Shirley would make her way to shops and David to the dentist. Liza and Clara were dropped off at the laundromat, where they unloaded the bags of washing they had brought with them. Sam Crown wanted to go to the Department of Indian Affairs office. Atsin and I parked the pickup and walked to a nearby cafe. We arrived at one o'clock. No one would be ready to go home before evening. The day stretched before us, and you never quite know what may happen once you are in town.

Fort St. John, with a 1981 population of nearly fifteen thousand, is large by northern standards. Its central shopping area covers approximately thirty blocks. It supplies a large hinterland and is a staging point for much of the region's industrial development. Fort St. John is both a prairie centre and a northern boom town. An old community lives in scattered family homes and gives some sense of stability to the place; but the rapidly constructed town centre, and the self-styled toughness of newcomers on the frontier, obscure evidence of permanence. In its way Fort St. John, and all towns like it, is friendly and welcoming. But the surface, the first impression, is marred by haste, confusion, and aggressive forthrightness.

As Atsin led me to the cafe, we passed shops and restaurants that anticipate the needs of farmers, cowboys, suburban residents, and new workers on what they call the oil patch. Its hotels cater to expense-account industrialists and bureaucrats on the one hand and the hardest of hard-hats on the other. The town sees large numbers of both these groups.

The town reveals itself most clearly, however, in its bars. After some lunch and a visit to two stores looking for marten traps, Atsin suggested we go for a beer at the Fort Hotel, where we might find Sam. The Fort is one of three hotels in the town's centre that demonstrate the styles and uniforms prevalent on the Canadian northwestern frontier. Atsin explained to me that he preferred the Fort bar; the other two have either too many cowboys or too many hippies. This categorization seemed a bit overstated, since people were plainly going from one to the other. But Atsin, and many others, often gave it as their reason for drinking in one or another of the bars.

As we entered the Fort we met two of Atsin's relatives standing in the doorway. They were broke, they said, and were happy to join us for a drink. They told us, as we went inside, that their table had been "cut off" by the barman, because someone who had been drinking with them dozed off and then, on being woken, smashed a glass. After some argument, they had all been thrown out. We would be allowed in now, they said, because the one who had fallen asleep and been the real cause of trouble had gone down the street to another bar. They were right. We found an empty table and a barman quickly came round with a tray loaded with glasses of beer, urging us and everyone else to keep drinking and buying. If there was something contradictory in pressing drinks on customers but condemning drunken behaviour, no one chose to mention it.

Throughout our day in town Atsin was uneasy. He anticipated difficulties and trouble, and repeatedly insisted that he was not drunk — as if to defy the expectations he read in the eyes of everyone we passed in the streets. This apprehensiveness affects the whole manner in which many Indians behave when in town. The rules are not familiar. Most of the town is an alien environment, with its own form of excitement and danger. For the sober and shy, unease produces an air of false purposefulness. They walk as if they were in a hurry, as if they were sure of where they were going, in order somehow to minimize or altogether avoid any anxious or incomprehensible exchanges with strangers. With a quick wave and unchecked pace, they avoid uneasy encounters. Fear of being judged and criticized causes a defensive abruptness of manner. Indians who fear others' judgements become overzealous in disciplining their children in cafes or other public places. In a stranger's territory, under his critical eye, they feel that every rule whether real, suspected, or merely imagined must be obeyed. For the drunk and adventurous, these same apprehensions result in buoyant, noisy, challenging defiance of all possible conventions. This awkwardness and the kind of drunkenness that goes with it reconfirm and reinforce the Whites' stereotypes of Indians.

Many seek to escape notice. At the same time, they need a place in town where they can drink, talk, doze, or just be themselves according to their own ideas of how it is best and most enjoyable to behave. They find this necessary privacy in patches of urban bush — house sites and lots where there are as yet no buildings — and inside abandoned shacks. In towns like Fort St. John, the very rapid and uneven progress of development leaves anomalous islands of scrubby vegetation in the form of these unsold or as yet unusable lots. There are even such places close to the town's centre. It is to these that many Indians withdraw, away from the criticism and safe from the hostility that are always to be feared from some Whites in town.

On unused lots or in empty shacks they light fires. Sometimes, even in winter, they spend the night there. They are not always comfortable, nor always safe. Heavy drinking leads to petty thefts by drinkers who are broke before their spree is over. But here, at least, an Indian can be in town without being directly under the disapproving eyes of the Whites. Yet by using such places, Indians who come to town confirm, or even inflame, the judgements of their critics. Patches of urban bush are dirty, littered with broken glass, and a dumping ground for city junk. More conspicuously than anywhere else in town these lots and shacks await development and rehabilitation. People who use them, even as temporary shelters, are readily viewed in much the same way as the lots themselves.

Yet when Atsin and others were in town that day, and were cold, tired, and broke, patches of bush and derelict shacks afforded privacy on the Indians' own terms. Late in the afternoon, when it was time to drive the eighty miles back to the Reserve, we picked up people from these places. We made a tour of street corners, drove twice in front of the most popular bars, passed a nearby cafe, waited a while at the entrance to a favourite grocery store, checked out the dispatch office of the taxi company (where we found that the clean laundry had been left in safekeeping), and scouted around the urban bush sanctuaries. We asked friends and relatives whom they had seen and where. The pickup gradually filled with people who wanted a ride back to the Reserve. There were some who had not travelled to town with us in the morning. Two of those who had could not be found.

We drove back along the sixty miles of Alaska Highway and the twenty miles of dirt road just as night was falling. It was not possible to see the new farmlands, but the gas rig was still flaring, bright orange and pink in the night sky, and it still stank. ("So how come you're still farting? Too much white man's grub?") The back of the pickup was loaded with groceries and the laundry. In the front everyone told stories of the day, exchanged gossip, laughed about petty misfortunes, and speculated on the whereabouts of the two who were missing. One man's shoulder was hurt. He had got into an argument with a group of white kids, and they had thrown stones at him. One woman had a rapidly darkening eye. She had quarrelled with a friend. Everyone was drunk, everyone wanted to continue drinking, and now that we were on our way home, everyone was in jovial mood. It was the end of a typical round trip to Fort St. John.

The Indians' Maps

The Indians' use of the land, like every other aspect of their way of life, is little known and less understood by outsiders. Stereotypes of the hunter, myths about so-called primitive economies, frontiersmen's self-serving ideas about Indians they encountered and wished out of the way, the Indians' own inclination to remain hidden — all these have contributed to drastic misunderstandings of the Indian economic interest. Events and notions that surrounded the signing of Treaty 8, the opinions expressed subsequently in support of the registration of traplines, have shown how myths and misunderstandings sustained white purposes in the Indian lands of northeast British Columbia. Since no one bothered to find out what lands the Indians' system depended upon, few facts ever disturbed the white man's myths, and no account of Indian economic needs ever challenged his purposes.

As we read about the way Indian societies were deemed to be destitute, if not actually defunct; as we see the extent to which the signing of treaties created a prospect for their confinement in tiny enclaves; and as we discover how trapline registration further undermined the Indian hunter-trapper's rights and freedoms, the demise of the Indian system comes to seem inevitable. Even if all previous such judgements turned out to be mistaken, surely the combination of attacks and pressures in the first half of this century did their work.

In many parts of northern Canada, however, such fatalism has been challenged by a series of surveys that attempt to describe Indian and Inuit economic life in the closest possible detail. The first of these land-use and occupancy studies (as it and its successors have been inelegantly named) was designed in 1973. It sought to document the nature and extent of Inuit land use, past and present, in the Northwest Territories. A combination of local oral history, early accounts of white explorers, and the results of archaeological excavations established a succession of Arctic material cultures. This primary information was then used as a general background for individual map biographies. These maps are the key to the studies and their greatest contribution. Hunters, trappers, fishermen, and berry pickers mapped out all the land they had ever used in their lifetimes, encircling hunting areas species by species, marking gathering locations and camping sites — everything their life on the land had entailed that could be marked on a map.

Following the study of Inuit use and occupation of the Northwest Territories, similar projects were carried out amount the Inuit, Settlers, and Naskapi-Montagnais Indians of Labrador, the Dene of the Mackenzie River basin, the Indians of the Yukon, the Inuit and Cree of northern Quebec, and two Ojibway communities in northwest Ontario. The methods used have varied. Some researchers strove for comprehensive data on wildlife harvests and the domestic economy. Others have paid close attention to the nature of internal colonialism and its effects on Indian life. Some have relied more heavily than others on conventional social scientific and legal methods and concerns, from questionnaires to analyses of the bases of aboriginal rights. But all of these projects have shared two main objectives: a demonstration of the extent of land use and the elucidation of the peoples' land-use systems.

In these two regards the studies in every case can be said to document, with irrefutable detail, what was already generally accepted. Few denied that aboriginal land use in northern Canada had once been extensive. But the results of the research showed something almost no one, including many of the scientists involved, expected: the peoples' systems endured into the present. Indeed, they more than endured. The studies echo one another in their revelation of the way the systems constitute a persistent basis for the material well-being and, therefore, for the cultural strength both of peoples and of individuals.

But the description of a hidden economic interest is not straightforward, and such discoveries in the social sciences encounter distinctive kinds of resistance. The Indians have supposedly been on the verge of disappearing since soon after they were first enountered by Europeans; hunters have been thought to have had no economic life since they first aroused European sympathy, or dismay. To have endured in the past is no guarantee of endurance in the future. What is more, politicians and administrators have again and again insisted that Indians need many kinds, almost any kind, of development. Without these, they say, Indian reserves and villages will slip from present poverty to inevitable destitution. The result of a land-use and occupancy study, however, is a crucial first step away from uninformed and stereotypic pessimism. The mapping project carried out by the Indians of northeast British Columbia yielded some remarkable results.

The majority of the men and many of the women in seven of the region's nine reserves drew maps of their land use. They also explained the seasonal round, shared knowledge, described changes over time, and indicated other aspects of land occupancy that underpin and interpret the information they drew on their maps. This book does not reproduce all of these findings. Anyone interested in more encyclopaedic data can find them in volumes 16 and 17 of the transcripts of the Northern Pipeline Agency's 1979 hearings. The details — animal species by animal species, hunting location by hunting location, activity by activity, hunter by hunter — are housed in the archives of the Union of British Columbia Indian Chiefs in Vancouver, and can be used for specific and technical purposes. But the way in which these details were collected and then aggregated, along with the general picture this aggregation yields, directly attacks the fatalism and scepticism that accounts of the region's history may cause in those who are concerned about the prospects for the Indian economy. The findings of such a thoroughgoing land-use and occupancy study cannot easily be denied. The Indians' maps are a strong affirmation of the peoples' enduring presence on the land.

The Doig River Reserve, along with its subsidiary community of Petersen's Crossing, lies to the northeast of Fort St. John. These two villages, with a combined population of 100, comprise a small community that has gradually been surrounded by farmland. Less than two miles away stands a compressor station, which serves a section of pipeline constructed across one edge of the Doig hunting territory. Fifteen years ago, contact between Doig River Reserve and Fort St. John was by covered wagon over mud-and-gravel trails that were impassable in bad weather. Today, all-weather dirt roads give access to new ranches, to oil and gas exploration camps, to pipelines that are already in place, and to the reserve itself.

The people living at Doig and at Petersen's Crossing mapped their land use during the autumn and winter of 1978-79. The base maps were 1:250,000 topographic sheets on which individuals marked everywhere they had hunted, fished, trapped, picked berries, and camped. They drew the outer boundaries of the areas they had used for these activities and, in the case of campsites, they marked particular locations with a small x. Map 6 shows one Doig River hunter's description of his total land use. When everyone

6

DOIG RIVER RESERVE: ONE HUNTER'S LAND-USE BIOGRAPHY

The original map was drawn in coloured inks on 1:250,000 sheets. This black-and-white copy follows all the areas as the hunter outlined them, and shows the campsites he marked. The symbols here are:

—·—·—·—	hunting
—————	berry picking
— — — — —	fishing
——··——	trapping
■	camping sites

The base map here is used throughout the following map series. It shows the main rivers and their tributaries, places that can conveniently and usefully be labelled, and all-weather roads (marked with a broken line) that appear on the most recent provincial maps of the region (in most cases, 1978).

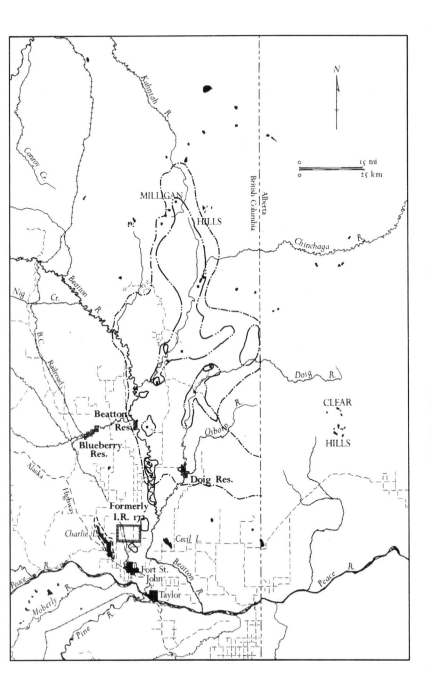

had drawn a similar map, the individual maps were aggregated. In this way a map was drawn to show all the Doig and Petersen hunting areas, fishing locations, campsites, etc. Separate composite maps (Maps 7 to 10), were made to show each type of land use.

The hunting areas would have been far more complex, and therefore more difficult to aggregate, if the hunters of northeast British Columbia set out on any given day with an inflexible resolve to kill only a particular species of animal. But they do not hunt like that; rather, they may choose their hunting area with a particular species in mind, but once there they hunt whatever they can find. The answer to the question, "Where have you hunted mule deer?" is the same as the answer to the question, "Where have you hunted moose? Black bear? spruce grouse?" In fact, because moose is the most highly valued and the most widely distributed of the species hunted, the outer boundary for moose hunting is indistinguishable from the outer boundary for all types of hunting — with the exception of goats and sheep, which the hunters seek high in the mountains. Within this hunting territory, there are particular areas where one species or another is likely to be abundant or especially accessible. The hunters of this region, however, see their main use of the land as a generalized hunt for ungulates: they are reluctant to point to special areas or particular locations for such hunting because, they repeatedly point out, you never know where you might find one of the locally important animals. For this reason, there is only one composite map for hunting, and it includes information about many large animals, including moose, mule deer, black bear, grizzly bear, caribou, elk, and mountain sheep and goats, along with the many smaller species that a hunter might encounter in the course of a day's walk or ride. With trapping, however, or fishing, or berry picking, they are much readier to be specific, and there is one map for each of these activities.

Men and a small number of women at Blueberry River, East Moberly Lake, and Halfway River reserves drew similar land-use maps. Residents of Prophet River, Fort Nelson and West Moberly Lake reserves also made maps, though proportionally fewer. The results, reserve by reserve, activity by activity, show the same patterns: there are concentrations of overlapping land use, which have a small number of remarkable extensions (see composite Maps 11 to 15).

The aggregate maps for each reserve can themselves be made into regional composites. These show the extent (but not the intensity) of all Indian land use throughout the region. The regional Map 16 shows only the outer limits of each reserve's combined hunting areas. Within these outer limits there are concentrations of activity and areas of critical importance. In a general way, the people of each reserve regard the whole region as their territory. A glance at the community maps will show how an individual's land use fits into an overall pattern. But it must never be forgotten that each individual has a neighbour or a relative who depends on, or has depended on, areas where he himself may not have travelled. Because everyone has depended on a collectively high level of harvesting and on sharing of meat, there is a widespread feeling of dependence upon lands that lie beyond any single individual's area of land use.

The men and women who drew their map biographies tried to mark all of the areas they had used during their lives. The total area of land use, the combination of the summary maps, shows where hunting, fishing, and trapping have been carried on within living memory. Some old people have lived and travelled over extensive territories. To some degree, then, composite hunting maps obscure changes in the pattern of land use that have occurred since the 1930s. Obviously it is important to know whether or not, and to what extent, these hunting territories are significant to the reserves' younger men and women.

In the Inuit land-use study, maps were drawn to indicate land use at different times. Three historical phases were identified for some communities: before the establishment of a trading post; after the establishment of a post, but before people lived in a permanent settlement; and the modern period. Most trading posts among the Inuit of the Northwest Territories were established in the 1920s and '30s, and only the oldest hunters could contribute information about

7

DOIG RIVER RESERVE: BERRY PICKING AREAS

The variation in size of circled areas here reflects both the extent to which individuals have travelled, and whether or not they mapped especially good places rather than all places they ever picked berries. The tendency to follow Beatton River emerges clearly on this map. The berries picked in these areas include saskatoon berries, strawberries, raspberries, and several species of *Vaccinium* (blueberry, bilberry, etc.).

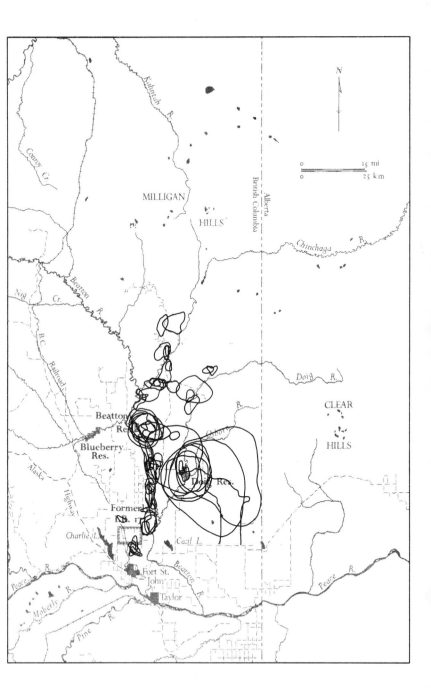

8

DOIG RIVER RESERVE: FISHING AREAS

Lines were drawn around obvious lakes or rivers; fishermen did not try to draw their areas exactly along shorelines. This is especially evident in the case of lakes in the Milligan Hills. But once again the concentration of use on Beatton River is shown.

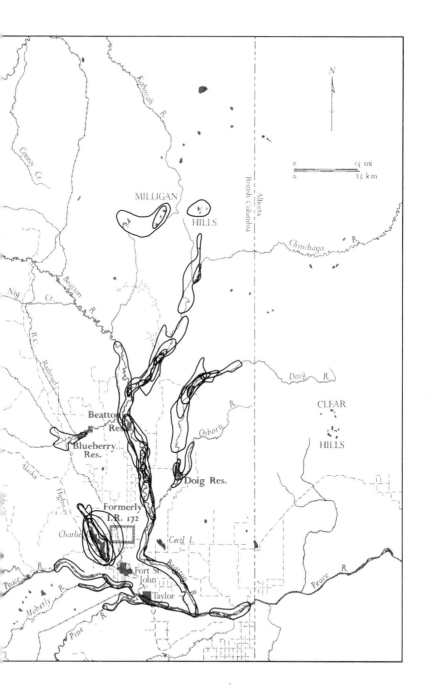

N

0   15 mi
0   25 km

Kahntah R.

Conroy Cr.

MILLIGAN

HILLS

Alberta
British Columbia

Chinchaga R.

Nig.

Beatton R.

Cr.

B.C.

Railroad

Doig R.

CLEAR

Beatton
Res.

Osborn

HILLS

Blueberry
Res.

Alaska

Highway

Doig Res.

Formerly
I.R. 172

Charlie

Cecil L.

Beatton R.

Peace

R.

Fort St.
John

Moberly R.

Taylor

Peace R.

Pine

R.

9

DOIG RIVER RESERVE: CAMPING SITES

The sites marked on this map are not merely overnighting spots. They represent, rather, all places that people have regularly used as hunting camps, trapping cabins, or even former village sites. The scatter of dots is in some cases a result of minor inaccuracy: clusters at the edge of Beatton Reserve and Osborn Creek represent a specific location of great importance to several Doig families.

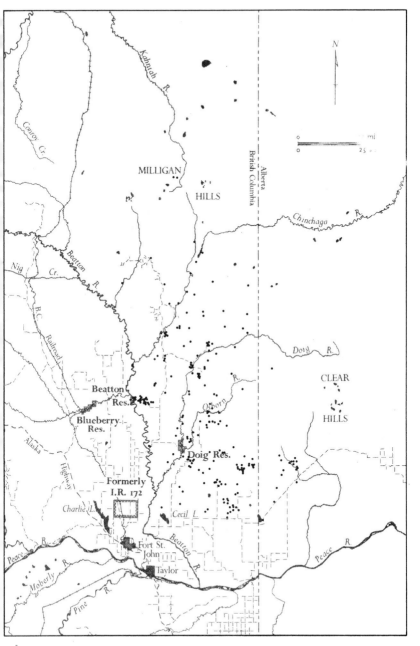

10

DOIG RIVER RESERVE: HUNTING

The large areas shown here indicate where hunters look for the major species — moose, deer, and bear. The flexibility of hunting, however, means that often no definite species is pursued: hunters follow whatever tracks they find. In this way, the hunting territory here is also important for all the minor species, including grouse and waterfowl, that are found in the region. It will be noticed that some of the berry picking and fishing locations on Maps 7 and 8 lie outside the areas marked here. This reflects the specific significance some individuals attached to those sites. In fact, berry pickers or fishermen would usually have a gun with them and be on the lookout for game.

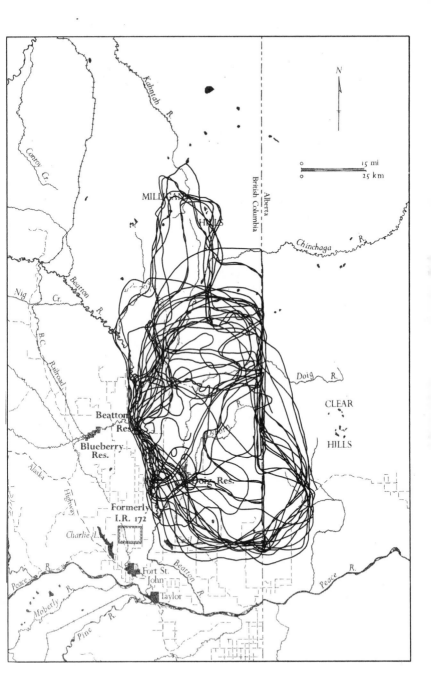

I I

BLUEBERRY RIVER RESERVE: HUNTING

A number of Blueberry hunters have exceptionally extensive land-use areas, but the map here shows the concentration of hunting west of Beatton River. The distinction between Blueberry and Doig hunting, in fact, can easily be seen by comparing this map with Map 10: the Doig hunters' western limits converge on or to the east of Beatton River. This is not a result of exclusivity of use but represents traditional concentration on particular drainages and river systems. Some of the small circles suggest that roads are used to reach areas which are then hunted on foot. This modern pattern of land use is very much a feature of younger persons' hunting maps from Doig, East and West Moberly Lake and Fort Nelson, as well as from Blueberry Reserve.

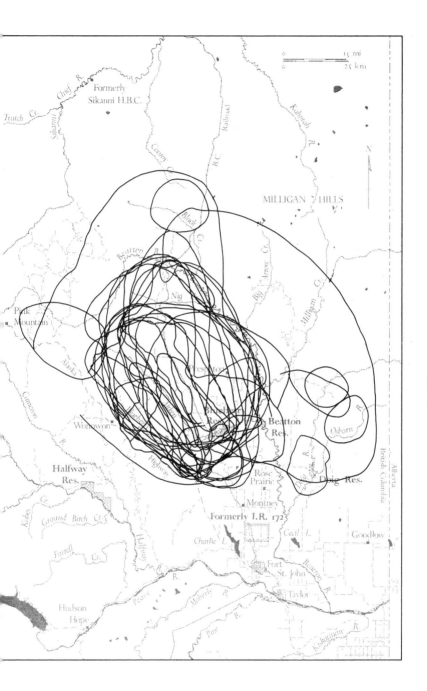

I2

EAST MOBERLY LAKE RESERVE: HUNTING

Seven hunters at East Moberly Lake drew separate maps for their land use before and since 1961. In this composite, all the hunting areas are included for both time periods. The extensive use to the south and west in fact represents the earlier period. East Moberly people have experienced great pressure on their land from white settlement and development: hunting has become concentrated in the areas marked here as the approximately 1,100 square miles (2850 km²) around the reserve.

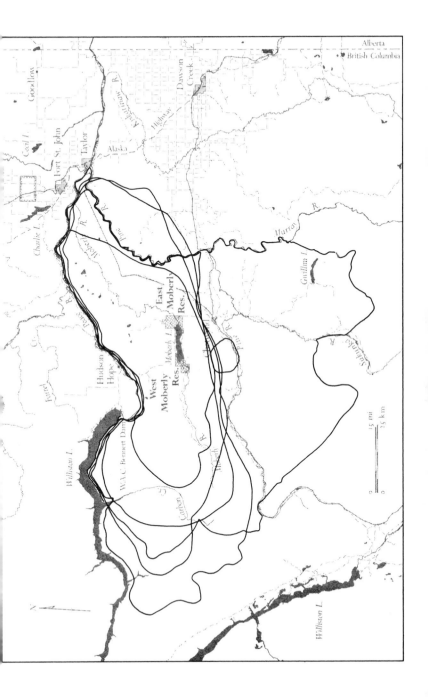

13

WEST MOBERLY LAKE RESERVE: HUNTING

A comparatively small number of hunters at West Moberly drew land-use maps. In fact, West Moberly is a small community, and in 1979 only two families lived on the reserve itself. (In 1980-81 the chief and three other households built new homes there.) Nonetheless, the hunting area is extensive and has some striking correspondences with the outer areas of East Moberly.

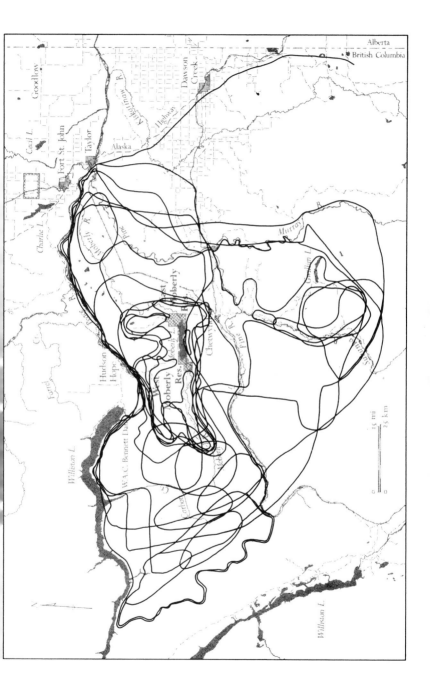

14

HALFWAY RIVER RESERVE: HUNTING

The hunting areas on this map show remarkable convergences at both their western and eastern boundaries. These are influenced by the Rockies and the height of the land along which the Alaska Highway runs. One hunter's area stretches remarkably far to the north, overlapping with the land used by Prophet River people. This is not so anomalous as may appear: one important Halfway trapline is to the north of Sikanni Chief River, and several Halfway families have close relatives at Prophet River Reserve. The Halfway Reserve area, however, is centred on the Halfway River and its several major tributaries which flow one beside the other from the mountains at the western edge of the region.

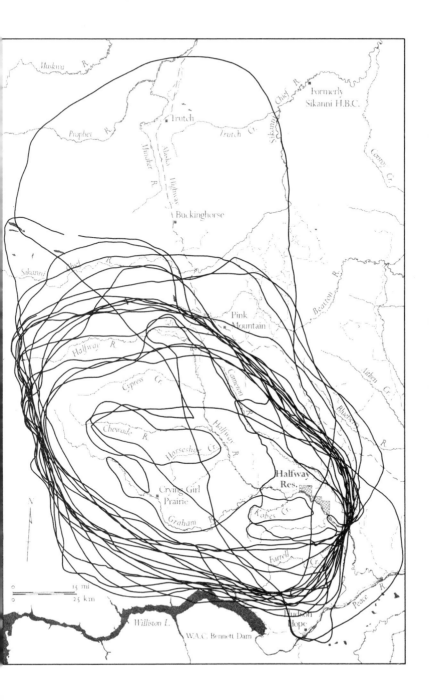

15

FORT NELSON AND PROPHET RIVER RESERVES: HUNTING

The main difference between Fort Nelson and other hunters' way of describing their land use is well illustrated by this map. Prophet River people drew wide circles to show hunting that is done without a sense of limitation by terrain. The Fort Nelson areas, on the other hand, quite closely follow a small number of important, and wooded, river valleys. The extensive muskeg (shown by the symbol ☀) in the north of the region is difficult hunting terrain. In this map the scale of the base has been slightly changed in order to show all the hunting areas for both reserves on one page.

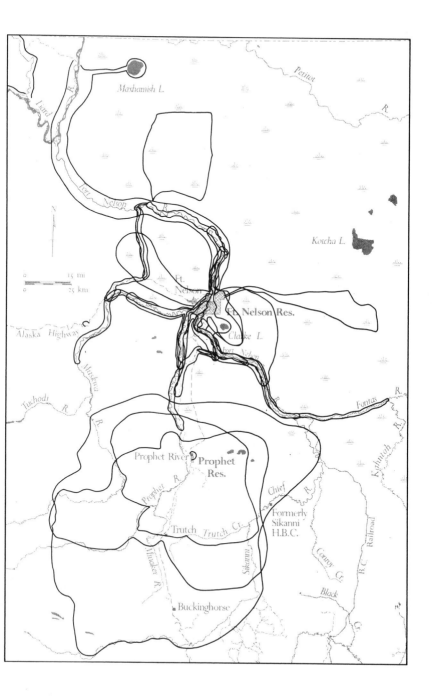

16

INDIAN HUNTING TERRITORIES IN NORTHEAST BRITISH COLUMBIA

The outer boundaries of each reserve's land use show how the Indian occupancy of the land extends throughout the region. They also show the extent to which the different territories do and do not overlap. Important boundaries are between the two Moberly territories and Halfway (on the Peace River), and between Halfway and Blueberry territory (at the Alaska Highway). Overlapping reflects both non-exclusivity among Indians vis-à-vis their land use and the extent to which members of different bands are related to one another.

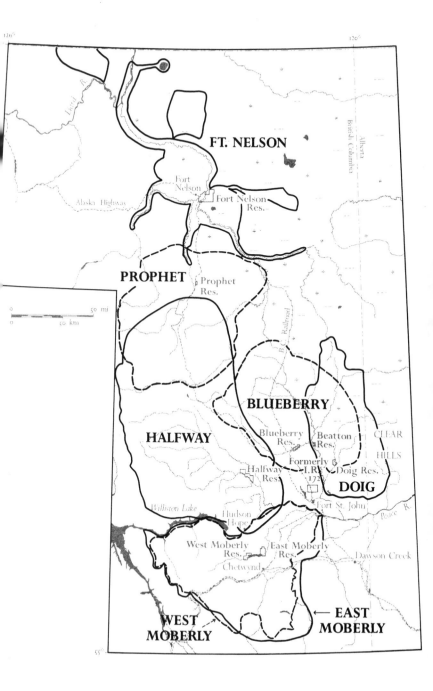

the earliest period. Many middle-aged hunters, however, drew two sets of maps — one for the time when they lived on the land, and one for the most recent period, during which they have lived most of the year in government-provided housing in settlements. Comparisons between maps for these different time periods make it possible to see, at least in a general way, changes in the extent of hunters' use of the land. Such comparisons of different time periods are also a feature of the Labrador Inuit Land Use and Occupancy Project.

When the northeast British Columbia project was under discussion, we assumed that Indian mappers, especially older men and women, would draw separate maps for different periods of their lives. However, this kind of mapping proved to be impossible: hunters saw no meaning in such distinctions. The fur trade and its posts have been established in the region for over a century, and Indians repeatedly insisted that the lands they used five years ago are the same as the lands they used thirty years ago. Their hunting system, which is based above all on the skillful tracking of animals that live all year round within a general area, requires a comparatively large territory. Hunters may use parts of this territory infrequently; some locations they may not have seen for twenty years. But no part is therefore dispensable: dependence is upon the territory as a whole. Successful harvesting of its resources requires knowledge of animal movements over the whole area, including places that are rarely, if ever, visited. This aspect of the system goes some way towards explaining why the people of northeast British Columbia did not see the usefulness of separate maps for different periods of time. The land-use maps show a pattern of harvesting that is flexible in details but surprisingly constant and extensive. The Indians say, with their maps, that they continue to use or need all of their territories.

It will be said that this land-use mapping is incompatible with the aims of scientific work and at odds with the need for objective data. Even if advocacy or self-interest is not seen as a reason for skepticism, the sheer difficulty of the task might well be. How can anyone be sure that these maps are accurate, given the vast areas involved, the many years of use that they include, and the unfamiliarity of the people with maps and mapping? Is everybody really able to recollect in detail all the uses of the land? Is no one going to mislead, even if unwittingly? Might the questions that go into the mapping project themselves be alien to hunters and trappers and result in distorted mapping results? And if not alien, might the whole objective be completely unmanageable? Might it, for instance, be like asking a lawyer to summarize all the memoranda he has written in the course of his career? There are answers to some of these questions.

Anthropologists and others have often pointed out the remarkable preoccupation among hunting peoples with literal truth. Precision and accuracy in all aspects of land use have obviously been integral to survival. It is not surprising, therefore, that among the Inuit, Beaver, and many other hunting peoples, there is great hostility towards any unreliability about resource-harvesting activities. It is striking that in some hunting peoples' languages there is no very clear distinction between making an error in judgement and telling a lie. In a society where information about the land and its animals can make the difference between life and death, there cannot be much tolerance for errors of judgement. This simple anthropological fact helps one to have confidence in the methods devised for land-use and occupancy research.

The accuracy of the maps is also supported by their internal consistencies. A considerable number of individuals did map biographies. If these map biographies are superimposed one upon the other, certain striking correspondences present themselves. There are lines that again and again appear in the same places. There are whole circles that neatly sit one on top of the other. Such coincidences suggest that everyone is telling either the same lie or the same truth. Since each hunter did his own map, often without ever having seen anyone else's, there is no reason for thinking that there was a conspiracy to distort data. Correspondence constitutes reasonable evidence of truth. Another striking consistency is to be found in the cabins and campsites. Again, if the individuals' maps are overlain, cabins appear in clusters that represent major coincidences of mapping. These overlays of cabins and campsites reveal patterns of use that distinguish one family's area of primary activity from another's. The patterns correspond with topographical features of the land, in particular with the river systems that are the heart of traditional land use.

The most important test, however, is the way each community's aggregated map fits alongside the others. If individuals have exaggerated their areas of use, then the communities' territories should overlap. Given the high degree of mobility of hunters and the incidence of intercommunity marriage, such overlapping would in fact be expected. It is all the more striking to see, therefore, that the composite of community hunting and trapping areas shows very distinct patterns. Moreover, there is an important correspondence between the results and the terrain. The Doig Reserve's hunting and trapping area is centred on a particular system of streams and rivers; so also is that of the Halfway and Moberly reserves. Between them the community areas cover most of the available ground; yet they do not impinge on one another. These maps were drawn community by community. There was no collaboration between mappers of the different reserves. The systematic pattern that emerges is a reflection of reality, and a reflection, therefore, of both the truthfulness and the accuracy of the men and women who drew their maps.

Of course there are inaccuracies, and some of the lines are approximate, but the internal evidence shows that they are good approximations. There are overstatements caused in particular by some individuals who have very extensive and elaborate hunting areas, which may distort the findings. This distortion can, however, readily be adjusted: by concentrating on collective ideas of land use, it is possible to minimize the part played by exceptional individuals.

Anticipation of possible challenges to the Indians' maps is defensive and may seem unnecessary. After all, the Indians' maps can stand on their own. They make their own case. But to refuse to anticipate criticism amounts to a more general rejection of social-scientific concerns. This may indeed be welcome. Few subjects are more broadly received with yawns of boredom and impatient expectation of impenetrable jargon than are the social sciences. However, exclusion of social-scientific discussion also denies a proposition that is anything but defensive: research done as part of a political process can actually be conducive to the most reliable results.

The Indians of British Columbia made maps, explained their system, gave detailed information about their economy, and took us into the bush with them. They did so because they believe that knowledge of their system will result in an understanding of their needs, and that this will in turn help establish and protect their interests. It is easy, almost habitual, for Indians to conceal their economic interests; and those who either unwillingly or merely passively go along with research projects will always obscure the facts. People whose economy is hidden are not going to facilitate its description unless they believe that they will serve their own interests by doing so.

The Indians' maps, like their explanations of them, are clear representations of their use of the land. The clarity comes from a wish to have others see and understand. There may be oversimplifi-cations — lines and circles on 1:250,000 topographic sheets can scarcely do justice to the intricacies of which they are a distant overview. But they represent a reality and have an integrity that social science can rarely achieve.

None of these thoughts will finally lay to rest the belief that however efficacious the Indians' system may have been even in recent years, the present-day extension of the industrial frontier is now totally undermining the very possibility of their system. The Indians' maps establish a claim to areas the people have used, and they demonstrate that the fur trade, gold rush, treaty signing, and trapline registration did not succeed in pushing the Indians off all of their lands. The incursions of industrial and energy frontiers, however, create yet new difficulties. The Indians' maps demonstrate that their system exists in the form of general and recent land use. The account of the compelling ways in which Indians have and have not coped with these attacks is yet to come. The fatalists have been wrong in the past. It remains to be shown whether or not their pessimistic view of the prospects for Indian life in the region may at last be turning out to be right.

To Quarry in Winter

After their return from Bluestone, Joseph and the family stayed at the Reserve. The men hunted all day long on or close to Reserve land, returning every night to their houses. By Christmas time, in the wake of Alan's sickness and the many accidents, and after the celebration of the midwinter festivities, Joseph began to grow restless. "Better to be at Quarry," he remarked, "far away from these flats."

It was at about this time that Robert Fellow took the three teen-age boys out to his trapline, where they would be kept out of trouble and learn the right ways to live. This mixture of prevention and cure was given authority by its having been recommended many times before by Indian elders eager to affirm their way of explaining and dealing with social problems. Some elders said even the police now agreed that nothing else would work. In any event, everyone seemed to think that the trapline was something of a local correctional institute. Joseph, along with all the other older people of the community, strongly endorsed the view that the best way to deal with such problems was to take offenders off into the bush. Every day conversation returned to the Highland Creek boys, as they came to be called — after the creek that runs through Robert Fellow's trapline. Imaginations drifted out in their direction.

"Wonder if they've run out of sugar? Pretty cold up there now, I bet!"

"Bet you lots of good meat on Robert's trapline. Those boys getting good and fat!"

"Maybe getting pretty thin, packing ice from the creek every day. We should go up and see if they're O.K. Stay up there a while."

Joseph had an additional reason for being delighted that the boys were trapping by Highland Creek. Robert Fellow's trapline was in the same area as his own, and his thoughts often wandered back to Quarry. "That's how to make life better," he liked to say. "Move to a good cabin where there are no neighbours. Lots of real work, and the best of food." It was no surprise, then, when he made it known that he would soon leave again for his cabin on the Quarry River, deep inside his registered line. Anyone was welcome to come along. If no one wished to be up there with him, all well and good. He would stay there alone. "No use down here, on the Reserve. Too much trouble."

Is Joseph too old for another winter's trapping? Too weak? Might his heart give out? His family asked these questions, sometimes directly, sometimes in the form of cryptic or discouraging remarks. Joseph himself stated the issue in characteristic fashion. With his hand over his heart, he shook his head and said, "Maybe no good. Not long now. Not long now." But his answer to his own and others' remarks was plain enough: "Better to be on the trapline, at Quarry. And even if you die up there, that's fine." That way, said Joseph, he would die in the place where his first wife and others with whom he had spent the best years of his life had already died.

These questions were asked many times in the week before Joseph actually set out. When the hunters returned after dark from their day trips, they liked to sit in Joseph's house, discussing by candlelight the day's hunt and hunting in general, and basking in the intense heat thrown off by the wood stove. Speculation followed speculation about animal movements and the prospects for trapping at Quarry. But there was the usual long hiatus between Joseph's declared resolve to set out and any outward sign of his getting ready. Then, one morning, as I sat visiting in another house, someone remarked that Joseph had been preparing to leave since daybreak. Maybe he would leave that same afternoon. Since we had agreed that he use the pickup to move his supplies to the Quarry cabin, I hurried to his house to help pack.

At Joseph's house small mountains of gear were already rising. Boxes of groceries, tarpaulins, snowshoes, axes, guns, a new stove for the cabin, clothing, bedding, pots and pans. After two or three weeks of inactivity, of sitting for hours every evening, dozing in the middle of the day, pottering here and there, Joseph was now a blaze of activity. Shirley and Tommy helped, searching for things that were lost and gradually shifting everything they wanted to take with them onto the general pile. At the same time Atsin and David carried their gear from Atsin's cabin to Joseph's home. As they sorted, packed, carted, and piled up everything they could possibly need, Joseph repeated his line of reasoning.

"Too much trouble here. Better go to the trapline. Maybe never return, but better to stay there than live here in this place."

The departure, however, was delayed. That day there was a heavy, overcast sky and continuous light snowfall. Impossible to see caribou on the hillsides in such weather; we should wait until the sky cleared. Which turned out to be the following morning. By midday we had loaded the pickup and set out on the journey. Not a very long journey, though much farther by car than by horse; roads quadruple the distance between Quarry and the Reserve. By car it is about a hundred miles.

We travelled by way of Robert Fellow's cabin. Joseph had been asked to visit the Highland Creek boys and take them some groceries and other supplies. We arrived to find them hauling river ice for water, and we learned that they had killed a moose the day before. It was a quick visit, hardly more than the exchange of a few words around the fire. We admired their marten furs, sleek and dry on their stretchers, and inspected the butchered moose meat, which Robert had spread in the comparative warmth of a tent to keep fresh but unfrozen. As we left, everyone remarked on how fat the boys looked — the greatest tribute that could be paid to life in the bush.

The rough road from Highland Creek to the Midden River was said to be good enough for a pickup. Close to the Midden, the road joined the trail to the Quarry River valley. Along this road the hunters sighted a cow moose browsing in the bush. We stopped and watched it for a minute, which seemed a long time to men who often must size up in a second how an animal can be shot. The moose chewed, hesitated, and stared back, but there was no question of making a kill. It was not the time. Farther along the road we met a confusion of three new cat trails which had been bulldozed off in different directions. None of them had been there two months before. After some puzzled discussion, we chose the trail that seemed to lead most nearly in the right direction. A little way along it we came to a bulldozer at work, clearing and levelling the new road. After asking the driver for directions, we eventually found the way. No one commented on these new roads beyond wondering where they might go and what other trails and link-ups they might eventually join.

Closer to Joseph Patsah's cabin, the roads had also changed. What had been a rutted and almost impassable route in the fall had now been turned into a good and easy road that was obviously much used. And only two hundred yards from the beginning of the trail that leads from the road through the woods to Joseph's cabin was a seismic crew's camp, a new airstrip, and another camp made up of no fewer than ten trailers surrounded by all the generators, trucks, and equipment that seismic crews depend upon. We had heard no rumour of these developments, but the people had become so accustomed to finding the paraphernalia of oil and gas exploration sprouting up everywhere that, once again, they showed neither dismay nor indignation. They just speculated about how far the new, good roads might now lead and whether or not there might be oil rigs higher than ever in the mountains.

From the road to Joseph's cabin is a half-mile walk through the bush. We had to carry or drag all of the supplies and gear this distance, along a narrow trail that twisted among the trees and, for its first hundred yards, led down the side of a steep ridge. At about the quarter-mile point we lit a large fire, and there we piled the stuff that did not need to be taken the whole way to the cabin that first evening. The carrying and hauling took several hours and was interrupted by our periodically resting by the fire. We finished long after dark. That night seven of us would be staying in the single-room cabin, with bedrolls for sitting and sleeping on, a small wood stove for heat and cooking, and cartons of groceries heaped in one corner. Scattered around outside were various sizes of traps, axes, and other items of equipment. Sam Crown mentioned that, while hauling gear, he had set three rabbit snares; everyone reviewed the tracks he had noticed. The crowded little cabin was warmed by the heat of the stove, half-lit by candles that made pools of brightness surrounded by the softest of shadows, and lulled by the tired and relaxed conversation that is made up of unhurried, murmured remarks. As the warmth spread out to the walls and corners, one by one we dozed off to the smell of old pine needles and rabbit stew. Outside, the forest was smothered by the deep stillness of the coldest nights of a cold winter.

During the first morning at Quarry, Joseph announced that he would like a fat cow moose to be killed. This would provide a supply of the best meat. In midwinter most bull moose are still lean and their meat is inferior. Two rabbits were found in the snares Sam set the night before, and a multitude of rabbit tracks showed that we were not likely to be short of rabbit meat. But the hunters wanted a moose — or, maybe, a caribou, though so far no one had seen any caribou tracks. During that day we found four sets of moose tracks close to the cabin. For a while we followed a pair travelling together.

In winter snow, tracks are comparatively easy to read. The texture and shape of a fresh hoof mark or of droppings clearly show just when animals have been in an area. The angle at which urine has hit the snow tells a hunter whether the moose he is close to is a cow or bull. The distances between hoof marks show an animal's speed and indicate, also, changes in speed. When Atsin set out to hunt the two moose close to the cabin, he gesticulated as he read the signs. With his right arm, he waved, pointed, and explained. The quick movement of his fingers showed the direction in which the animal was going. Opening and closing his hand, his arm stretched out level to the shoulder, he showed the direction the wind was blowing (here, in winter woods, hardly more than the drift of a breeze). The sweep of an open palm echoed the undulations of the terrain. Finally, with decisive pointing he established — given the lie of the land, the way the animal was moving, and the wind's direction — the particular course that he was going to take. Those behind him could follow if they wished.

With much excited signalling — he had deduced from tracks and droppings that a large cow was only minutes away — Atsin attempted to circle around to catch up with the moose from the side, and to surprise it from down wind. Three times he turned off from the animal's track. Twice he circled too late: the moose was deeper into the woods than Atsin had expected. The third time the manoeuvre was almost exactly right, but Atsin came so close to the moose that it was alarmed before he had a clear enough view to take a shot. That night we ate rabbit stew again.

On the second day we drove to Clay Flats, a small, open, and grassy area a little to the west of the cabin. Atsin and Sam hoped to find marten or lynx tracks and so decide where they might best set traps. Of course, everyone was on the lookout for moose. Only a mile or two from the cabin we spotted a magnificent bull. The hunters watched it for a few moments, as it browsed within easy range; then we continued on our way — Joseph had said he wanted a cow. After inspecting Clay Flats, we drove for some miles to the southeast, in the direction of the Alaska Highway, to take a look at Juniper Flats, another place important to the people, and where Atsin's family had always trapped. This took us away from the mountains towards the most settled land in the Quarry area. We were heading towards ranch and ranchers. These are established but small-scale ranchers, some of whom supplement their incomes by trapping. The Indians who once lived at Quarry know them well and think of some of them as neighbours. There are pleasant memories of helping and being helped by one another.

When we approached the ranches, a matter of no more than four or five miles from Clay Flats, the hunters put their guns away — even insisted that they be more or less hidden. Too many farms this way, they said. It would be better not to do any hunting here, even though these small farms are on or at the edge of lands on which the Indians hunt and trap just as much as they do anywhere else in the neighbourhood of Quarry. There was an immediate and pervasive sense of conflict. It may be all right to trap beaver in the spring on Crown lands near the farms, but it is as well not to hunt too close to them in fall or winter. More specifically, it is best not to be seen hunting there.

Some way down the valley, Atsin proposed that we visit one of the ranchers. There was a household of old-timers only a little way ahead, he said, and we would be sure of a warm welcome there. He had known them for twenty years, and he always liked to call in on them, to recall old days, see and hear what had been happening in the area. Atsin particularly hoped to talk about his suspicion that strangers had been poaching his old trapline. Everyone agreed, and we turned off the snow-packed road into a driveway that led to a cluster of shacks and farm buildings. To one side of these, on the wide bank of a frozen creek, stood a small but well-finished log house. Atsin led the way; but before he got to the door, it was opened by a short middle-aged woman, who, recognizing the Reserve people, pressed us to come inside for coffee. There, in a warm and comfortable ranch kitchen, the Indian visitors, nervous but full of curiosity, sat in a ring of chairs at one end of the room. In an armchair facing them sat a heavy-set man. He was a neighbouring rancher, also visiting, well known to the hunters. The man of the house sat at the kitchen table.

He joined his wife in urging everyone to accept the offer of coffee and to help themselves to slices of a large cake that was passed around.

The ranchers teased the Indians. "Trapping out of a pickup these days, eh? Don't suppose you guys bother to do much walking no more!" Such remarks were addressed to men who hunt and trap on foot or horseback, who only occasionally have the use of a pickup, and whose home community has never had more than a total of two functioning vehicles. But the Indians did not explain or contradict. They did not even tease back. They simply laughed along with the jokes. Sam was complimented on the particularly nice pair of moccasins he was wearing, but then one of the ranchers commented that Sam must be the only person left with such footwear. "I guess nobody makes them things. Forgotten how, eh?" This remark was not made in jest, but as an observation of undeniable fact. Once again, no one resisted the implications or reacted to the assured tone of the question. They kept laughing along with their hosts and, with this show of amusement, may even have reinforced a stereotype of modern Indian life. Yet every Indian in the room belonged to a household where moccasins are made. All the hunters in the cabin at Quarry River wore moccasins nearly every day of the year.

Even in the kitchen of a family that the people had known for twenty years, the Indians' identity was somehow effaced. They accepted the condescension, the barely concealed air of superiority. At one point the visiting rancher commented on the fact that the girl with us, Joseph Patsah's daughter Shirley, was pretty. He spoke of her in the third person, as if she were not there: "Yeah, I heard about her the other day. She's a good-looking gal, too." His remark was addressed to everyone and to no one, a thought out loud. The girl blushed, and later she said that she had been angry. But no one replied to the rancher, just as they had not bothered to challenge remarks about pickups and moccasins. The Indians observed, accepted coffee and cake, waited on the ranchers' conversation, and presently left them with their ways, opinions, and attitudes unruffled. Much as the Indians' land is taken and cleared, so also were the people themselves overridden by the settlers, whose assumed dominance the Indians seemed to have granted.

Within minutes of our leaving, conversation in the pickup turned to the Whites we had just visited: to the details of their homes, their life styles, and what they had said. Some of their remarks were considered to be lies, others were laughable. Some of their jokes and teases were picked up and exchanged within the Quarry group. The visit had been an entertainment, a spectacle — not an occasion for participation. The ranchers' homes were living theatre. Their stereotyping of Indians appeared to reach no deeper than that. And on the way back, at the edge of the farmland, Atsin spotted a cow moose among the trees. After a brief hunt he killed it.

The afternoon was unusually cold, even by the standard of sub-Arctic winters. As usual, we built a large fire as the hunters began the butchering. The intensity of the cold gave some reason for haste, and the men felt an additional urgency because of our proximity to the ranches. Atsin kept repeating what we all knew: Indians have the right to hunt for game, even on land that belongs to a farmer. "We have to get meat. Out trapping you have to kill your meat. This is all Indian land. We can go any place to get our food." He spoke in apparent defiance, but he could not entirely conceal his apprehension and nervousness.

The moose was butchered hurriedly but properly. As always, virtually every part of the animal was taken: the digestive system was cleaned out, the intestines separated from other entrails, the liver and heart carefully set aside. Despite the cold, and whatever uneasy feelings were inspired by the thought that others might say we were trespassing, the hunters observed the rules and conventions that govern the butchering of a moose. On this occasion they observed also the conventions that surround the treatment of an unborn calf. First, they prepared a thick bed of partially digested browse which they poured from the animal's stomach. Then, painstakingly, they began to remove the foetus. Each part of the surrounding reproductive system was disconnected from the womb and set aside. Then the womb itself was placed on the bed of the cow's stomach contents and sliced open. As the amniotic fluids flowed from it, Atsin very carefully guarded against their running onto the snow. His son David, who had been building up the bed of stomach contents, almost allowed a trickle of amniotic fluid to escape. Atsin leapt forward and, with his butchering knife, remoulded the mushy, half-digested grasses into a better barrier. "You've got to be careful," he shouted. "If the water goes on snow, then right away the weather will go hard and cold. And pretty soon we'll all be frozen to death!" Finally, Atsin pulled the tiny calf from the womb.

A well-developed foetus is used as food. This time there was some discussion about whether or not it should be taken, but the hunters in the end decided that it was too small. So the foetus was carefully laid on the mat of stomach contents, protected with more digested grasses and some membranes, then covered over with spruce boughs and a few dead branches. Only when all the remains were entirely hidden away was the butchering finished. Such respectful treatment of the foetus was as automatic as any other part of the butchering. Even if it did cause some delay, there was no question of its not being carried out.

Eventually we packed the meat, along with the skin, brains, organs, and intestines, out to the trail. Most of the meat was finally stored under the snow about a mile from the cabin, but we took some with us for immediate consumption. The cached meat could be retrieved as needed.

During the next days the hunters had more opportunities to kill moose. One morning, Joseph and Atsin left the cabin after breakfast to find a large cow standing within easy range of the cabin. Another morning, Sam discovered a bull resting even closer. That same afternoon Thomas Fellow surprised a dry cow moose, dozing within fifty feet of him. Such mature females that have not calved are usually fat and highly prized for their meat. But none of these shots was taken. There was enough meat for now. Joseph had wanted only the one cow moose. Along with rabbits and occasional spruce grouse, there was plenty to eat. When three of the men returned to the Reserve, they took a moose quarter along with them. They said that some households might be short of fresh meat. But there was no question of killing another moose at Quarry until meat was needed.

We spent much of the next days eating and resting. Every morning there were three or four rabbits in the snares. Sam walked each day looking for caribou, or whatever he might come across. But the weather was bitterly cold. The temperature was never above -25°F, and often was as low as -40°F. Too cold, everyone said, for more than short, quick walks. Moreover, the trapping was poor: there were hardly any marten tracks and no sign of lynx. On the nearby creek, there was one spot where a family of mink had dotted and scuffed the thin snow on the river ice, coming and going to their den in the bank. But even the mink were too canny, or too few. The coldness of weather became the focus of pessimism and a justification for a prolonged but untroubled inactivity, which had their real source in the failure of that winter's trapping.

Conversation began to turn towards the Reserve. Is everyone O.K. down there? Do you suppose they have enough meat? Maybe the kids are hungry. Maybe no one is doing much hunting. No doubt it is even colder on the flats. Maybe some of the good hunters have gone out to work as slashers on the new seismic cuts. And there could be problems, too. There is still some meat in the cache up here at Quarry. Perhaps someone should take it to the Reserve, help people out. Joseph rarely joined in these conversations. He busied himself with the firewood, made bannock (a slow-fried bread), cooked grouse and rabbits, checked and prepared his traps. Trapping might not be much good right now, he seemed to be saying, but that gives us time to get ready for the spring beaver hunt. The talk of returning to the Reserve went on around him, it was never directed at him. Yet its purpose was probably more to secure his agreement to a return than an expression of any great anxiety about the folks at home. If Joseph resolved to stay at the Quarry cabin, someone had to stay with him. Whatever he might insist to the contrary, however often he declared a willingness to live alone at Quarry, however much he assented to the risks his independence might necessitate, the others would never agree to it: someone would have to stay there with him. As the cold, inactive days wore on, and all hope of busy and profitable trapping was given up, no one much wanted to be the one.

Eventually Sam volunteered to stay with Joseph, at least for a while. Greatly relieved, everyone else set off the next morning for the Reserve. Only one trip from the cabin to the trail was required to move everything we were taking back. Much was left behind, either for Joseph and Sam or for hunting and trapping trips later in the year. The return was quick and easy, and belied the great social and spiritual distances that had to be crossed. But these were revealed by other changes. The talk turned to speculation about what might have been going on at the Reserve while we were away at the cabin. The quiet, delicately balanced, and gently paced relaxation that prevailed at Quarry was interrupted, or layered over, by quick replies, hasty gestures, small tensions, and very different topics of conversation. By the time we arrived at the Alaska Highway, forty miles east of the cabin, at the end of winding, narrow valley trails and access roads, everyone was excited. We might have been going to a party.

At the Reserve there was a party, though not a protracted one. We learned that people there had experienced difficulties, but nothing serious. There were some minor shortages of meat. About a week later Joseph and Sam returned. They had hitched a ride from a local rancher. Joseph was not well, and Sam had become alarmed by the possibility that Joseph might fall seriously ill so far from help. Joseph himself insisted he had returned only because Sam was so worried. He would, he declared, spend the next weeks at the Reserve getting ready for the beaver hunt. Soon it would be time to go back to Quarry. By then, he remarked, as if to justify another stay "down on these flats," the horses would be in good enough shape to be taken up there. There would be adequate grazing around the cabin and up the valley slopes. Better, in any case, to have the horses at a real hunting place. Yes, that was how it was going to be as soon as it was time to hunt beaver. He and all his family would move up with the horses, and they would stay there, of course, through the whole spring and summer. It is always best, said Joseph, to be on the trapline during fine weather.

12

The Indian Economy

It is hard to believe that an Indian economy could have survived the succession of frontiers and accumulated change that are the history of northeast British Columbia. The genius of frontier technology, concentrated in the wizardry of resource extraction and transportation, is not easily opposed or evaded. A hunting society must make many adjustments to accommodate it, and even then the hunters' ways of using land are never secure. The people's maps demonstrate the extent of Indian interest in the land, and are a starting point of any account of these accommodations. But they cannot do justice to the sophistication of an economic system involving varying patterns of movement at different times of year, shifts from one kind of resource harvesting to another, and a knowledge of the land — and its animals

— whose richness is astounding. Nor can maps show the degree to which the Indians continue to base their economy on wild meat and furs.

The present strengths and weaknesses of the Indian economy come from a mixture of income and resources that is closely bound up with a seasonal round. Over the past fifty years this round has changed in detail, but not in broad outline. It can be divided into five activities: the fall dry-meat hunt, early winter hunting and trapping, late winter hunting and trapping, the spring beaver hunt, and summer slack (Fig. 1). Each of these has its own pattern and its own areas of land use. People have followed this seasonal round from the early days of the fur trade, and it is still the basis for hunting that is carried on from the fixed base camp or the permanent campsites that housing on a reserve represents.

Most of the species hunted, especially moose and deer, tend to be dispersed. In their hunting, the men either follow the game's seasonal movements, or they travel to areas where a specialized habitat supports particular species in abundance. In late summer and early fall, the bands split into small groups to begin the dry-meat hunt. This is a period of dispersal to camps that may be as little as five and as much as thirty miles from summer locales. The people travel to areas in which, based on their knowledge of animal behaviour and distribution and their understanding of the current population levels of the major resource species, they predict animals will be numerous enough to provide their winter supply of dry meat.

Until recently, the Prophet River people travelled by horse to fall hunting camps on the Minnaker River near Trutch, and on the Prophet River. Some of the Blueberry hunting groups followed trails along Blueberry River or Aitken Creek to hunting camps near the headwaters of the Blueberry. The Halfway River people went up valleys into the foothills and to the headwaters of streams that flow into the Halfway River. Similarly, some hunting groups from Doig Reserve rode north to Milligan Hills and other groups went to the Clear Hills in Alberta.

It would be difficult and exhausting to compile a list of all the areas that each band uses during the fall hunt. Nor are these the same each year. At times of great need, when moose and deer populations are low, they may move to distant areas to hunt for mountain sheep and caribou. The Halfway people, for example, have used the region of the headwaters of the Sikanni Chief River as a reservoir of game when animals were scarce in their usual hunting areas. Everywhere, moose and deer have long been the main animals hunted; although, wherever possible or necessary, fish, goose, whistler (hoary marmot), sheep, goat, bear, elk, and caribou are taken too.

In late September or early October, the small groups return to base camp with their supply of dry meat and grease. Until recent times, the women often remained in base camp while the men travelled to one of a number of trading posts for an outfit of basic store-bought staples (such as flour, sugar, tea, baking powder, tobacco) and the tools of trapping (snarewire, traps, twine, ammunition). This journey could take a few days and was sometimes made on foot or with dogs. Nowadays the frequent coming and going to nearby towns often includes everyone and is accomplished by hitch-hiking or in one of the few local vehicles.

This was also the time of year when many hunters left their horses at winter pastures. The Doig and Blueberry bands once left their horses on the former reserve at Montney, near Fort St. John. The Halfway people used clearings and meadows in the foothills above Chowade River. In the 1940s and '50s, Prophet River men travelled to the Hudson's Bay Company's post on the Sikanni Chief River, southeast of the present reserve, taking their horses along the old Fort Nelson-Fort St. John trail to Montney, where they left them with local farmers to board for the winter. The men then walked the 150 miles back, using their dogs to carry all supplies and equipment in backpacks. Nowadays, hunters who have horses use winter pasture on the reserves.

After autumn trading, trapping groups dispersed to their traplines. Some of these are now difficult of access, and trappers share lines or trap on and close to the reserves. Although the main beaver hunt is in spring, some beaver are snared and trapped under the light ice cover of early winter. As the ice on streams and ponds thickens, trappers turn their attention to marten, lynx, fisher, and wolverine. The trapline out from the main winter campsite frequently follows the hunting trails of the predatory fur-bearers from one stream bed to another in a circuit that leads back to camp. Sometimes at Christmas and New Year, trappers travel to a trading post to sell furs and join others there and at reserves for the midwinter festivities that take place during the Christmas celebration. Present-day proximity to towns has made this journey less of a winter highlight, but it continues to be an important time in the seasonal round.

Early spring sees the next major movement. After trading, visiting, and, if necessary, fixing up their cabins, hunters move to their beaver hunting grounds. In most cases these are the same as or close to winter trapping areas. They stay there hunting beaver, moose, and deer until the end of May, a period as important now as it was fifty years ago. At this time of year, while the ground is still moist, hunters used to set fires in carefully chosen locations. These fires encouraged new undergrowth to provide browse for moose and deer and, by warming the soil, extended the growing season of important plants. They also burned away deadfalls on paths and trails and renewed pasture for horses. The Indians' spring burning continued in northeastern British Columbia and nearby Alberta until recently. Forest management regulations have now suppressed the practice.

Following the spring beaver hunt, people once again traded their furs. Then, in June, they gathered at their summering sites. Some of these are the present-day reserves, and the pattern is therefore much the same today as it was before the construction of permanent housing. During summer, people periodically travel out to nearby hunting, fishing, and berry-picking spots for short camping or day trips. Early August was, and still is, the time for rodeos. Many Indians have incorporated them into their seasonal round. Then, in late August or early September the seasonal round begins again. It is a pattern that originated in aboriginal times, was adapted to accommodate the needs of the fur trade, and still underpins economic life. Everyone thinks of this system as "traditional."

Most of the bands moved into permanent housing on the reserves in the early 1960s. From that time on, their pattern of residency can be said to have changed from semi-nomadic to semi-sedentary. The traditional round of movement was modified. Those who continue to hunt and trap do so from a single, permanent base camp. But the animals harvested and the seasonality of the harvests — the Indian Year — have stayed the same. For some bands, this change has increased their reliance on the occasional and seasonal wage labour that has been part of their economic mix since the early days of the fur trade. For other bands, notably those at Moberly Lake and Fort Nelson, it has meant a more regular commitment to wage labour. Hunting and trapping are undertaken after work, during holidays, on weekends, or by other members of the family.

Late summer and early fall is still the season for dry-meat preparation, with hunting aimed at moose and deer. Today, the dry-meat hunt entails a division of time between residence on the reserve and the use of hunting camps in the bush. The people from Blueberry Reserve, for example, hunt from camps on several family traplines off the Mile 73 Road along the valleys of Blueberry Creek, Aitken Creek, and Nig Creek. The road is busy with people on their way to and from camps or bringing meat back to the village. Until the early 1970s, some of the Doig people still travelled the 35 miles by wagon to Clear Hills, Alberta, hunting and camping as they moved, and other Doig people went into Milligan Hills. Since then, the fall activities of this group have been concentrated on lands immediately to the east of the reserve. Some of the travel camps on the former route became the main camps of today. From late August through October and even into November, a number of the men are away from their families working as guides for outfitters who cater to white trophy hunters.

Late in the fall, the guides and hunters come home and hunting concentrates on lands near the reserves. Small game is important, especially rabbits and grouse. On November fifteenth, the trapping season officially opens. Some trappers move to their trapline cabins, but most harvest fine furs during short trips to traplines close to the reserves. Many traplines, however, are too distant for short trips, and their owners — if they lack transport, have children in school, or have other jobs that make long trips difficult — must either use friends' and relatives' traplines or trap only on the reserve.

After New Year, trips tend to be longer. Some trappers stay at their trapline cabins for several days or weeks. Hunting continues close to the reserves, especially for moose. Winter is also a time when Indian men work away from home for extended periods as slashers, cutting new seismic lines and rights-of-way. With the rapid growth of the oil and gas industry, this source of income has assumed a great importance in the economy. Nonetheless, the trading of furs is still remunerative. Most Indians sell furs to local small-scale buyers who then auction them at Prince George, Vancouver, or Winnipeg; and furs still find their way into the European and Asian garment markets.

The spring beaver hunt also has its old importance, and here again there is a mixture of long- and short-term trips. The Doig people walk along the streams and rivers of their traplines; the Fort Nelson people travel by boat and on foot along the Muskwa, Fort Nelson, and Fontas rivers and their tributaries; the Halfway people trap around the streams and ponds that drain into Halfway River and its main tributaries.

Summer, for many bands, is a season of hunting and seasonal wage labour. Much of the wage labour is on the reserves, and includes working on the bands' ranch, and constructing or renovating houses. Some of the Fort Nelson band do seasonal work in the town of Fort Nelson. Most early summer hunting and fishing trips are short.

In all this description of the Indian Year, I have tried to point to changes in its details without losing sight of the basic pattern. The nature of these changes can be shown by refinements of the general diagram (Fig. 1) into two diagrams showing the Indian Year pre- and post-1960 — the approximate date at which people received permanent housing on reserves (Figs. 2 & 3).

Some understanding of the system by which the Indians' life is patterned suggests that several kinds of economic activity affect everyone on the reserves. It is easy to describe this in general terms, and to insist, accordingly, on the vitality of the Indian economy. Yet in order to grasp the relative importance of the several sectors and to assess the value of the whole, there is a need for numbers — for a statistical breakdown of the economy. Statistics, as everyone knows, can be obfuscatory and misleading, even when based on large samples. In this case populations are small and many Indian people are understandably reluctant to give any details about their hunting and trapping harvests.

Also economic well-being among northeast British Columbia Indians, as among all hunting peoples, depends on both a separation and overlapping of men's and women's work. The separation has several aspects. Men hunt large game animals; women hunt smaller species. Men's work is concerned with killing and butchering; women's work is centred on distribution and preparation of food and skins. Men hunt very intensively for short periods; women work all the time — and have complete responsibility for young children. At times the separation appears to be very sharply marked; but appearances are somewhat qualified by everyone's ability, if not always willingness, to do just about any kind of work. Men often hunt without women, and when they camp must prepare meat, cook, and fix clothes. Women often hunt in company with a husband and then share all the work. Some women work their own traplines in winter, when they snare, trap and skin as well as prepare hides for sale. However, the economy really does have two domains of activity that tend to be kept apart: the prosperity of a household depends on both, but there is often dependence without obvious collaboration.

The account of the hunting economy with its reliance on the meat of large ungulates distorts reality. The work of women is concealed; its produce is even more difficult to quantify than is the men's — with the one exception, perhaps, of handicrafts. Moreover, it was the men who explained the system, and who on the whole took control of the research. The continual and essential work of the women, less conspicuous precisely because it is a matter of steady routine, should be kept firmly in mind when looking at the numbers used in this

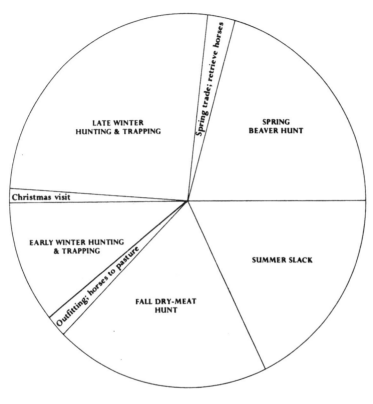

Fig. 1
The Indian Year: A Seasonal Round

chapter. Nor should it be forgotten that the author of this book, and most of those who worked on the research, are men. Women drew maps and made direct contributions of all kinds to the project. But their contribution is not adequately expressed here. Doubts and difficulties notwithstanding, during 1978-79 the Indians of three of the northeast British Columbia reserves offered detailed accounts of their economic lives. From these data I have been able to sketch a rough-and-ready statistical outline of the Indian economy.

The three reserves are East Moberly, Doig, and Blueberry. They

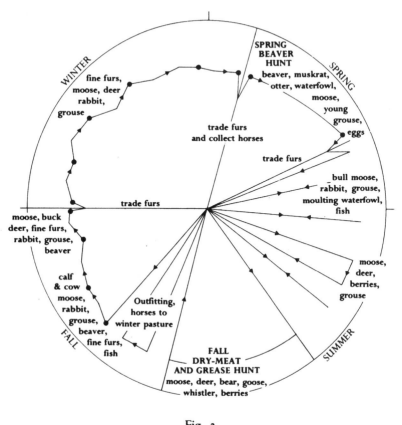

Fig. 2
The Indian Year, pre-1960

(Figs 2 & 3): The centre of the circles represents the summer
meeting place, and the black dots represent cabins on traplines.
The arrows indicate movement. Back and forth arrows on one
line indicate short-term hunting trips. The principal resources
and activities of each season are indicated near the perimeter.
On Fig. 3, seasonal wage labour is marked outside the circle.

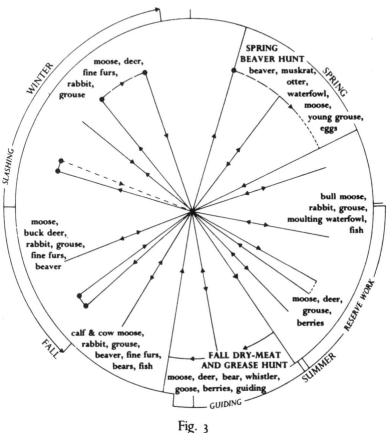

Fig. 3
The Indian Year, post-1960

have four kinds of income: hunting, trapping, wage employment, and transfer payments. East Moberly is close to Chetwynd, a town that offers work in the logging industry. The members of this reserve are often said to have moved a long way from dependence on traditional resources and activities. On the other hand, Blueberry is a reserve where everyone agrees that local and traditional resources play a dominant part. If these two reserves are placed at opposite ends of a spectrum between wage labour and hunting and trapping, Doig Reserve might well be situated somewhere in the middle. The three

communities cover a wide range of economic possibilities. None of
them is as heavily dependent on income from the bush as the Fontas
and Kahntah reserves in the Fort Nelson area, or Halfway Reserve in
the Fort St. John area. Nor is any of them as proletarianized (an ugly
but useful word) as the West Moberly or Fort Nelson bands. The
three reserves chosen are samples, but none of them represents an
extreme.

It is not easy to gather statistics for income from all available
sources. The reluctance of hunters to give full details about their
hunting, the fact that Indian trappers within the Treaty 8 area are not
obliged to file fur returns, and people's imprecise recollection of
exact numbers, even when volunteered, make quantification elusive.
Accused, as they repeatedly are, of overharvesting, waste, and defiance of game laws, Indian hunters suspect that numbers may be
used against them. Yet they also know that they stand accused of no
longer needing to hunt. Local Whites, and even some game management officials, have often said that Indians have ceased to use the
bush. Conventional methods of calculating the Indian economy
reinforce this notion. Wage employment and transfer payments
(pensions, child allowances, unemployment cheques, welfare benefits, etc.) are recognized as income; earnings from the bush are not.
Full-time hunters are, therefore, officially classified as unemployed.
Their earnings from the hunt, and even from trapping, are taken to be
minimal or nil or unavailable. Conventional economic analyses thus
systematically misrepresent the Indian economy.

An example of this misrepresentation is found in the tabulations of
the Indian economy given in the 1966-67 report published by the
Department of Indian and Northern Affairs, where the Indians of
northeast British Columbia make a brief appearance under their old
name, the Fort St. John Band. Their total earnings from trapping,
fishing, guiding, and farming are given as $161 per household per
annum. This figure is based on estimates provided by local Indian
agents, and is perplexing. Even in the 1960s, guides earned relatively
substantial wages; and this was a time when every household earned
money from the selling of furs. The real error in these data does not,

however, spring from underestimates of wage employment or cash earnings, but from a failure to recognize that the domestic economy is a source of income. By this means, Indian income is persistently misrepresented, and the poverty of hunting bands is either grossly overstated or mistakenly identified as a direct result of hunting and trapping activities. It was to combat distortion that hunters and trappers of northeast British Columbia decided to give data for the domestic economy, information they usually keep secret. They decided to make this available as a part of their insistence on the strength of their economic system.

The starting point of the analysis is meat. This calculation depends upon the average weights of edible meat from major species harvested (Table 2). Waterfowl and fish were not included; their numbers are too variable and imprecise. Lynx and squirrels were assumed not to be eaten, though they sometimes are.

Table 2
Average weight of edible meat for major species harvested

Species	Meat per animal (in lbs)
Moose	450
Deer	80
Black bear	150
Beaver	18
Hare	2
Grouse	1

Using these figures and harvest information that hunters gave, it was possible to calculate the total meat supply for each of the three reserves. These figures are remarkable. Every man, woman, and child at East Moberly had available an average of more than one pound of meat a day. For Doig and Blueberry, the averages are higher: 1.13 pounds and 2.24 pounds respectively. Fresh meat is the primary strength and most important item of the hunting economy.

There is reason, however, to think that these figures are too high.

Some Indians in the region prefer not to eat bear meat. They associate the omnivorous black bear with poison baits that white game managers at times used to kill wolves, and with the many garbage dumps that ranches, drilling camps, and settled populations create at the edges of and even near the heartlands of Indian hunting territories. Bears are often hunted, therefore, only for their furs, and some part of the bear harvest should be represented as a component of the fur and not the meat economy. A similar consideration applies to beaver. As the seasonal round showed, the important beaver hunt is in the spring, when they are taken for their furs. Hunters then kill more beaver than they need to eat. If they are hunting in camps far from the village, surplus meat cannot easily be returned there and some must be wasted. The figures can be adjusted by making the conservative assumption that none of the bear meat and only 50 per cent of the beaver meat is eaten. When these adjustments have been made, East Moberly Reserve has available for consumption just under one pound of meat per capita per day; Doig Reserve, 1.1 pounds; and Blueberry Reserve, just over 2 pounds.

The value of this meat needs to be translated into terms that permit comparisons with the returns from other economic activities. To attach a conventional economic value to the produce of hunting is abhorrent and, at least to many Indians, misleading. To do so would seem to imply that these returns can be understood and — worst of all — compensated for in dollars and cents. Dollar values are given here only to help demonstrate the place and scale of meat in the Indian economy. These values are only an aid to understanding and positively not a guide to potential loss for which compensation could ever be paid. The figures here do not suggest ways of overcoming or of ameliorating the destruction of the traditional Indian economy.

Setting dollar equivalence to meat is not easy. Hunted meat has no real or even hypothetical market value. Non-Indians regard some of it as unpalatable, and the sale of any game has long been illegal in Canada. Given these constraints, the only way to arrive at equivalence is to assess the cost to Indian families of buying produce of the same nutritional value, using, for example, the price of beef as the value equivalent of wild meats. There are still complications. The price of beef varies from store to store and according to the scale of a purchase. Do we use the price per pound of packaged steak at the local store or of the whole carcass in a bulk order from a meat market? A home economist might buy the latter, but in fact Indian families nearly always buy the former. A per-pound dollar equivalent must be chosen from a range of prices that differ by as much as 75 per cent.

The difficulties do not end here. Store-bought meat and wild meat do not have the same nutritional properties. So, should the dollar replacement costs be calculated pound for pound, per unit of protein, or perhaps according to calorific value? To arrive at reliable figures that are adjusted for protein and other factors would be extremely difficult and vulnerable to many objections: nutritional analyses have not led to any final agreement about the merits of such different kinds of meat for the human body.

For simplicity, the calculations below are on a pound for pound basis. The dollar equivalent given is the price Indians would have to pay for the same weight of meat they provide for themselves by hunting. The price itself, moreover, is that of bulk-bought meat from Vancouver in the summer of 1979 (Table 3). The choice of this low price is a concession to the possible argument that hunted meat may be great in quantity but variable in quality. If there is to be error in these calculations, let it be on the conservative side. If the replace-

Table 3
Dollar value of hunted meat
if priced as bulk-ordered domestic meats

Species	Dollar value
Bear	1.85 (price per lb of side of beef)
Moose	1.85 (price per lb of side of beef)
Deer	2.39 (price per lb of whole lamb)
Beaver	2.00 (price per lb of 50-lb pork packet)
Rabbit, fish, grouse	1.00 (price per lb of chicken)

ment values here are wrong, it can only be because they are too low. In fact, the price of bulk-ordered meat is just over half the price charged in local stores. To adjust the figures to show how much the Indians would, in reality, pay to replace meat that now comes from their hunting economy, the dollar equivalents should be doubled.

A range of figures is used because, in the absence of hunted meats, people would continue to have variety in their diet. They could not be expected to buy only sides of beef. Because the mainstay of the traditional diet is moose, it seems sensible to consider moose equivalent to the commonest of bulk-bought meats, and regard deer and beaver as equivalent to lamb and pork. Using these minimum prices, the value in dollars of the meat harvest for the three reserves is impressive (Table 4).

Table 4
Average potential annual value (in dollars) of meat per household

Reserve	Bear	Moose	Deer	Beaver	Small species	Total
East Moberly	168.35	3,028.45	133.84	267.96	120.00	3,718.60
Doig	197.76	3,110.77	234.22	572.04	240.00	4,354.79
Blueberry	74.00	5,392.01	206.97	464.04	360.00	6,497.02

The figures in Table 4 represent potential rather than real replacement income, not only because they are for produce that cannot legally be marketed but also because they include produce that is not actually consumed. If these figures are adjusted by subtracting all the bear and 50 per cent of the beaver meat, as was done for meat supply, then we reach real income equivalents for meat, again erring towards an underestimate (Table 5).

The domestic economy also includes money from trapping and the sale of handicrafts — including moccasins, gloves, jackets, and some beadwork. Furs are sold to a few local buyers on a limited number of occasions each season, and trappers have little difficulty

Table 5
Adjusted annual value per household
(in dollars) of meat harvest

Reserve	Total
East Moberly	3,182.97
Doig	3,388.83
Blueberry	5,648.35

recalling what they were paid for each species during recent years. Handicrafts too are mostly sold locally and many women can recall the quantities of different items they have sold. The dollar returns from trapping and handicrafts are shown in Table 6.

The replacement value of meat plus earnings from sales of furs and handicrafts give the total monthly household income from the land. This total indicates the approximate value of what is called the traditional economy, but is probably better thought of as renewable-resource harvesting or, in the language of modern social science, as the domestic mode of production.

Although this income is given here as a monthly average, actual levels of production vary greatly from season to season and from household to household. At certain times of the year, very little meat comes into the communities; in addition, some households hunt and trap far less intensively or far less successfully than others. This kind

Table 6
Average annual value (in dollars) of fur and handicrafts

Reserve	Winter fine furs (per household)	Beaver (per household)	Handicrafts (per household)
East Moberly	635.75	176.40	45.60
Doig	1,428.46	328.80	97.20
Blueberry	3,405.33	270.72	188.40

of unevenness is offset, to some extent, by preservation and sharing of meat. To a lesser extent, cash earnings from trapping and other activities are also shared. People feel free to ask one another for cash, but, more importantly, some money received from traders is turned into supplies for the next hunt. These individual purchases benefit everyone who participates.

So far the figures have omitted earnings from guiding. Northeast British Columbia is a favourite area for both big game sports hunting and trophy hunting. White hunters come from all parts of Canada as well as from the United States and Europe. Out-of-province and non-Canadian hunters often made use of outfitters' services. The region's outfitters (only one of whom is Indian) have registered territories, many of which are high in the mountains, where they provide trophy hunters with accommodation, horses, and guides. The success of these hunts, as well as the skillful removal of antlers and hides, depends on guides, most of whom are Indians.

All of the reserves in the region have a long history — almost a tradition — of guiding. In late August or early September, men leave for outfitters' camps, remaining there until October or November. A much smaller number of men also work as guides in spring, at which time there is a short bear-hunting season. Payment for guiding is on a per diem basis and in the 1979 season varied between $50 and $65, on top of which there can be substantial tips (in the range of $150 per week) if the hunt is successful and the hunter generous. In a good year a well-respected guide can be "in the saddle" (as they put it) for twenty or thirty continuous days. Compared with other sources of cash income, guiding is the most lucrative sector of the Indian economy.

Guiding rarely produces meat for domestic consumption on the reserves. In fact, most of the meat taken in trophy hunting is left in the mountains where the kills are made and — to the incredulity and dismay of the Indians — is wasted. Money earned from guiding comes into the community in lump sums, and it does not, therefore, contribute to the routine maintenance of domestic economic life. On the other hand, guides are proud of their skills, and they take pleasure and satisfaction in the respect accorded them by the outfitters for whom they work and by the hunters whom they guide. Economically, work as a guide is a long way from traditional Indian life or the domestic mode of production. Culturally and psychologically, however, it requires and reinforces many of the skills and activities essential to the hunting and trapping economy — riding, tracking, and skinning.

If income were rigidly divided into the traditional and modern economic sectors, it would not be easy to place guiding in one or the other. In fact, income from guiding illustrates how misleading such a dichotomy can be. In theory, the Indians' earnings can be broken into the equivalent gained domestically (meat from trapping and hunting, fish, berries), and wages from working for others. In practice, these cannot readily be disentangled. Guides work for others, but in separating them from the traditional sector, cultural and historical associations are lost. It is the dichotomy of traditional and modern that creates this confusion.

Income from guiding proved difficult to estimate. Calculations for the three reserves were attempted in two different ways: men who had worked as guides gave their own estimates; these figures were then adjusted on the basis of known rates of pay for guiding and the number of days worked (Table 7).

Table 7
Annual income (in dollars) per household from guiding

Reserve	Hunters' estimates	Adjusted estimates
East Moberly	644.52	339.12
Doig	169.20	260.76
Blueberry	471.96	434.76

Sources of income that are not based on hunting and trapping include both direct and transfer payments. Many men work occasionally and seasonally as slashers, clearing pipeline rights-of-way and cutting seismic lines. Reserves also generate work locally. Three of them have ranches or farms — although only one of these is economically successful enough to provide even two or three regular jobs. All reserves hire their own men to build new houses. A small number of men and women have full-time jobs in town but live on reserves. One reserve has its own small forest products industry.

This mixture of kinds of work reveals the difficulty and the pointlessness of any clear distinction between traditional and non-traditional activities. Households do not depend on a single source of income, and the various activities that make up a yearly round of economic life rely heavily upon one another. As new opportunities for work have appeared, many Indians have used them in conjunction with and in support of established kinds of work. The new has always been used in ways that were reconcilable with the old. If reconciliation with the old proved to be impossible, new opportunities were rejected or avoided. Indians became trappers, but did not trap to the exclusion of hunting or with an eye to maximum fur returns. Similarly, they took occasional wage labour, but often would leave, and lose, a job in order to hunt or fish. Despite their great interest in horses and their skills as horsemen, few northern Indians have been prepared to farm or ranch on a full-time basis. Nor have they bred horses for sale. Also, horses are owned by individuals, but all pasture is communal. The economic mix is not a neat sequence but a flexible and changing system.

The way the Indians of the region describe one another's sources of income provides a local perception of the economy. People were asked to go through a list of men over eighteen years of age and to say what each one did for a living. Was he a hunter, trapper, guide, farm worker, slasher, or did he depend on some other kind of wage employment? In the case of East Moberly Reserve, of 39 men living on the reserve, 34 were considered to be dependent on hunting and trapping. The same number of men were also said to be dependent on wage employment, while 11 were said to work as guides. At Doig Reserve, all 23 men were considered to be dependent on trapping and hunting, 15 on guiding, and 9 on wage labour. At Blueberry Reserve,

10 men were said to be guides and 16 wage employees out of a total of 30; but all 30 were considered to be dependent on trapping and hunting. At Halfway Reserve — not one of the three sample communities, but where this part of the survey was also done — every man over 16 was said to be a guide, hunter, trapper, and wage labourer.

At first, these figures may seem absurd. Yet the extensive overlap of activities is the basis of a mixed economy, and the declaration that virtually everyone is a trapper and hunter simply reflects the immense cultural and economic significance of these activities in all the communities. Such perceptions do not contradict the other economic data and, as a matter of cultural and social life on the reserves, they are reality.

There are important differences in the degree to which hunting and trapping, along with dependence on horses and sale of furs, are central to the Indian economy. These differences are partly the result of variable local circumstances — it is harder for some men to hunt and trap successfully simply because of the reserve's position within the white frontier. Doig Reserve is almost encircled by farms; Fort Nelson and the two Moberly reserves are well placed for men interested in full-time wage labour. Such differences are significant in the balance of elements in the traditional economy.

Variations among the reserves may be less interesting and less important than variations among individuals and families. On the apparently nontraditional reserves there are influential individuals who depend totally on traditional skills. Such individuals can all too easily be overlooked. At most reserves spokesmen and translators tend to be educated and sophisticated young people who express the traditional point of view reluctantly and incompletely. Also, in their dealings with white authority almost all Indians efface their own culture. For generations they have found the role of welcoming suppliant to be the most useful both in dealing with and protecting themselves from Whites. But the truth is expressed in the Indians' perceptions of economic life. All adult Indians on reserves consider themselves to be, in some ways and to some degree, traditional. This is no more and no less than to consider themselves Indian. "Traditional," for the purposes of consideration of self, signifies the preference for country foods, ability to hunt and prepare meat or hides, capacity for finding one's way in the bush, and willingness to share what one has. For many it also means knowledge of one or more Indian languages and, in the southern part of the region, considerable skill on horseback.

The wage employment sector of the economy should not be too sharply distinguished from activities that are usually regarded as traditional. Nor should unemployment insurance, pensions, child allowances, and occasional welfare cheques (Table 8) be separated from the maintenance of the overall economic mix. They all contribute cash which facilitates hunting and trapping.

Table 8
Average monthly cash income (in dollars) per household

Reserve	Wages	Pensions	Child allowance	Unemployment insurance	Total
East Moberly	422.25	45.00	40.00	20.83	528.08
Doig	175.19	46.15	38.20	75.96	335.50
Blueberry	144.65	60.00	45.20	46.79	296.64

With figures from Tables 5, 6, and 7 — the value of domestic economic production, wages from guiding, and other wages plus transfer payments — the returns from different activities can be compared. The relative value of renewable-resource harvesting against the value of other kinds of activity plainly refutes any suggestion that the renewable-resource economy is defunct or impoverished. For every dollar earned from all other sources, renewable resources provide 63 cents at East Moberly Reserve, $1.30 at Doig Reserve, and $2.67 at Blueberry Reserve. East Moberly Reserve is widely regarded as an Indian reserve where "traditional" life has almost completely given way to a modern wage economy. Yet even there families would, on average, be between a third and two-thirds worse off if they had to get along without hunting, fishing, and trapping. Blueberry, the most traditional of the three reserves, appears to earn over twice as much from renewable-resource harvesting as from all other activities combined.

These figures are subject to qualifications. They are not exact; they do not claim to be comprehensive; and they are based on replacement value calculations. But they conclusively contradict any attempt to dismiss harvesting of renewable resources as of past or passing economic importance; and they invite skepticism about the kinds of material benefits that industrial development is supposed to bring to Indian communities. The figures show the scale of what the Indians stand to lose. The intricacies of the economic mix show how difficult must be any attempt to calculate the balance of gains and losses that the white man's frontiers may bring.

Most important of all, the figures show that the succession of frontiers has not yet proved fatal to the life Indians regard as traditional. There is a strong Indian economy in the region, but it is hidden. None of the white officials who contributed to the 1969 government report, which gives total returns to Indian economic activities as a few hundred dollars per annum, could have ventured an even remotely plausible estimate of the value of the renewable-resource sections. Nor do the figures given in this chapter represent the harvest when hunting is at its best or most intensive. In three weeks of the 1979 spring beaver hunt (during which time deer, moose, and several smaller species were hunted), the harvest amounted to more than five pounds of meat per day per man, woman, and child. This level can be sustained when hunting is going well; when the hunters are living full-time in a bush camp; and when surplus meat is dried, smoked, and distributed among families not able to hunt. This is not a level that could be sustained every week of the year. I give it here only to indicate that the averaged daily per capita figures, large as they may seem, still underestimate the potential of the Indian economy.

How can the strengths of this economy be reconciled with the fact

that many homes on the Indian reserves of northeast British Columbia look poor when viewed through non-Indian eyes? Houses do not
have much furniture, and they are not in good repair. The people do
not own many cars or other consumer goods. There is a tendency
among Whites to think of many households and even of whole
communities as disaster areas — places of intolerable, frightening
poverty. And there is poverty. In some households it is extreme. But
to regard Indian homes as poor and destitute is often to fail to take
into account the hidden economy. Peter Usher, the Canadian social
scientist who has done the most work on the northern renewable-
resource economy, has said that one of the most striking things about
Inuit is that they are poor people whose tables are always laden with
meat. The same could be said of the Beaver, Cree, and Slavey Indians
of northeast British Columbia. There is a great difference between a
poor household that has a reliable and large supply of meat and a
household that experiences the remorseless and debilitating effects
of urban poverty.

Per capita incomes for different economies and societies have
sharply differing meanings, and can all too easily fail to take account
of public as opposed to private wealth. One advantage of using
replacement values for meat is a partial moderation of distortions
caused by indifference to the kind of economy in question. On the
basis of data presented here, the 1978 average per capita income per
month for East Moberly Reserve was $148.84; for Doig Reserve
$132.36; and for Blueberry Reserve $187.60. The 1978 Canadian
average per capita income per month was approximately $550.

Another aspect of the Indian economy needs to be addressed.
Cash earnings are not always spent in ways that would please social
workers or Indian agents. Ready cash is often spent on spree-buying
or on parties. Why do people spend money on "things they do not
need?" When they have so little, when they appear so clearly to be in
need, when their families are "hungry at home," why do they spend
money in ways that do them harm?

The statistics here, however, indicate that most of the families are
not hungry at home. Spending patterns are not based on a disregard

for family, nor on indifference to the pitiful cries of hungry children. Rather, spending is shaped by the confidence and security that comes from a belief that there is food, that there always has been food, and, all things being equal, that there always will be food that people can get for themselves. It also comes from an ideology: beyond the essentials of shelter and meat, few goods and services are indispensable to hunting peoples. Here we confront the paradox that is fundamental to all understanding of this kind of economy. Living off the land in general, or by hunting, trapping, or fishing in particular, is associated with poverty; but a shift away from such harvesting creates the conditions for poverty.

The Indians' dependence on a hunting and trapping economy has entailed many kinds of uncertainty. The availability of most species fluctuates, in some cases dramatically. Rabbits in the sub-Arctic forests, for example, have an eight- to eleven-year population cycle at the peak of which they number as many as three thousand per square mile but at the low point of which their population drops to as few as thirty-five per square mile. Moose, caribou, and waterfowl have annual migrations or seasonal redistribution within the region, as well as long-term population fluctuations. The prices paid for furs have gone up and down, according to distant and uncontrollable market forces. Finally, the agricultural and industrial frontiers impinge upon and increasingly destroy Indian lands. Yet Indian hunters and trappers have skills and qualities that have made the persistence of their economy an undeniable reality. The economic data, vulnerable as they may be to methodological attack, imprecise as they no doubt are when viewed with statistical precision, consolidate what the Indians' maps illustrate and an explanation of the system helps to understand: that there is enduring strength in the Indian economy throughout the region. It is the future of this economy that is now in doubt.

13

Beaver and Spring

One day towards the end of April, a day when winter was at last softened by the light if not the warmth of early spring, Abe Fellow leaned against the rails of the Reserve corral and stared thoughtfully into the distance. Abe is one of Joseph Patsah's adopted sons, and each year he has the job of checking, branding, and clipping the hooves of Joseph's horses. Inside the corral younger men were riding broncs. Suddenly Abe shouted and pointed straight above him: a skein of snow geese was flying northwest, in the direction of Quarry. But Abe's attention was not on the geese: behind them, and much higher, were twelve golden eagles — wide-winged blurs in the sky. He pointed to this astonishing number of eagles and said, "Looks like we better get going. The beaver will be swimming all over the place pretty soon."

Joseph, however, was in no hurry. We could not begin the journey until the rivers were clear enough of ice for horses to be able to ford them. The timing of a spring hunt is critical. During early May, beaver leave their lodges and swim around in the dams before they move along rivers and creeks for the summer. They are easy to trap and shoot then, and their fur is still in good condition. Once the melt is fully under way in the hills and mountains, rivers rise quickly and run in spate for several weeks. This usually happens in late May. By that time hunters should have recrossed the rivers on their way back home with their pelts. Between the break-up of river ice and the late spring run-off is the time for hunting beaver.

Meanwhile, there was cowboy work to be done. Every morning groups of men rode down the Reserve, looked for horses in woods and hidden meadows, checked foals and colts, and drove some of them to corrals to be broken and trained. In their wide-brimmed hats, chaps, and stitch-patterned riding boots, lassos tied to saddlehorns, long bridle lines held high, these men and their work evoked the Wild West of the movies. But the work was in preparation for the beaver hunt: cowboys in order to be Indians.

On the third of May, Joseph decided it was time to set off. We would begin the hunt at a deep but narrow beaver dam close to the cabin at Quarry. Joseph and his family would first camp there and then move to other areas. Robert Fellow, along with two other family groups, decided to camp at a site a few miles away. Seventeen people, almost twice that number of horses, and one pickup loaded with provisions and camping equipment travelled to Quarry. Joseph and his immediate family arrived at the Quarry trapline on the second day of travelling. A storm of sleet had caught us the evening of the first day, and the trail became slick with a treacherous mixture of ice and mud. The pickup slid off the road to sink at once axle-deep in a run-off that formed an oozing lake over twenty yards long. We were all wearied by such setbacks; we repeatedly had to jack up the pickup and try to build up the road surface with logs and brush that the older men cut and hauled. Joseph and Atsin finally decided that a camp should be struck at the roadside. With the help of a rest and a dry night, we were able to finish the journey the next day. The men with horses followed the valley bottom, and they also took two days to arrive. After a long and cold winter, even this slow pace exhausted some of the horses.

Once at Quarry, there was excitement. The oil and gas industry's construction camps that appeared during the winter had now disappeared, although a large garbage dump and a muddy airstrip were reminders and tokened their possible return. The trails were impassable for most vehicles and, for the time being, intruders into the area would be very few. The men walked short distances along the paths above the cabin, noticing with equal satisfaction the absence of vehicles and an abundance of animal tracks. Earlier that day a black bear had walked past with a young cub, which had been chased but not caught by a wolf. That morning a large grizzly bear had made its way along the trail heading for an area of muskeg farther up the valley. And there were plenty of moose.

By the time camp had been set up it was late afternoon. For a while everyone relaxed around the new fires and we talked about tracks we had seen. Joseph decided that, if possible, we should kill a bull moose — no calves or cows. He also told the hunters not to shoot elk: never before had they come so near the cabin at Quarry, and he insisted that their numbers now be allowed to increase. A deer or caribou, said Joseph, would be welcome fare, but beaver were on everyone's mind. Soon the men went to inspect the nearby dams and set the first traps.

I went with Atsin and his son David as they followed the river downstream and then made their way back through the forest south of the Quarry cabin. Small, spring-fed creeks run through these woods, at the low western edge of which they join the Quarry River. These are the small streams that beaver can most easily dam and, if they are lucky as well as true to their proverbial industriousness, they can cause a small and shallow flow of water to become a wide, deep pond.

Atsin and David soon found places where beaver had been moving and feeding: worn trails over the undergrowth which had yet to regrow and the freshly chewed stumps of trees that beaver had felled. Atsin paused at the trails and sniffed patches of dead grass. If freshly used, grass along these runs often has the distinctive tang of beaver urine. By following the most worn of the runs back into the forest, he soon came to an enormous lodge. Here was the place to lie in wait.

The earthworks and the lodge were prodigious. Once the beaver had blocked the flow of the stream, the water had found new ways around the dam. The animals had then blocked these flows with ever widening and more elaborate walls. The animals scrape at the mud and heap it up towards the crown of a wall, on which they pile sticks and branches. The higher and thicker the wall, the larger the branches. The main wall of this new dam was over eight feet high and had incorporated boughs several yards in length and as much as a foot in diameter. A man could walk along this wall, which stretched in a semicircle for some fifty yards. At one end, alongside the deepest part of the dam, stood the lodge, a pile of logs and earth that included the dam wall itself and rose another five feet above it. Smaller dams twisted away into the forest in every direction. The whole structure covered many hundreds of square yards and the pond formed by it was no less than eighty yards in length.

Atsin scouted the area of the pond and wall downwind of the lodge. He explored until he had found a place where he could sit well concealed behind stumps and saplings. There he leaned his back against a large spruce to wait for beaver to leave their lodge to swim and feed in the pond. If he kept out of sight and downwind, the beaver would be likely to swim in his direction. Their feeding begins before dusk and continues until nightfall. Atsin judged that a beaver would soon leave the lodge and swim close enough for him to shoot. The lodge was visible, though not plainly, and he, with David beside him, settled down to wait.

This is the only hunting done by Indians of northeast British Columbia that entails a silent wait. They often track game with great stealth, but even the most cautious tracking does not allow the sounds and sights of the forest to close over the hunter. Atsin and David sat beside the dam, their eyes watching the surface of the water for giveaway ripples and bubbles, and their ears straining for the sounds of a beaver's nervous movements that will cause the water to lap at the pond's edge. At the periphery of their vision and hearing, birds called and rattled and rustled. Whenever Atsin thought he saw a head, or merely sensed a beaver's movements, he dropped his chin onto his chest and half-raised his .22 rifle in readiness.

Once a beaver did leave the lodge, but chose to swim upwind towards the bank farthest from Atsin. It splashed loudly, thwacking its tail on the water's surface. Then it clambered out onto the bank where it began to feed in dangerous ignorance of a hunter's proximity. There the beaver stayed, just out of sight or out of range. When the light was too dim for a good shot, Atsin and David got up from their place of hiding, and the beaver at the other end of the dam, suddenly aware of danger, slid almost silently into the water. Atsin glared in its direction and muttered his resolve to be back the next day. On his way to the cabin he set a trap along the trail that the beaver of this lodge were plainly using to reach some poplars they had cut down to feed on.

At first light the following morning Atsin and David once again walked downstream along the river bank. I went with them. Along our route, Atsin set a series of traps, concealed in the mud and undergrowth of freshly padded beaver and otter trails. He concealed the jaws of each trap just below the surface of the water, where the trails followed the very base of the bank, at places where animals would be about to swim. He attached each trap by a chain or stretch of string (or both) to long, strong poles that he cut and shaped with his axe. He laid these poles cunningly over and alongside the trap so that it disappeared altogether among the tangles of driftwood heaped everywhere by the riverside. When Atsin had set all his riverside traps, we returned through the woods, checking moose tracks and beaver runs along the way, and came again to the hiding place Atsin had used unsuccessfully the night before. The trap he had set on the dam was sprung but empty. A beaver had had a narrow escape. It was duly reset in the same spot. Atsin laid a second trap at the other end of the dam wall. Then we went back to camp for breakfast, checking and resetting two beaver snares in well-worn runs beside our trail.

In this way Atsin established a series of beaver and otter traps and snares — a trapline. He checked this line each morning during the coming week. Each evening he waited in hiding, usually with David, near one of the beaver lodges he had located within a mile or two of the cabin. Sometimes he spent the evening waiting near a lodge on one of the creeks that drained into the other side of Quarry River, and sometimes he waited near a lodge that was too far away to walk, especially if he had a beaver or two to carry home. On these occasions we went on horseback, and rode home, at the very close of twilight, with kills tied behind our saddles.

Atsin killed several beaver at their dams, shooting them in the head as they swam. Accuracy is important: a wounded animal can dive and find the safety of its lodge. A head shot is almost always fatal, and so long as the beaver does not sink it can easily be retrieved. In fact, Atsin twice succeeded in hooking sunk beaver off a pond's bed, and once killed an animal that he had already wounded, when it climbed onto the bank after failing to dive for its lodge. On these occasions the end of the hunt was protracted. Usually, the sharp crack of a .22 rifle is followed either by catching a dead, floating beaver with a long stick, pulling it in, and hauling it on shore, or by the splash and swirl of an animal that has been missed. A hunter who aims at the head rarely wounds his target. If a shot is missed, it is often a very long wait before another chance arises: beaver are wary once the sound and smell of rifle fire has disturbed them — although sometimes hunters took two, and even three, from a pond in one early morning or late evening.

During the middle of each day everyone rested. Liza, together with the men who had been successful the previous evening or on that morning, sat a little away from the fires, skinning animals. They pegged out beaver pelts on boards that are kept at the cabin, but they stretched otter skins on slim, flat wedges pushed inside the complete, tubular skin. The pegged and stretched furs were laid to face the sun. In fine weather they would be ready for sale within two or three days. Liza also prepared beaver carcasses, paring the meat and skillfully arranging it above the fire.

On some afternoons a group of men went hunting for moose,

deer, or any other animal whose tracks they came upon. On the third afternoon of the spring hunt, in fact, Jim Wolf killed a bull moose. He had found its fresh tracks high on a hillside to the west of camp and, after circling around, he got the animal within easy range. But just as he was about to shoot, he heard the sound of a 30-30 rifle shot some way in the distance. He realized that the sound of a large-bore gun probably meant that another hunter was firing at a moose; given the distance and the direction of the sound, it could only be someone from Joseph's camp. Joseph had said that one bull moose would suffice; it was now possible, he thought, that one had already been killed. Jim waited, with the bull at close range, for more shots, and to give himself time to decide whether or not he should risk killing another. The bull, barely conscious of danger, stood still, ears and nose twitching apprehensively. It also waited for more signs. Finally Jim decided to shoot.

Later he learned that one of the men in the camp had indeed fired at a bull moose. Three of us had at that moment been on our way home, and had just crossed a narrow meadow by the side of the Quarry River. We had surprised a bull resting there in the long grass. The startled animal jumped to its feet within thirty yards of us and ran across the river into willow thickets on the other side. There, believing itself to be safety hidden, the moose paused and locked back at the horses and riders. One of the men had by this time dismounted, taken his gun from its scabbard beside the saddle, and while the animal stared towards us he aimed and fired, but missed. The bull then fled into the safety of the forest. We galloped after it, across the river and into the trees, searching for its tracks, trying to come round on the animal from a different angle. But the forest was very dense; we rode on with increasing difficulty. In the end we gave up.

By this time Jim Wolf had made his kill. When we got back to camp it was late afternoon. We joined the others as they set out to butcher and pack the meat. The whole animal was loaded onto two pack horses, mostly in two pairs of panniers, though each rider also carried a sackload of small pieces of meat behind his saddle. The ribs and head were carried on top of the filled panniers, tied in position by the ropes holding the panniers in place. As usual, the hunters left nothing of the animal behind except the lungs and a few inedible entrails. These were scrupulously piled together and then covered with branches.

Liza took over the preparation of the meat once it was all at the camp. She cut the flesh from the bones, and soon there were long folds of it drying and smoking around the main fire. At the same time, she began to cook a stew of tripe and small chunks of back meat. Some of the men meanwhile speared neatly split fillets on sharpened willow sticks and roasted them at the fire's edge. In the coming days, Liza kept the meat in perfect — indeed, improving — condition: turning and arranging pieces on the poles, and recutting large pieces so that the flavour of smoke, wind, and sun could reach them all the time, permeating the meat with flavour and protecting it against flies and decomposition. The stews and barbecues became ever more delicious.

Now that Jim had killed a bull moose and we all had a good supply of meat, even more time was devoted to the beaver hunt. On the day before Jim made his kill, Joseph had asked me to ride with him several miles upstream to look over an area of beaver dams and lodges that he had not hunted for several years. When he came near to the dams, he dismounted and walked slowly from one to the other, making his way through a tangled profusion of trees which the beaver had felled. It was a landscape signposted by the pale freshness of newly gnawed stumps and the dark decay of older cuttings. Joseph read these and other signs. He was checking his fields, counting stock, reviewing assets. The analogies of other economic orders spring to mind, though none does justice to the massive body of information that eyes such as his could see in these trails, stumps, dams, and lodges. Towards the end of his walk he listened with great attention to the splashing noises of beaver coming from distant points.

When this noise began, Joseph found a sheltered spot a short distance downwind from a lodge that rose on the opposite side of an unusually small pond. It was, rather, a neck of dam, where the flow of

water narrowed between two large hummocks. One of these hummocks was the base of the lodge; we squatted behind the other. The
surface between was still partly frozen, but an area of ice was broken
and worn — almost frayed — where beaver had repeatedly surfaced
and climbed onto it to get to an adjacent feeding area. Open water
flowed slowly between thin shelves of shore-fast ice, and a dark and
inaccessible expanse of open water extended towards the wider end
of the dam.

Soon after Joseph took up his position, a beaver surfaced just in
the spot he had anticipated. Its head appeared near the beginning of
the trail at the edge of the worn ice. But instead of climbing out, the
beaver paused and would go no farther. Joseph waited, rifle at the
ready. The beaver was getting nervous — somewhere at the edge of
its senses it knew there was danger. Then, just as it began to turn
back, Joseph fired — and missed! As the beaver plunged off towards
its lodge, Joseph muttered that perhaps it was better to miss: had he
not killed the beaver instantly, it would have slipped away to die in the
water still bordered by thin ice and been irretrievable.

Joseph then led me in a circle back to our horses, checking dams
and lodges on his way, and we returned to camp. He had decided that
this was an area that should not be hunted this year. Better to leave it,
he said, for one more year: its beaver would then be very plentiful.
Instead, he suggested, some day all the hunters should gó ten miles
farther up the valley to a complex of beaver dams that had been left
unharvested for even longer.

That "some day" came sooner and more suddenly than expected.
Two days after Jim killed his moose, we heard a vehicle as it passed
slowly along the trail a quarter of a mile above the cabin. It was
heading up the valley, though well out of sight. All the roads and
trails, by this time, were awash with meltwater, and in many places
were deep in mud. We had neither seen nor heard any vehicles since
our arrival at Quarry. We had even arranged that our own pickup be
taken back to town. The absence of cars was one of the pleasures of
the spring hunt, and was evocative of a time when there were no
roads into the Quarry area. So what was a vehicle doing on the road

now? Its noise caused alarm, even when it had passed and could be heard no more.

After anxious and hasty discussions, Joseph decided we should trail the vehicle on horseback. Probably it was heading in the direction of Mule Creek, the area to which Joseph had suggested we might some day go. Within two hours, everyone in the camp set out. All the horses were put to use, although Tommy had to make do with an old, worn saddle and poorly broken three-year-old.

Joseph led the way, keeping his horse at a fast walk and riding in his characteristically upright, very correct style. Behind him rode the other men, with Liza and Tommy at the back. All the hunters carried their basic gear: gun, axe, and a small pack that contained knives, file, kettle, tea, sugar, and some bannock. The younger men wore wide-brimmed cowboy hats and cowboy boots; the older men, their usual odd assortments of peaked caps and old coats or rain parkas.

As we followed the tire tracks, the hunters watched the trail and gathered information. It was a four-wheel drive pickup, with a power winch in front. There were three occupants, two men and a woman. One of the men — but not the driver — was large. At several places they had gotten stuck. At one of these, the men had pushed, while the woman drove. Twice they had winched the pickup through long mudholes. They were heading towards Mule Creek. This much the hunters gleaned from footprints, tire marks, and scuffs on trees. In every discussion of these signs, speculation returned to the trouble-some question: What could these people be doing on the Patsah trapline?

Joseph was darkly suspicious, perhaps because this intrusion came at a time of year when he and the other hunters believed that no one — not even oil-rig workers or loggers — could break into the people's lands. He guessed that they might be poachers after his animals; or that they might be squatters, trying to take over his lands; or that they might be hippies planning to use his woods to grow marijuana. He raised each of these possibilities many times as he followed them to see who they really were.

After several hours of riding we found the empty pickup parked on the trail. Its owners were not to be seen, but their tracks were soon discovered, and we turned into the woods to follow them along a worn path. It was not the first time that people had walked that way. Soon we saw why: the path led out into a clearing in the middle of which stood a large, new log cabin. One of Joseph's guesses had been right: there were squatters in his woods.

While Joseph and the older men rode up to the cabin, Liza and Tommy and the younger men lingered at the edge of the clearing, more or less out of sight. Everyone dismounted, hitched their horses, then waited, sitting on the trunks of large deadfalls. Silence from the cabin. Joseph eventually strode to the door and knocked once, a single thump.

A middle-aged white man opened the door. Behind him stood a young couple. They were surprised and alarmed. They, too, probably had thought that no one would visit their remote spot so far along impassable trails. They looked out towards us apprehensively, staring at the ring of horses loaded with guns and all the gear of the hunt, and at the Indians. Joseph took quick advantage of their amazement. While the three stood speechless, he walked past them into the cabin. In his own way, he conducted a search. He looked along the walls, under a bed, and behind the stove. He was looking for trapping equipment in places where he, and trappers he knew, usually kept traps, guns, and stretcher boards.

As he looked, he asked a few questions. How long had they been there? Was it cold in winter? Didn't they find it a damp spot? Hadn't they built in a wet hollow? Had they seen much game? Did they like fishing? A list of questions like this gives a wrong impression: Joseph took his time, and there were silences that, given the tension of the visit, seemed long and heavy. The occupants of the cabin gave fumbling answers, but Joseph could not or did not bother to react to these. Perhaps he had difficulty in understanding their nervous, rapid English. Or perhaps he preferred to stand aloof from any discussion with squatters on his trapline.

Joseph had nearly finished his inspection of the cabin when Robert Fellow, after some hesitation, joined him in the cabin and carried out his own very similar search. Finally Joseph left the cabin, and walked slowly around the clearing in which it stood. He found an unfinished homemade paddle on the ground. "Maybe you crossed the river to see the beaver over there?" He climbed up to an elevated storage platform. "Good place to keep meat and furs up here?"

The occupants of the cabin gradually became more talkative. No, they insisted, they never hunted. They only did a little fishing. Certainly they did not trap. One of them at this point asked Joseph if he knew whose trapline the cabin was on. When Joseph gave no answer, the older of the two white men said he had heard it belonged to a Mr. Patsah. Then Joseph did react. He was Mr. Patsah! For a moment he ceased his relentless pacing and searching. He opened his arms wide in the clearest of gestures, and said, "This land, all round here, is mine. My land."

Satisfied, at last, that there was no evidence the squatters had been trapping, but still unhappy and suspicious, Joseph turned to the rest of us. "Let's go now." The cabin, its three occupants, the clearing and all that it represented suddenly vanished from the conversation.

Everyone remounted. Then Robert remarked to Joseph: "Some of us will go to the dams across the creek. We'll hunt over there."

"Good," said Joseph. But he, along with Liza, Tommy, and Atsin rode back along the trail they had followed from the road. Robert and the others headed west, towards the Quarry River and beaver dams that were known to be a mile or so away. The two groups of riders parted and disappeared — from the point of view of the squatters — back into the forest. The two men and the woman stood outside their cabin, watching.

The new cabin did not, however, disappear from the Indians' thoughts. They had long suspected that hippies and white trappers might be spending time in the area. And though this direct evidence was no great surprise, Joseph and his companions were troubled. The Patsah trapline lies well beyond white settlement. Once the Indians had left behind the last ranches along the valleys of the Quarry and Midden rivers, they expected to be beyond the white man's frontier. Logging activity and the search for oil and gas were reaching ever deeper into their land, and winter roads were pushing farther and farther into the wilderness. But they had believed that during spring, when Indian ways of travelling and using the land were the only ways, they could still be safe. But cabins? Squatters? Even Quarry might be occupied, and by residents who would no doubt want to hunt and trap there. Conversations during the next weeks continually returned to the cabin. What could be done to get rid of it? How could they protect their land against these intrusions?

After the journey to Mule Creek, the beaver hunt settled into a steady and productive rhythm. Sam Crown and Jim Wolf hunted an area across the Quarry River. Atsin and David daily followed their line downstream to the southeast of the cabin. Joseph trapped the creeks and dams closest to home. Others roamed more distantly, taking whatever direction seemed promising to them. Meanwhile, other families from the Reserve had set up farther down the valley to trap and hunt on the Fellow and Crown lines. The distances between all these camps were small. Every day there were visits among them to share news and meat and to exchange information and ideas about the condition and movements of animals, the weather, the search for horses that had wandered back towards the Reserve and must be tracked down, and possible ways of spending the rest of the spring hunt.

One day, Joseph decided that we should all move downstream to the Bluestone area. He had asked each hunter how much he had killed and found that the total came to over twenty beaver, two otter, and several muskrat. Enough had been taken at Quarry. After half a day of arranging gear, loading up pack horses, and dismantling tent frames, the entire camp was on the move. For the rest of that day our line of saddle and pack horses travelled southeast, down the river, across a ridge of hills to the Midden River, across it and into the woodland between the Midden and Bluestone Creek, and close by the cross we had visited the previous fall. Along the way we met the Robert Fellow camp, who also were moving to Bluestone Creek. Now there were nine of us and some twenty horses threading our way along a network of overgrown trails to within half a mile of Bluestone

Creek. Suddenly the riders in front stopped. Ahead of them they could hear the roar and hiss of a forest fire.

Judging by the noise and smoke, the fire, though not large, was very close to the campsite to which we were headed. A slight breeze seemed to be wafting the flames towards our trail. Everyone was nervous. Three men rode ahead to locate the fire and assess its dangers. Everyone else rode on slowly. Our eyes were now on the smoke and, as we came closer, we could see occasional columns of flame leap high above the treetops.

The campsite that both Joseph and Robert had in mind is in a large meadow on a plateau between two areas of dense woodland. One side drops a sharp and muddy twenty feet to a small creek. Sheltered, with good water and fuel close to hand, and excellent grazing for horses, the meadow is a perfect camping place and, according to the elders, generations of Indians have used it. The fire was burning the woods directly south of the meadow. These woods are very close to the last of a line of ranches that presses towards the core of several Reserve families' hunting grounds. It was now angrily declared that the ranchers must have set the fire with a view to clearing land and extending pastures.

The scouts had concluded that the fire offered no danger to us: between it and the meadow lay marshy ground — a natural firebreak which the flames would not cross. By the time the last of the horses and hunters had arrived, the first camps were already set up. At dusk, our fires seemed like small echos of the forest fire beyond them. In the night, as the people had predicted, the fire died down. By morning only patches of smouldering ash were left. The Indians had not feared for their safety. They completely and rightly trust their judgement of spring fires, if only because they used to set them themselves in order to improve the browsing habitat for horses and moose. They were less comfortable with the proximity of farmers. This favourite campsite now lay at the meeting point between hunting and ranching.

During the next days, the beaver hunt continued at dams and lodges within a walk or short ride of our new camp. Conversation returned repeatedly to who was responsible for the burning of woodlands, and to whether or not it was illegal. When the hunt was over, camps were broken for the last time, and we had begun the journey to the Reserve, everyone was deeply conscious that only a mile or two down the valley the long trail through farms and along ranching roads would begin.

This movement along the edge of a frontier is a troubling experience. It is not possible for hunters to return from Bluestone Creek without passing through cleared farms, along old and new logging roads, and by way of trails that have been upgraded into dirt roads for the oil and gas industry. As far as possible, the Indians skirt the edge of farms and stay on trails that take them by more direct and less conspicuous routes from their traplines to the reserves. For the last fifteen or so miles, however, they cannot avoid a valley road that serves a succession of large ranches. Wherever possible, the horses then follow a thin path a few yards off the dirt road. Where no such path exists, the horses (none of which is shod) must walk on the loose stone surface of the road itself, and riders and horses must both suffer the clouds of dust and the hail of pebbles that passing vehicles cast up as they pass.

Within an hour of leaving the Bluestone Creek campsite, the year's spring hunt reluctantly ended. In a long line, we crossed a rancher's meadow to approach a crossing place on the creek itself. On the other side we stopped to rest. Fires were lit, tea was brewed, and some meat was quickly roasted. But Joseph paced restlessly about the fires. "No good this side of the creek," he muttered. "White man's land here." We could still see the woods that guard Bluestone and Quarry; but the ease, good humour, and joy of the hunt was already overshadowed. We were now on land where the Indians felt like intruders — even though they say that these lands are still their own.

Everyone was relieved finally to turn through the gateposts and see the first houses of the Reserve. Smoke rose from out-of-doors fires which people had built alongside their homes to smoke a moose hide, heat drums of water to wash clothes, or simply sit beside. It was not Quarry, but, after the rough and dusty road from Bluestone, its own kind of peace was welcome: a small outpost, perhaps, but one with some of the serenity and well-being that had been found in abundance thirty miles higher up the valley.

Along the road, just before we came to the entrance of the Reserve, David pointed to the willows. Their leaves had just begun to unfold and were lightly touched with the palest green. A sign of spring. But for all the Indian households of the region, the spring hunt had already ended. By the time the tourists and sports fishermen had begun to push their way in early summer up the Midden and Quarry valleys, there would be no sign at all that Indian families had been living there only a few weeks before. The Indians, by then, would have sold their beaver pelts and be resting in summer camps on the reserves. And, if Joseph may be seen as an example, they would already be mentioning places where it might be good to hunt for beaver next spring.

14

Causes and Effects

The sports hunting season opens at the beginning of September. It continues, with some local variation, until November. During these months, particularly in the early, warmer weeks of the northern autumn, hunters stream into northeast British Columbia from all directions and then pass easily along the Alaska Highway to promising-looking hunting spots. Their vehicles are often conspicuous, especially as they depart for home triumphantly displaying the antlers of a fine moose or elk tied to the roof or not quite hidden under a tarpaulin in the back of a truck. Some hunters with a special sense of display, perhaps in emulation of a stag in rut, charge along the Highway with the antlers of a prize kill tied to the front of the radiator.

Sports hunting in British Columbia is controlled by licences issued on a two-tier system. For people who live outside the province licence fees are high — $100 for a moose, $300 for a grizzly bear, $100 for a caribou, plus a $75 general permit — and such hunters are required to be accompanied by licenced guides. These restrictions do not discourage foreigners — they travel from all over the United States, Germany, France, and even from Japan to enjoy the sport in northern British Columbia — but they are not conspicuous intruders. They are usually met at airports and flown at considerable expense, if not always great comfort, to camps in the mountains. These are trophy, not meat hunters, who rely on guides, usually Indians. The Indians, who feel that they both control and derive some economic benefits from these foreign visitors, do not resent them.

British Columbia residents, on the other hand, are subject to few restraints. Any resident may buy a licence to kill one of each species of large game. These licences are not expensive. Since 1960, the right to kill a moose or caribou has cost a resident $10; the price of a grizzly has been $35; a deer or a black bear only $4. General permits and licences to kill migratory birds, grouse, and rabbits cost a total of only $10.50. Anyone holding the required licences is entitled to hunt anywhere on all Crown lands, subject only to game management regulations. The cheapness of permits and the availability of Crown lands make sports hunting one of the most popular of British Columbian hobbies.

The autumn spate of campers and pickups along the Alaska Highway has its primary source in Vancouver and Victoria, but collects volume from all the smaller towns of the province. These hunters, out for a day or weekend if they are local, or for as much as a week or two if they have come from more distant parts of the province, are not usually preoccupied with a trophy for the sitting room wall. They are on a hunting holiday; but their main object is, increasingly, a freezer full of cheap meat. The region's reputation for moose attracts them. The moose season in the area is long and includes periods when cows as well as bulls may be shot. For the resident meat hunter, the chances of making a kill are said to be at least as high in northeast British Columbia as anywhere else. Many claim that the region has the best moose habitat in the world. Thousands of meat hunters turn right and left off the first two hundred miles of the Alaska Highway (which begins at Dawson Creek, forty miles south of Fort St. John), and then turn again along roads that lead into the hunting and trapping territories of the Beaver and Cree Indians.

The secondary roads, usually gravel-topped or packed dirt, lead to ranches and logging camps, or, more recently, give access to sites where oil and gas rigs have been or are soon going to be. Not long ago movement beyond these roads into the hinterland of forests and footpaths was possible only for the intrepid White who had the confidence to abandon his vehicle and the skill to navigate cross-country. Now, however, hunters can follow new trails that are being cut or bulldozed into the bush as a result of the burgeoning frontier: seismic lines and pipeline rights-of-way that have been slashed ever deeper into the foothills and forests. Four-wheel drive pickups can often follow the roughest of these cutlines, which therefore offer safe trails for Whites who might otherwise soon be lost in lands they would not normally dare to enter. This network of trails and access roads also means that the hunt need not be too arduous. The hunter will not have to pack his gear on foot or pack meat any great distance from his kill to his car. The popularity of so convenient a sport is evident on any Saturday afternoon at the peak of the meat-hunting season, from mid-September to early October. Then it is not surprising to come across a dozen hunters' vehicles or camps in a single fifteen-mile stretch of promising terrain on the dirt roads within twenty miles on either side of the Alaska Highway.

Virtually all sports hunters adopt a lie-in-wait strategy beside a trail or cutline where they expect game will travel or feed at dawn and dusk. There, usually within fifty yards of his parked vehicle, sometimes in a blind or maybe on a raised platform but more often just hidden in the bush, a hunter waits for an unwary animal to roam his way. Some sports hunters walk along the cutlines, in the hope of meeting a particularly incautious deer or moose that is using the same route or feeding a little way off the trail in the forest. British Columbian resident meat hunters are not required to hire guides, and very few of them will venture any distance from easy trails. This means that they cannot track animals as the Indians do. It also means that few of them will follow an animal they have wounded for much more than a hundred yards into the forest. Some dare not go that far.

The Indians have much to say about sports hunters. They dislike their coming unguided into Indian hunting territories and traplines. Whenever possible, they avoid them. At the same time, they carefully examine their old campsites, and interpret vehicle tracks and even sports hunters' footprints. They note their numbers, the recency of their presence, directions they have taken, equipment they have used, the kinds and quantities of booze they drank, whether or not they made a kill, their skinning and butchering methods, and how much meat and skin they have wasted. Indians are very quick to put together this kind of information, even picking through litter that the Whites have left, sometimes in conspicuous piles, sometimes in shallow dumps.

The Indians are glad that few sports hunters go any distance into the woods, but they are nonetheless appalled by the Whites' consequent unwillingness to follow and find wounded animals. They say that many sportsmen are trigger-happy, that they wound moose and deer they are unable to track, and that they fire at other species — ones that are not legal quarry. Almost every Indian hunter tells of beaver, lynx, moose calves, and other animals that have been found dead or dying during the sports-hunting season. Many also tell stories about dead horses and even cattle shot, they assume, in an abysmal extreme of ignorance. The abuse of wildlife disgusts and alarms the Indians. It represents a dangerous failure to respect the animals and the land, a respect that is essential for the Indians' own continued supply of food; essential, that is, for their security.

The sight of a white man, rifle in hand, trudging noisily and conspicuously along a trail, with very little of the understanding that Indians regard as integral to any hunting activity, is a cause of anger and despair. If there is one white hunter, there are no doubt others like him within a few miles. They ruin the hunting. Even when they notice only vehicle tracks or footprints in an area they have chosen, Indians abandon their hunt. It is as if an area has somehow been polluted; or more simply, is felt to be unsafe. Although some Whites are cautious, competent, and skillful in the bush, too many sports hunters are so anxious to make a kill, say the Indians, and so unskilled in the bush, that they might shoot a person, believing that anything large and moving in the woods can only be a moose or deer. A sports hunter may not go far from a trail, but his rifles are high powered and, in inexperienced hands, can be fatal even to people who try to keep well out of the way. If white hunters are around, most Indians go somewhere else — or go home. In so doing, they leave the forest and the animals to an intruder who, from their point of view, has no clear right to hunt freely on Indian lands.

The Indian hunters, angered by this annual intrusion and disturbed by the way many of the intruders behave, are also alarmed by both the numbers of white sports hunters who now come to the region and the number of moose they manage to kill. In 1978, an elder at the Halfway Reserve said he was sure that as many as one thousand Whites had hunted on his trapline the previous year. This "thousand" may sound like an angry exaggeration, but it has turned out to be an underestimate. When it comes to numbers of animals sports hunters kill, the Indians' fears also turn out to be more than justified.

The relevant figures can be calculated from official statistics. Each year, based on spot-check and roadside estimates as well as questionnaires, the provincial government publishes estimates of the numbers of hunters and kills made in each game management unit. These game management units are small and do not coincide with the Indians' pattern of land use. But this problem can be overcome by aggregating the figures for each of the units that falls within a band's or family's hunting territory. The figures for the management units can be seen on Map 20. Table 9 shows the extent to which each of the region's reserves is affected.

The table and the map illustrate how the intensity of meat hunting is related to the extension of access roads. The hunting territories

Table 9
Numbers of sports hunters and moose kills
on Indian hunting territories, 1977

Hunting territory of reserves	Number of sports hunters	Number of moose taken by sports hunters
Blueberry Doig	1,520*	660
Halfway	2,436	920
West Moberly East Moberly	1,349*	500
Prophet River	487	220
Fort Nelson	686	230
In all parts of region	10,099	3,625

*Where the hunting territories of two reserves overlap greatly, the total is given for the combined areas.

that lie beyond all roads and trails are comparatively untouched by white hunting. Those that are now within easy reach of a four-wheel drive vehicle are hunted very intensively. The new frontier has allowed hundreds, even thousands, of Whites to hunt or fish deep inside the heartlands of many Indian hunting territories and traplines. The prospective boom in the region's energy economy promises to give even more Whites access to the few areas they have not yet reached.

This access causes the most direct threat to the Indian interest in northeast British Columbia. The Indian moose harvest is small when measured alongside the numbers taken by white sports hunters. In the Halfway Reserve territory, for example, Whites take in two months a little over four times the number of moose the Indians take in the whole year. The Indians' dismay and indignation about the presence of so many white hunters is an indication of their reliance upon and belief in their own economic resources. Many reserves are bordered by farms. All the region's Indians have withdrawn from, or

simply lost the use of, much land that fifty years ago was important
for hunting and trapping. The effect of a succession of frontiers has
been a succession of withdrawals. Now at or very close to the limits
of further withdrawal, but maintaining in these lands a productive
hunting economy, they experience sports hunting as an ultimate
threat.

The intrusion of sports hunters, and their slaughter of animals on
which Indians depend, is a culmination of many years of frontier
settlement and development. The way in which different sectors of
the white man's economy have affected Indian use of the land can be
demonstrated graphically by superimposing maps showing resource
development in the region on the Indians' maps of their hunting
territories.

The gradual occupation of Crown lands by white settlement,
spreading westward along the Peace River valley, pushed the Indians
out of some of their best lands. This was well under way by the time
today's oldest hunters and trappers were children. The Indians'
hunting maps reveal that these traditional heartlands have long been
abandoned. A map showing all alienation of Crown land to white
ownership and occupancy, drawn onto the Indians' hunting territories, illustrates this withdrawal (Map 17). It also shows how more
recent alienation of Crown lands has been reaching deeper and
deeper into the Indians' lands.

Forestry activities at both the northern and southern ends of the
region create a patchwork of connected incursion into Indian hunting
lands. The prospect for continuing forestry can be seen on a map of
all harvestable timbers in the Indians' territories (Map 18). Similarly,
prospective coal and hydroelectric developments provide a further
set of forces potentially destructive of wildlife habitat and, in the case
of coal mining, promise an accompanying boom in urban development and white population. Finally, the oil and gas industry in
northeast British Columbia has spread far and wide through Indian
hunting and trapping lands. Were a map to be drawn showing all the
seismic lines that have already been cut through the region's forests,
extensive areas would appear as solid black. The activity that de-

velopment of the region's oil and gas resources has generated can be summarized in a map showing proven reserves and pipelines in the Fort St. John area (Map 19). But these summaries do no more than highlight some important features and convey a general impression: behind them is a mass of detail — rigs, trails, dirt roads, camps for seismic crews — that must be left to the reader's imagination. All these trails give sports hunters access to Indian lands (Map 20).

The maps show a succession of frontiers impinging upon lands where the Indians of northeast British Columbia continue to hunt, trap, and fish. By now it should not be hard to understand the many ways in which these frontiers threaten Indian economic and cultural well-being. There are still extensive areas where this progressive incursion has not destroyed the wildlife upon which Indians depend. But is it really possible for such a combination of frontiers to avoid, in the end, a final destruction of the way of life that the Indians say they must be able to pursue? The latest effect of the frontiers has been to produce the conditions under which sports hunting can thrive and expand.

Social scientists and others who have spoken out on behalf of the Indians' needs and rights in this and other regions have pointed to the cumulative impact of industrial and frontier developments. It is to this idea of cumulative impact that I now turn. Its consideration will lead directly into some of the difficulties that bedevil many discussions of northern development.

The concept of cumulative impact directs attention from a limited focus on individual projects to a consideration of the whole process of which any single project is only a part. Impacts are thus seen to be interconnected and cumulative. A given project may have minimal or limited effects; but seen as part of all the projects that will follow it, the cumulative effects may be severe. The point is, if we look at the process as a whole, then the cumulative significance of many impacts can be better grasped. From the Indians' standpoint, cumulative impact may be a question of context. The effects of mining development on a people whose hunting territories have already been altered and restricted by agricultural clearance or ranching will differ from

•

17

ALIENATION

The section by section purchase and use of Crown lands cannot be shown on a map of this scale. (Maps 17, 18, and 19 have been scaled down from a large and detailed original.) This map, therefore, gives a visual impression of the way white settlement has spread into northeast British Columbia from the southeast. In time, newcomers, moved along fertile valleys towards the northwest. The hunting territories show how the Indians had by the 1940s withdrawn from prime lands around the Peace River. The recent period of settlement shows Whites moving deeper and deeper onto the lands on which the several Indian bands now depend.

Source: Data and map compiled by Community Information Research Group for Union of British Columbia Indian Chiefs.

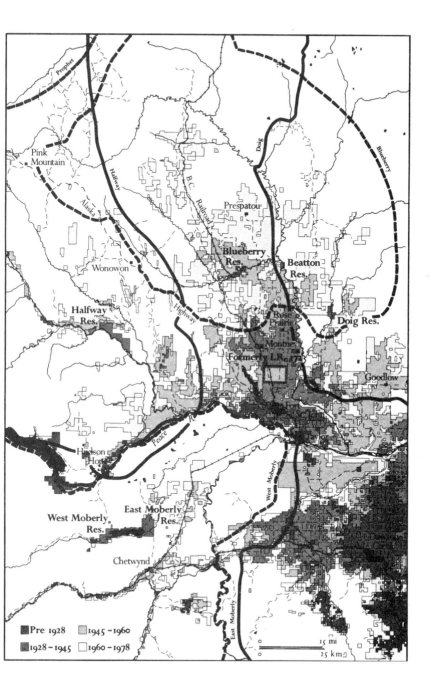

Prophet

Pink
Mountain

Halfway

B.C. Railroad

Doig

Prespatou

Alaska

Wonowon

**Blueberry
Res.**

**Beatton
Res.**

Blueberry

**Halfway
Res.**

Highway

Rose
Prairie

Doig Res.

Montney
Formerly I.R. 172

Goodlow

Peace R.

Hudson
Hope

West Moberly

**West Moberly
Res.**

**East Moberly
Res.**

Chetwynd

East Moberly

☐ Pre 1928   ☐ 1945 – 1960

☐ 1928 – 1945   ☐ 1960 – 1978

15 mi

25 km

18

FORESTRY

The extent of harvestable timber in this, the southern part of the region, represents the geographical potential for logging. Locations where logging was being carried out in 1978, or was at that time planned for the near future, indicate the pressure on timber in the hunting territories of the Moberly Lake and Halfway River reserves. A comparison of this map with Map 17 reveals the way in which logging is most intensive in areas that were just beyond white occupancy of Crown lands by the early 1950s. The cut sites, shown by black dots, are linked by new logging roads, giving access to land that was previously beyond the reach of vehicles.

Source: Data and maps compiled by Community Information Research Group for Union of British Columbia Indian Chiefs.

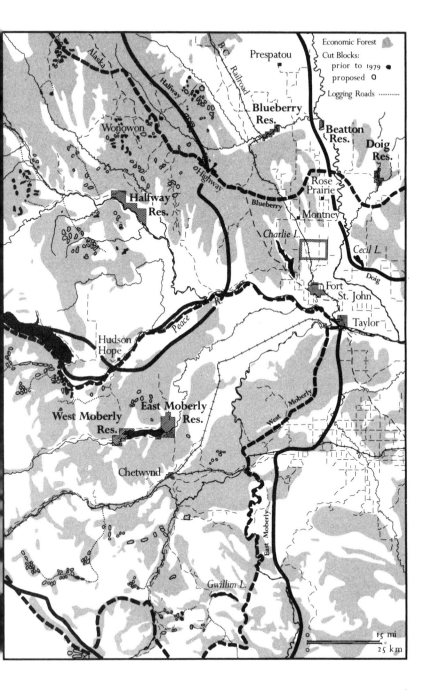

Economic Forest

Cut Blocks:
 prior to 1979 ●
 proposed ○

Logging Roads ··········

Prespatou

Blueberry
Res.

Beatton
Res.

Doig
Res.

Wonowon

Alaska

Halfway

B.C. Railroad

Highway

Rose
Prairie

Blueberry

Montney

Halfway
Res.

Charlie L.

Cecil L.

Doig

Fort
St. John

Taylor

Peace

Hudson
Hope

West Moberly

East Moberly
Res.

West Moberly
Res.

Chetwynd

East Moberly

Gwillim L.

15 mi
25 km

19

OIL AND GAS

The oil and gas fields shown here are proven deposits. The regularity of their shapes and distribution are consequences of the ways in which deposits are proven up and then specified. In fact, the probable (and widely anticipated) extent of both oil and gas is far greater than indicated here. Present exploration in the eastern foothills is yielding prospects for a very much more extensive map than this one. Similarly, the wells marked here do not include ones that have been drilled and capped, or are found to be dry; and the data base, being 1978, understates their present proliferation. Seismic cuts are not marked. If they were, the whole map would be crosshatched with indecipherable lines. As in Maps 17 and 18, this one shows only the southern part of the region. Oil and gas are, of course, scarcely less important in the Fort Nelson area and lands to the north.

Source: Data and map compiled by Community Information Research Group for Union of British Columbia Indian Chiefs.

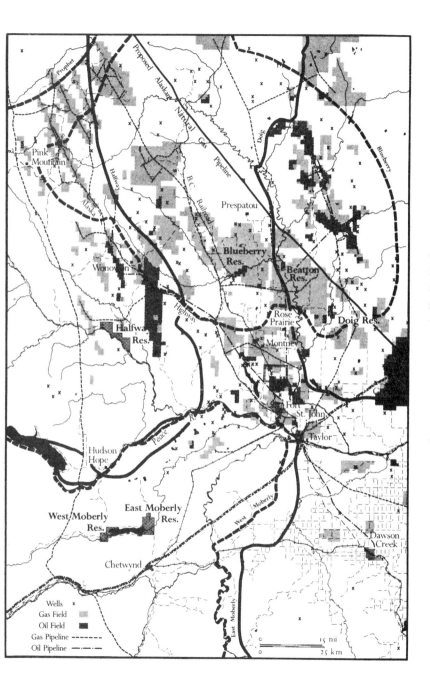

Wells   x

Gas Field

Oil Field

Gas Pipeline   - - - -

Oil Pipeline   -·-·-

0   15 mi

0   25 km

Prophet

Pink
Mountain

Proposed

Alaskan

Natural

Gas

Pipeline

Doig

Blueberry

Halfway

B.C. Railroad

Prespatou

Alaska

Blueberry
Res.

Beatton
Res.

Wonowon

Rose
Prairie

Doig Res.

Highway

Montney

Halfway
Res.

Fort
St. John

Peace R.

Taylor

Hudson
Hope

West Moberly
Res.

East Moberly
Res.

West Moberly

Dawson
Creek

Chetwynd

East Moberly

20

SPORTS HUNTING FOR MOOSE IN NORTHEAST BRITISH COLUMBIA,
1977

The areas outlined on this map show the British Columbia government's wildlife management districts. The numbers are of sports
hunters who hunted in each district in 1977 and, in parentheses, the
number of moose they killed. The high numbers coincide with areas
close to the Alaska Highway (shown by the dotted line), or along
access roads leading from it. The districts that include the Rocky
Mountain foothills, and which go off the base map, are hunted
intensively at their eastern and hardly at all at their western edges.
The intrusion onto Indian hunting territories that these figures
represent is discussed and tabulated on pages 234 and 235 of this
chapter.

Source: Department of Fish and Wildlife, Government of British Columbia.

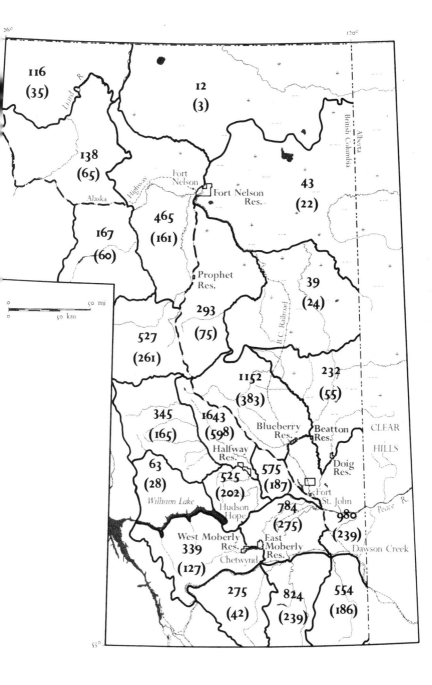

its effects on a people whose hunting territories are still largely intact.

The concept of cumulative impact is easily related to the series of developments experienced in northeast British Columbia. From the Indians' perspective the long history of the region's development can be understood only as a progressive loss of lands by a people for whom mobility has always been at the heart of economy and culture. A simple analogy may convey the result of cumulative impact on such a people. To shove, be it gently or forcibly, a person who stands in the middle of a field is one thing; but to shove someone who stands at the edge of a cliff is quite another. Developments that serve an industrial economy are usually interconnected by stages of economic growth and by infrastructure. To understand the effects of new developments then, we must understand what has passed and been experienced before. The idea of cumulative impact invites this kind of understanding.

Yet it is an idea beset by difficulties. It is not always easy to specify the process of which any project is part — unless the process is described in very general terms as industrialization or frontier development. If the process is described in this general way, however, its cumulative impact may be similarly described. Such generalizations may be useful in looking at how damage to wildlife or to the environment has occurred and may be minimized, but may be of little use in prescribing specific remedies for specific ills. Nor is a general description of the effects of industrialization as a progressive deterioration of the environment any less discouraging: large and general processes occur with anonymity and remorselessness. The forces that press them forward transcend the merely national, and often seem too many or too abstract to be related to regional needs or fears. The imagination stumbles and falls when presented with the idea of turning the relentless course of history from its path. When impact is seen as process, those most directly and personally affected, confronted by the horrifying magnitude of it, are likely to give up in despair.

An overenthusiastic use of the idea of cumulative impact can thus lead to a hopeless fatalism. It can also imply a troubling degree of passivity among the peoples who are impacted. The idiom of social science, pointing as it does to strong socioeconomic and historical forces and to their general or inevitable consequences, often suggests that people upon whom these forces act are helpless victims who have neither the wit nor the freedom to influence events. There is a narrow and difficult path between a social science that denies human freedom, and naive or romantic ideas about individual or even collective will. The trouble with the term "impact" is its connotations of passivity. No one will deny that Indians, like all too many other minority groups, have been victims of strong and perhaps irresistible pressures. Yet they have not merely endured impacts. To suggest such helpless passivity is as much a historical error as it is an insult.

Indian groups in northern British Columbia have already lost the use of areas that were once at the centre of their hunting system. They are continuing to suffer many different kinds of incursions upon their territories. Step by step, field by field, road after road, new pipelines, dams, and even whole new towns — this is the accumulated impact of a century of white frontiers. During this same period, however, the Indians became involved in the fur trade. They adopted many items of new technology, including guns, steel traps, and horse tack, and they developed a flexible, mixed economic system. They now regard many of these innovations as elements of traditional life — proof that the Indians have not been passive in the face of change. They have welcomed and made their own some of the innovations brought to or urged upon them by Whites, and they have rejected many others. Early colonialism was far from benign: the Indians lost land; critical habitats were destroyed; infectious epidemic diseases were recurrent and widespread; the Indians, as a people, were much despised. But flexibilities in the Indians' society and their economy meant that sometimes they sought to benefit from forms of colonialism, and sometimes they were simply able to avoid them. A century of change has included economic and cultural transactions that were, in some ways, on the Indians' own terms.

In British Columbia, governments and industrialists have long dreamed of a permanent boom based on the export of energy. The proponents of the energy frontier are single-minded in their determination to exploit energy resources wherever they might be found. Many feel that this single-mindedness will have effects on Indians that are unlike any they have so far experienced. Yet such effects must certainly be seen in the context of an Indian vulnerability that is a consequence of the progressive restriction of their land base by earlier frontiers. As an example of the accumulated effects of a combination of such activities, consider the case of Moose Call, part of the West Moberly Lake Reserve and an area of vital importance to that reserve's hunting and trapping economy. Almost every development in the region has affected Moose Call. A pipeline cuts through it. Logging has destroyed a substantial proportion of its climax forest of evergreens. Transmission lines from the W. A. C. Bennett Dam cross it. The hydroelectric development at Site 1 on the Peace River threatens to flood a large part of the area — and may have done so by the time this is published. If such impacts have not yet proved devastating to the wildlife of the area, this is because the West Moberly Lake Band has gone to great efforts to monitor and protect the animals that live there. Every Indian band has its Moose Call. These are areas that they have depended upon and cared for over many years, and that are acutely sensitive to intrusion. Not all of them have yet been so badly damaged by industrial developments.

The prospect of a protracted and intrusive oil and gas frontier, potentially active throughout all the reserves' hunting and trapping territories, obviously threatens all the Moose Calls that have been maintained (or withdrawn to) in the face of other, earlier developments. But even here we must be wary of shrill and fatalistic cries of imminent and final destruction of the Indian economic interest. The Indians' lands and resources are terribly threatened, and there may be nowhere for the people to withdraw to. It does not follow that they are *bound* to be destroyed. There is here a difficult tension between insisting, on the one hand, that Indians are surprisingly flexible and saying, on the other hand, that they are now economically and socially threatened as they have never been before. Chapter 16 pursues this tension; but before any attempt to resolve the problem, it is important to consider the way environmental and social effects are linked.

Environmental effects, good or bad, are inseparable from the social and individual well-being of a people whose domestic economy, historical experience, and sense of identity are focussed on the land and its resources. Even though the precise links in the causal chain from environment to society are not easily spelled out, the effects upon individuals of divorce from their traditional activities are clear to see.

This brings the discussion towards matters that are both problematical and uncomfortable. The discomfort is moral as well as scientific. To reinforce racist stereotypes in any way would be irresponsible as well as misleading. To discuss social pathologies in general, or to discuss the alcohol question as a particular example, is to risk strengthening the opinions of those who despise and disregard Indian people. On the other hand, such issues must be addressed directly, together with the source and validity of the stereotypes these problems have helped to sustain. No one pretends that the social problems of Indians are pure fiction. Indeed, an important part of the argument here is that these problems could easily become much worse.

Chapter 4 described the ways in which the Indians of northern British Columbia have been stereotyped. Drunkenness is an important part of the stereotype. George Simpson, one of the first Europeans to describe life among the Beaver Indians of the Peace River region, wrote in the 1820s:

> They are now however excessively addicted to Spiritous Liquours which they use immoderately and unadulterated. Their constitutions are delicate, most probably owing to their want of attention to personal comforts and unrestrained use of ardent spirits; few attain the age of Fifty years, and pulmonary complaints make dreadful ravages among them.

Simpson's view has been echoed by almost all Whites who have since visited the area. The long-established stereotype has reinforced the general tendency of Whites to believe that, however marvellous they may once have been, Indians are now doomed, their drunkenness, ill health, and poverty being sad symptoms of ubiquitous causes of irreversible decline.

Before their contact with Europeans, the northern peoples of North America neither made nor used intoxicants of any kind. Abnormal states of mind were induced in shamans by drumming, singing, and dancing; visions were part of spirit-quests and related shamanistic searches for power and for the causes of misfortune. None of these skills, rituals, or private spiritual activities depended on drugs. When alcohol came, then, it was a very major innovation — though in the case of the Athapaskan hunters, it never became a part of spiritual life. Rather, it was used by traders to encourage Indians to come more frequently to trading posts and to become more dependent on Whites. Traders soon recognized that they had an almost ideal trade commodity in alcohol: it is soon consumed and tends to be addictive. They exchanged drink — traditionally rum — for furs, or sold it for the money they had paid for furs, or simply gave it away. The Indians promptly drank it all. The traders were left with the furs and the Indians were left with as great a need as ever — if not an increasing need — for trade goods. Trading, thus helped by alcohol, led to more trading. At the same time, rival trading companies used alcohol to make a visit to their particular posts more attractive. Of course, all this resulted in many Indian trappers spending time very drunk. But they could be relied upon to return to the bush to trap once their means were exhausted, and to return again to the post when they needed to do so — with more furs.

The history of Indian use of alcohol in the North is therefore as old as the history of the fur trade. Alcohol, and spree drinking, are part of the Indians' involvement with traders and trading. Moreover, since traders did not want to cause drunkenness so much as to nurture dependency, they created a situation in which the Indians recurrently made requests for help. And the pattern continues: anyone who has lived in northern British Columbia has encountered Indians who seem to fit Simpson's description, already 150 years old.

When Whites describe Indian drunks and bums who are chronically dependent on handouts from the government or other institutions, it is worth asking very simple questions. When do Whites meet Indians? In what circumstances do they get to know them? The answers to such questions show how the stereotype is reinforced. They meet Indians in the bars, on the streets of towns where Indians do not live, in many situations that involve a plea for money, for a ride, for a sympathetic ear. Alternately, they meet Indians in places of employment where, in order to be a success, the Indian must somehow demonstrate ability at many non-Indian social and technical skills. In all these settings, Indians are forever being judged and found wanting by the standards of the dominant society. They are vulnerable to these standards when they are away from home and are conspicuous. They wander in the streets or sit in bars. Visits to town are often an aspect of spree drinking, and visibility strengthens the white man's idea that Indians spend much of their time, maybe most of it, drunk. The way of life that Whites bring to their frontiers, as well as the racist's familiar inability to see individuals rather than examples, thus nurtures the stereotype.

Ever since trading posts were first established and Indian hunters became trappers and guides, periodic visits to white establishments have been part of the Indian's pattern of mobility. Because of the way alcohol was introduced and used, these visits have always been associated with festive parties. In the early days of the fur trade, Indian trappers would bring their skins in to trade only once or twice a year; as the trade developed, the visits became more frequent. But however frequent they may have been, the only times Whites regularly saw Indians were at trading posts. The origin of the negative stereotype is easy to see.

The stereotype has been reinforced in recent years, precisely because the association between drinking and dealings with Whites has persisted. For administrative reasons reserves are located near towns. Whereas twenty-five years ago trading visits may have occurred four or five times a year, many Indians now go to town once every two or three weeks, and some stay in town a week or more. The porportion of time that Indians spend in town has grown, whereas the idea, the tradition of how time in town should be spent has stayed much the same.

Whites who meet Indians in town, at the local grocery store, in the bars, or along the highway find it all too easy to believe that the Indians have lost their self-reliance and self-respect, and to suppose that all traditional strengths and skills are things of the past. Those who hold these views, based as they are on personal experience, are impatient with any suggestion that they should take the Indian interest into full and careful account. They regard the future of the region as their own, the Indians who live there as relics of the past and a liability in the present.

The few Whites who spend any time on the reserves find further evidence to confirm the stereotype. Reserves in northern British Columbia are strange places. Conceived, located, designed, and built by Whites, the reserve has little relation to the social, domestic, and economic life that their residents have traditionally regarded as good and proper. Perhaps in the case of reserves to the west of the Rockies, which have been placed near fishing resources on which the people depend, there really is an association between homeland and reserve. But this is not so for the hunting bands in northern British Columbia. Here the people have very little obvious employment connected with the reserves. It is no secret that they are places where there is a good deal of drinking, and where drunks are often more conspicuous than their sober relatives.

The Indians do not pretend that alcohol is not a problem. Indeed, they are deeply worried by it. However, they know the extent to which their lives go beyond anything that outsiders get to see. Many aspects of Indian culture and economy, especially those most valued by the Indians themselves, are concealed from critical and moralistic eyes. In the family, in homes, in the privacy of the bush, in the very shyness that often pervades Indian dealings with Whites, in that stillness, almost a withdrawal, that is considered a mature, wise, and thoughtful presentation of self — here is the Indian life that the people themselves value most. And here it is that the stereotype of the drunken bum can be discredited. Yet outsiders cannot enter easily into these places. The hidden qualities of life and personality are barricades directed against outsiders and against all forms of unfriendly intrusion.

Thus to be hidden may in some way draw on cultural tendencies that are beyond historical understanding, that are as old as the cultures themselves. To be hidden may also be related to ideas of wisdom, and to the manner in which Indians raise their children. It may be a corollary to the flexibility of the Indian system. But this readiness to withdraw has been powerfully reinforced, and perhaps distorted, by colonial history. Indians have been driven, or have found it best to retreat, out of sight.

The effects of colonial pressure, of the frontier, and of the very presence of the white man are escaped in the bush. All of the indicators — poor health, accidents and injuries, violence, and, of course, drunkenness — very rarely occur in the bush. That is why Joseph Patsah and many other hunters and trappers like to take their families to the bush when there are disruptive intrusions in the everyday life of the Reserve. That is why environmental effects feed directly and frighteningly into all adverse social disruptions in Indian life. That is why a resident of a northern British Columbia reserve said at a public hearing in 1979: "The answer to the alcohol problem is to be found in one word, the *bush*."

Among the most compelling features of Indian life in this region is the transformation in people when they leave reserves or towns to go on hunting trips. When they set out for the bush, to hunt and trap, they do not drink, are not violent. They are, instead, supportive of one another, attentive, and cautious. Tense people relax; the uncertain and shy become more confident. Everyone feels a sense of well-being that comes only with tasks and activities which they find deeply satisfying, which they know that they know best.

The contrasts are astonishing. The ability to track animals, to make fires, to travel through dense forest in the worst conditions without getting lost — these skills are shared by young and old alike. None of this is conspicuous to outsiders. Even Whites who have lived in the region for many years, perhaps all their lives, may never have had an opportunity to see Indians away from the reserve or to share Indian life in the bush. And those most fatalistic or pessimistic about the prospects for the Indian interest will always find it difficult to believe that life is other than they themselves can see.

Now think again of the sports hunter and the way he embodies so many of the influences that press on Indian communities. In the sports hunting season the white man has changed his clothes and left his drill rig, work camp, shop, farm, or office building to go into the woods. He can do so because he and others have cut roads and seismic lines into Indian territory. From the point of view of both frontiersman and suburban visitor, this access to the wilderness is a welcome and proper addition to his personal hinterland. He may never have heard of Treaty 8 or trapline registration. Sports hunting represents his rightful use of the province in which he lives and pays his taxes. In their own small ways, seismic lines and new trails cut in the eastern foothills of the Rockies are a hint of what is still new in the New World. Basements and garages all over northern America are full of hunting, fishing, and camping equipment. Nearly every Canadian feels, as a special part of his national identity, a closeness to the wilderness; and many a Canadian's personal identity is bound up with the pleasure he takes in wilderness activities. A sense of personal freedom, an escape from the metropolitan rat race, feelings of national pride, these and many related ideas are reflected by these basements and garages full of bush clothes and boots, canoes, sleeping bags, racks of hunting rifles. Of great importance also is the real conviction of most Canadians that the wilderness is part of their heritage, that everyone has a right to enjoy it in his own way. This may be less clear in Canada than in the United States, where nervous and competitive trading companies did not try to keep the wilderness under close control, and where insistence on the right to carry a gun is a carry-over into the suburbs of an old frontier ethic which became a constitutional right. But Canadian sports hunters feel this sense of rightness deeply and without question.

The sports hunters' use of Crown lands reveals, from the Indians' point of view, the collision of interest between Whites and Indians in the hunting territories of northeast British Columbia. There, the causes and effects are very plain to see. The richer, stronger, and more ignorant of the Whites are sure that they can push the Indians into the mountains, or oceans, or some lowly slot in the wage labour economy. Right, justice, common sense, and the forces of history, they will say, are all on the side of the white man's frontier. His dreams are far more urgent than Indians' maps — and as for Indian dreams, well . . . they are nothing more than that. The use of lands for sports hunting is an extension and an apotheosis of the frontier. The Indians see it as such. If the bush ceases to be a place into which Indians can withdraw, and whose resources they can rely upon, then they have lost their economy and are exposed forever to the stereotype that portrays them as impoverished. Such loss and exposure would mean that, finally, the stereotype would become the truth.

15

A Hearing

In June, Joseph and his family set up their summer camp on the Reserve. Four small households camped together in a patch of woodland only a few hundred yards from Joseph's house. There Atsin and David stretched a small tarpaulin between the trees and a sloping ridge pole. This provided shelter from rain, but, being open-sided, was cool. Sam Crown and Jimmy Wolf, Joseph and Liza, and Reza, Shirley, and Tommy all pitched tents around a central fireplace. Atsin had a fire in front of his camp, but he and David — along with everyone else who lived or visited there — spent much of their time sitting, chatting, and eating by Joseph's fire.

The hot days of summer had their own special mood. Every morning one or two of the younger men went to find the horses, following their tracks along the riverside or into the hay and oat fields where they liked to feed. Once they had chased them back to camp, the hunters tethered the ones they thought they might need during the day. But it was often too hot to hunt; days slipped by without much activity. The men lay for hours, a short distance from the fires, half asleep, getting up to eat, visit a neighbour, or play cards. Liza, Reza, and Shirley fried bannock on the campfire above which they carefully hung meat to smoke and to protect it from flies. On very still days they also built smoke fires to keep away the flies and wasps that persistently bit the horses. Children roamed the hillsides and river banks looking for berries, swimming, or hunting rabbits and grouse.

Thomas and Abe Fellow worked almost every day on the Reserve ranch, riding off to herd cattle, move a bull from one meadow to another, or look for horses that had strayed into the surrounding woods. Some days Sam and Atsin suggested a hunt, and then we would ride down the Midden River valley or drive to promising areas within fifteen miles of the Reserve. In summer, bull moose and buck mule deer are in prime condition, and hunting spots were chosen with them in mind. But tracking in great heat and through thick undergrowth and clouds of mosquitoes is hard work. Although enough kills were made to maintain an adequate supply of fresh meat, we spent most days dozing in the shade of the campsite.

In early August, almost everyone on the Reserve went to the Fort St. John rodeo. In mid-August, Joseph's brother and sister-in-law visited for two weeks, camping with us in the small wood by Joseph's house. At this time berries were ripening in abundance — first strawberries, then gooseberries, blueberries, and saskatoon berries. Everyone picked them as they found them, the children sometimes returning to camp with hats or plastic bags full of blueberries. Thomas's sister-in-law stewed panfuls of them in fat; that way, everyone said, you can eat as much as you want without any risk of diarrhoea.

In August, the heat was often intense. During the middle of the day even the mosquitoes kept to the cool shade of the undergrowth. The stillness was broken only by groups of children who walked and rode to a deep swimming hole a mile from camp. There they splashed and swam, sometimes riding into the water until their horses were out of their depth and then clinging on as the animal swam, or plunging off when a horse lunged and bucked in protest. A few older men and women at times came and watched these games, but many people spent their days in almost total inactivity. Summer is a time for resting.

So July and August passed quickly, quietly, and pleasantly. We twice moved camp from one part of the woodland to another. A porcupine, one or two mule deer, and grouse contributed to the excellence of our diet. From time to time someone went fishing within a half mile of the camp and returned with a sucker or a few rainbow trout. But there were also mishaps. Joseph was stung on the face by a wasp and spent two days with a painfully swollen cheek. Jimmy Wolf cut himself on the leg when angrily swatting at a bee with his hunting knife. One of the horses developed sores on its back and could not be ridden. These and similar events lent small features to a hazy, undifferentiated passage of time.

Then, in early September, thoughts turned yet again to Quarry and Bluestone, and the need to build up stocks of meat. Joseph spoke of the marmot that would be easy to shoot as they basked, fat from a summer of feeding, on rocks high in the foothills. He also said they might now find caribou in the mountains. It was at this time that the Blueberry Reserve was evacuated. A pipe in a nearby gas-cleaning plant had fractured and the reserve had been enveloped in the middle of the night in a cloud of hydrogen-sulphide gas. Thanks to haste, nobody was killed; but the community was forced to live temporarily in summer tents a few miles east of the Alaska Highway. This alarming event caused much discussion. Joseph and others at the Reserve had relatives who lived at Blueberry, and there had long been rumours of impending drilling for oil or gas on the Reserve itself.

But as summer turned to another autumn, the events at Blueberry were overshadowed by talk of the Alaska Highway pipeline, and about a plan to hold hearings in each of the communities that might suffer some of the consequences of this enormous project. An employee of the Northern Pipeline Agency (an office set up by the federal government to prepare social and environmental conditions as well as to facilitate pipeline construction) visited the Reserve. He left a sheaf of papers at the house of the Chief. Then, some weeks later, a long and difficult document was also left, which set out, in provisional form, the terms and conditions that might govern the pipeline's construction. Finally, a notice was fixed to the door of the meeting hall that announced a date on which a public hearing into these terms and conditions would be held.

It is possible that a few people on the Reserve saw, or even tried to read, the documents, although no one did at Joseph's camp. If they had tried, they would have made little sense of the tortured bureaucratese by which every idea in the documents was obscured. Perhaps agency officials had attempted to discuss the ideas that they were advancing. If so, the people's interest or understanding was too slight for such ideas to become topics of conversation in our camp. The Alaska Highway Pipeline was seen as a vast, unwelcome, and perplexing menace. But no one knew quite where it was supposed to go; few knew what it would carry; no one knew if its possible dangers had been considered. The construction project that developers had hailed, and environmentalists bewailed, as the largest and most significant in the history of free enterprise was little more than a vague and distant enigma to the people who were supposedly to be its first and absolute victims.

Some chiefs and other representatives of the Indians of northeast British Columbia had visited Ottawa the year before to appear before a parliamentary subcommittee, where they had spoken out against the pipeline. But the connection between that visit and the papers left in the Chief's home was not clear. White officials were always saying that bits of paper were of special importance, but right now there were other important matters at hand: the beginning of the autumn hunt, marmot, caribou . . .

In September, Joseph's household, along with several others, returned to Quarry for the first autumn hunt; but the weather broke and for two weeks the hunters endured almost continuous rain, eventually returning to the Reserve. By this time the hearing had become a more pressing issue. Northern Pipeline Agency officials had drawn up a provisional timetable, and political anxieties about how the whole process was to be effected were becoming intense. Yet the many meetings and disputes about the hearing took place in offices in Vancouver, Calgary, and Ottawa, and did not bear in any direct way upon the people. In early October, however, the Indians were told that representatives of the company planning to construct the pipeline, officials of the Northern Pipeline Agency, political and legal workers from the Union of British Columbia Indian Chiefs, along with an independent presiding chairman, and the press would converge upon the Reserve in November. Then, they said, they would listen to the people. A schedule set out the dates on which a hearing would take place at each of the reserves and at several of the towns and white communities throughout the region.

These community hearings were characterized by the Northern Pipeline Agency as an opportunity for the Indians and others to respond to the terms and conditions which they, at the agency, had already drafted. This limitation would not be rigidly enforced, since it was bound to result either in endless misunderstandings or a reduction of the hearings to discussion that, for many people, might well be unintelligible. The preparation of terms and conditions — the rules that were supposed to reflect the Indian interest — had also taken place before any close attention had been given to the Indian point of view.

The people at the Reserve nonetheless anticipated their hearing with great interest. Doubts may have arisen in the minds of their political representatives. Reports and papers left in the reserves by various officials may have gone unread. But the people themselves insisted that the coming meeting was of great importance. There was an ever-growing sense of occasion. No one had taken much trouble to ask the Indians what they thought about pipelines or any other frontier activity, and a hearing seemed to many like the first real chance to express their long-neglected points of view. As the event came nearer, the Fort St. John radio station repeatedly announced the days and times of different hearings. Everyone at the Reserve including Joseph began to look forward to the occasion.

The morning of the hearing was sunny and cold. No one was quite sure when it was supposed to begin. The notice on the door of the Hall gave the time as 10 A.M., but some people insisted that nothing much was going to happen before noon. At Joseph's house there was some excitement. On the previous afternoon, Atsin and Sam had discovered the freshly prepared den of a black bear. Branches and earth had been piled up around the den's entrance: the bear was about to bed down for the winter. The way the branches had been pulled and heaped left the men sure that they would be able to force the animal from its den and kill it in the entranceway, where it could easily be dragged out. The sooner they went back to the new den, said Atsin, the better. At this time of year, after a whole summer of feeding and the early autumn cold, the meat and fur should both be in excellent condition and there would be plenty of fat. Joseph added that he could use some bear grease, the best thing for softening and protecting the leather of his saddles and bridles.

Joseph, Atsin, and Sam were adamant: we should go and get the bear right away. Maybe we would be able to get back in time for the meeting; maybe the meeting should wait until later in the day; or maybe we could get the talking over with quickly, and be on our way to the den by early afternoon. It was a perfect day for hunting. Who could possibly want to spend it listening to talk? What was there to say about the pipeline anyway? After a long discussion, we finally agreed that the bear hunt could wait until first thing the following morning. Joseph and Atsin decided to stay for the hearing. Sam Wolf, however, said he would never listen to talk when he could be out hunting. He pointedly prepared his equipment and set off on foot to look for moose. Brian Akattah and I went to the hall to put up the maps the people of the Reserve had drawn to show the extent of their hunting and trapping territories. Everyone else patiently waited at home for the hearing to begin.

It was a long wait. The chairman came early, to be shown the

Reserve, but it was midday before a busload of officials drove up to the hall. Specialists on social and economic impacts, a secretary to oversee proceedings, people whose job it was to record every word that was spoken, all climbed out and began to assemble their equipment. In separate cars came the men from West Coast Transmission — the company that would build the British Columbian section of the line — with their diagrams of the pipeline, the press, and representatives of the Union of Chiefs.

Inside the hall, chairs and tables were arranged, maps pinned on the walls. In the kitchen, beside the main meeting room, the women of the Reserve were cooking. They had prepared two kinds of moose stew, venison steaks, and a bountiful supply of bannock. Rich aromas filled the hall and indicated that however numerous and alien the outsiders and their technology might be, the Reserve was going to do its best to turn the hearing into its own kind of occasion.

By the time the hall was finally ready for the hearing to begin, there were at least as many outsiders to listen, report, or observe as there were Indians prepared to speak. The visitors were talkative and jovial and quickly chose their seats. The Indians were quiet and reluctant even to enter the room. The chairman took his place at the altar-table on which, just over a year ago, Stan had drawn his hunting map. The two transcribers sat among a tangle of equipment. The Reserve women stayed in the kitchen, out of sight and busy with their work, but able to see and hear through a hatch and doorway which opened into the hall. Joseph, Jimmy Wolf, Abe Fellow, Robert Fellow, and Clare Akattah, with other community elders and leaders, had been urged into sitting at a table to one side of the chairman. They looked uncomfortable. No doubt they were wondering what was expected of them and were puzzled by the microphones an official kept rearranging in front of them — technology that hardly seemed necessary in so small a room.

In this unpromising way, the meeting at length began. The chairman started by trying to explain its purpose. He spoke about the Alaska Highway pipeline and sought to give some rudimentary history of the litigation by which it was being facilitated. Nervously, in an attempt to overcome the problems of language and culture, and conscious of the extreme lack of background information among the people who sat there trying to make sense of it all, he laid out the reason for the hearing. He talked about terms and conditions and explained what kinds of rules there would be. He tried, also, to describe the differences between the roles of the governments, agencies, and construction companies. And he emphasized his wish to hear all that the people of the Reserve might have to say about the pipeline, or any of the other developments to which it related.

The elders at the table watched and listened. They quickly felt some sympathy for the chairman, an elderly man with a quiet voice and gentle manner, who was wearing beaded moccasins. By keeping their focus on him, they lessened the disturbing effects of the other strangers and could feel that they were able to talk and be listened to in a personal, human way.

But it was not easy for them. The chairman was followed by the Northern Pipeline Agency's secretary and a representative of West Coast Transmission who introduced their colleagues and said what each of them did. The introductions were not translated into Beaver. At this time, in any case, only a small number of the people had come to sit in the hall. They continued to stand in the doorway, in the kitchen, or to wait outside. When the chairman did at last ask the Indians to offer their points of view, Joseph began to talk. His clarity and confidence filled the hall and transformed its atmosphere. He spoke in Beaver, with an interpreter. The unfamiliarity of the sounds and the richness of his tone cast a spell over the proceedings. The absurdities and awkwardness of the event faded away. Here, at last, was an Indian voice. After every few sentences, Joseph paused and let the interpreter translate. In English, the words were not easy to grasp, and its being rendered in the third person made the sense no clearer. But the points were not lost:

> He was saying in our country there was no such thing as money before the white man came; our only way to make a living is to hunt and there is no such thing as money to get from one another and big bulldozers that come over, go across our country.

He is saying as long as there is the sun that goes over, that he shall never stop hunting in this country and wherever he likes to do, as long as the sun is still there.

He is saying that the white man pushed his way into our country, that he stakes up all the land and a long time ago there was no people and then now there is so many. . . .

He is saying if the pipeline goes through, the game will never be here and is there no way that we can stop this pipeline from going through and when the game goes away how would the people make their survival for meat?

He says if the white man makes more roads, what if they get on my trapline and if they cut all the trees down, where would I go for hunting and where would I get the fur?

Then another of the elders made his statement. Again the Beaver language filled the room. Again the translation was uncertain, but the hesitant and broken English combined with the resonance of the Beaver to powerful effect.

One after the other the people spoke. Atsin tried to convey the importance of Quarry and, determined to speak in English, made a cryptic, struggling, but moving statement. Robert Fellow spoke in a mixture of Beaver and English about the progressive destruction of the timber on his trapline and tried to explain how this is driving away the squirrel, marten, and lynx. Clare Akattah talked about her ten-year-old son and the happiness he gets from trapping. Brian Akattah explained the significance of the people's hunting maps and pointed out that his family — like others on the Reserve — needed to have their trapline. His mother spoke in support of him and, in one sentence, encapsulated what everyone had been trying to say: "There is no way you can make paper into moccasins."

After the Reserve people had spoken, the representatives of West Coast Transmission explained their project. With the use of a pipeline map, they gave numbers, routes, scraps of history: 444 miles of 56-inch diameter pipe along a 125-foot right-of-way; nine construction camps at 50-mile intervals; four compressor stations, the nearest to be 46 miles away; at Mile 92 of the Highway there is already a compressor station. West Coast Transmission's other pipelines were built in the area in 1956, 1961, and 1964. Several gathering lines have been built around Fort St. John and Fort Nelson to connect the main lines with scattered gas fields. The proposed Alaska Highway pipeline, permissions granted, will be started in 1982 or 1983; the section on muskeg would be built in winter, the other parts in summer and fall; pipe would be brought into the area by the British Columbia Railroad, and off-loaded at Fort St. John, Beatton River, or Fort Nelson; this would be done in winter and the pipe then stored at compressor station sites to be distributed to construction points along the line.

Then the Northern Pipeline Agency representative spoke. Pipelines cause problems. There must be rules; the people here, and in all the other communities in the region, must say what rules they think they need. West Coast Transmission will have to follow the rules. Problems with traplines or any other issues can now be voiced. The job is to finalize rules, but there can be more discussion. "Our purpose in being here," he said, "is to listen to you so that we can set the best rules possible, but at the same time, recognizing that those rules have to be reasonable."

These men did not speak for long. Perhaps they sensed the impossibility of their task. Their statements were not translated. They may have been untranslatable. The divide between the details they offered and the people's voices was too enormous. West Coast Transmission and the Northern Pipeline Agency men came as employees of remote organizations to discuss a pipeline. They were on a business trip, doing a job. The men and women of the Reserve spoke of their homes, their lives and, moved to do so by profound apprehensions about the future, they struggled against language barriers and nervousness.

By 2 P.M. everyone had spoken. Joseph and Abe Fellow made final statements. The chairman expressed his thanks and admiration and adjourned the meeting. The West Coast Transmission men began packing up their map. Agency officials bantered cheerfully with one another. The transcribers coiled up their wires and packed away their machines. The Union of British Columbia Indian Chiefs' representatives and organizers exchanged the happy opinion that the hearing had been a success. Meanwhile, work in the kitchen continued. A few individuals had slipped in there to eat. Children crowded around their mothers, curious to glimpse the proceedings in the hall without being caught by the strangers' eyes. When the hearing adjourned, everyone was urged to help themselves to steaming dishes of stews, steaks, bannock. It was a lavish welcome, an invitation to share. If speeches and explanations had not captured the attention of the visitors, or had caused them to be at all uneasy, here was a feast to reassure everyone and, in its way, to give special emphasis to the importance of what the Indians had said.

It was all very convivial. The chairman and his associates, however, were eager to be on their way. Tired and satisfied, they regarded the hearing as ended. Once the social niceties were over and done with, the visitors could return to their homes and hotels in town satisfied that a job had been well done. Another hearing was scheduled for the next day. The formal business of making statements and placing them on the record was over. Children now ran in and out, and the two worlds of kitchen and hall had become the combined setting for a feast.

But the people had more to say. The Whites may have completed their work, but now that everyone was eating the Indians' food and talking to one another without agonizing and distorting formality, the hearing could get under way on the Indians' terms. Relaxed and scattered around the hall and kitchen in small groups, the visitors and officials failed to notice when Jimmy Wolf's brother Aggan and Aggan's wife Annie brought a moosehide bundle into the hall. Neither Aggan nor Annie had spoken earlier in the day, but they went directly to the table at which the elders had sat. There they untied the bundle's thongs and began very carefully to pull back the cover. At first sight the contents seemed to be a thick layer of hide, pressed tightly together. With great care, Aggan took this hide from its cover and began to open the layers. It was a magnificent dream map.

The dream map was as large as the table top, and had been folded tightly for many years. It was covered with thousands of short, firm, and variously coloured markings. The people urged the chairman and other white visitors to gather round the table. Abe Fellow and Aggan Wolf explained. Up here is heaven; this is the trail that must be followed; here is a wrong direction; this is where it would be worst of all to go; and over there are all the animals. They explained that all of this had been discovered in dreams.

Aggan also said that it was wrong to unpack a dream map except for very special reasons. But the Indians' needs had to be recognized; the hearing was important. Everyone must look at the map now. Those who wanted to might even take photographs. They should realize, however, that intricate routes and meanings of a dream map are not easy to follow. There was not time to explain them all. The visitors crowded around the table, amazed and confused. The centre of gravity had suddenly shifted away from procedural concerns, pipelines and terms and conditions, to the Indians' world.

A corner of the map was missing and one of the officials asked how it had come to be damaged. Aggan answered: someone had died who would not easily find his way to heaven, so the owner of the map had cut a piece of it and buried it with the body. With the aid of even a fragment, said Aggan, the dead man would probably find the correct trail, and when the owner of the map died, it would all be buried with him. His dreams of the trail to heaven would then serve him well.

Prompted by the map, the elders spoke again about the way their life is changing, and the extent to which frontier developments have damaged their lands. They complained, too, about the weakness of dreamers today: would the young people be able to use these essential skills? Some of these thoughts had been spoken into the microphones and, in inchoate form, had become part of the official record. But now there was no recording, nothing that made the words official. The people now spoke in their own ways, and with real confidence. Most important of all, they said what they wanted and needed. The officials and visitors expressed delight and interest, but it is difficult to know how much they understood. Did the dream map come from too remote a cultural domain? Did the fractured and hesitant English in which the Beaver people spoke too completely obscure their points? Or, taking place after the hearing had been adjourned, off the record, was the conversation around the map seen as no more than a further display of agreeable hospitality? It is never easy to judge the political significance of informal events. Evoking a strange and distant world, the Indians who showed the dream map could have failed to make their point simply because they were now using their own, very unfamiliar idioms.

All the men and women who spoke, whether at the microphones, in seemingly sociable conversations over plates of food, or while the dream map was being shown, said that their lives depended on traplines. They said that logging should be carried out in such a way as to leave enough habitat for squirrels and marten. They said that sports hunters must be kept out of the Indians' hunting territories. Many also insisted that the Alaska Highway pipeline either should not be built at all, or should somehow be built in a way that would not drive away the region's moose. They spoke of oppression in the past and disregard for their interests in the present. The substance of their remarks, along with the gentle tones they used, made it clear that the people had not given up hope, either of being listened to or of leading the kind of life that strengthens their economy and culture. They had tried to explain their concerns in many different ways. They took part in the outsiders' hearing and used it to explain their point of view, but they also prepared moose meat stew and showed a dream map. Despite a century of experience that might urge them to do otherwise, the Indians took the hearing seriously.

Many of the Whites who spent the day in the Reserve hall said they were deeply moved. The chairman repeatedly thanked the people for their words and generosity, and thanked the elders for sharing their wisdom. Yet discussion of the dream map soon petered out, and the officials hurried into their bus, anxious to drive back to town. The people of the Reserve were puzzled. Where had their visitors gone? The meeting was just getting under way. Thinking that there must be some misunderstanding, they asked everyone to come back into the hall, though representatives of the pipeline construction company had long since driven away.

Inside the hall, the elders explained that whenever a dream map is taken out, someone must play a drum and chant. The visitors would, of course, want to share in this. And one of the elders made the room echo with the soft but insistent rhythm of the drum, and sang. No one understood the words, and the singer was too shy to explain. He sat in a corner and relied on the power of the rhythm to hold everyone's attention. At the end of the first song he stopped and looked up. Perhaps someone else would now drum? The evening was just beginning.

But as soon as the drumming stopped the officials expressed their thanks and escaped again to their bus. They were tired, they said, and it really was time they were back in town. From their point of view, the meeting had ended more than an hour before. The people in the hall let them go. Perhaps they were no longer surprised by this demonstration of the white man's haste and incomprehension. No one criticized or complained. The drummer began another song. The sound of the bus driving away broke into the music, but soon the noise of its engine faded into the distance. When the second song ended, the men said that it was a pity there had been no time to play the stick game. They had looked forward to it.

People lingered in the hall. A young man visiting from another village drummed and sang for a while. Others ate. The elders talked about dreams and dreaming, and the maps of the Indians' hunting territories were taken from the wall. The hall began to seem very empty. It was still early. Outside a group of men talked about the meeting and the weather. "Tomorrow will be fine and cold," said Joseph. "We'll go and look for the bear early."

By the next morning it was hard to remember all that had happened at the hearing. Atsin led us to the bear's den. He and Sam Crown judged the lie of its interior by the shapes and textures of the ground, and then they dug and pounded until the animal appeared at the entrance. Sam shot it. Joseph and Robert Fellow skinned and butchered the bear while the others set off on a moose hunt. The sports-hunting season was over. The people again had the woods to themselves. No one said whether or not they felt they had gained anything by all the talk of the previous day. It is difficult to mix hunting with politics. But when they discovered a sports hunter's equipment cache and old campsite a few miles from the bear kill, their expressions of indignation were nothing if not political. As he uncovered cans of fuel, ropes, and tarpaulins, and looked around to see if a kill had been made, Atsin declared over and over again that white men had no right to hunt there, on the Indians' land. When Joseph heard about the cache he said: "Pretty soon we'll fix it all up. We've made maps and everyone will see where we have our land."

16

A Possible Future

Five weeks before the northeast British Columbian hearings, I went with Joseph, Atsin, and several of the young men to hunt at Copper Creek, an area of mixed forest only ten or so miles from the Reserve. On our way there we met a white sports hunter who asked Joseph where deer might be found. It was a request for help and advice and, somewhat to my surprise, Joseph seemed happy to answer. He said, "West. All over there to the west."

"Oh," replied the sports hunter, "you think I should try farther towards the mountains?"

Joseph continued: "Deer, moose, chickens, cattle, pigs, everything gone to the west. Pretty soon everything will be gone. All the meat. Then the white man will understand what he has done."

Several times in the following months, Joseph Patsah reiterated his foreboding of the end of the world to me. But he also said he was sure that the people's maps would make a difference to the future. This oscillation between pessimism and optimism was reflected in his periodic resolve to return to Quarry, the place where he could be away from the changes that he sometimes believes are about to engulf even his own family. Joseph, no more or less than the other people who live on the Reserve, is apprehensive, yet at the same time cannot quite believe that his way of life is in real danger. He expressed this with his own kind of rhetoric. His optimism is tentative, almost mystical. His pessimism often springs from anger about much that he sees around him and resonates with his sense of change. This pessimism, opposed as it is by a no less rhetorical optimism, is strikingly similar to the rhetoric that bedevils discussion of the future of our own way of life almost as much as the Indians'. Apocalyptic apprehension, lit by moral fervour and a collective self-reproach, is fashionable, compelling, and hard to avoid.

Canadian Indians, however, are not disappearing. Their numbers are greater now than at any time since white settlers and frontiersmen spread European diseases and began to take the land. However vicious the stereotypes or gloomy the predictions, Indian cultures and communities will continue to play a part in North American life. Indeed, many Indians — albeit not Joseph Patsah — say that their contribution to the ways in which we all live in the future might be far greater than can now be imagined. With limited needs and a careful protection of their resources, they are the peoples who have prospered. Perhaps it is not entirely fanciful to echo the thoughts of every important Indian leader since the first treaties were being negotiated: in the end, they may have to teach us the crucial lessons of survival.

Even if these lessons are never needed, there is no reason why the Indians, clothed in a vestige of Indian culture, should not continue to exist as long as anyone else. Group after group has shown that they can withstand generations of attack upon their cultural distinctiveness. And both liberal and conservative governments in Washington and Ottawa have encouraged local culture, with celebrations of costume, handicrafts, even giving some limited support to native languages. Discussions of Indian rights, land claims, and compensation for past injustice and loss suggest many different ways in which Indians and Inuit might win new political strength, and secure larger enclaves within the United States or Canada. But neither cultural distinctiveness nor political institutions can alone ensure that those Indians who wish to continue to live by hunting, trapping, and fishing will be able to do so. Concessions are made to Indian leaders so long as they do not demand a real recognition of the Indian economy. Pluralism is a North American ideal, but in practice it does not have room within it for a multiplicity of economic systems. Exotic languages do not get in the way of pipelines; hunting and trapping economies might.

The white man's inability or refusal even to see the existence of Indian economic systems is the one theme that threads its way through the story of the New World. European beliefs that hunting peoples occupied the bottom rung of an evolutionary ladder, together with contrary views of the hunter as an ideal of human existence alongside which contemporary European or American destruction of the Noble Savage could be judged and condemned, are two of the rhetorics that, in different ways, consign hunting peoples to the dustbins of history. There are others. Most ideas about aboriginal peoples in general and hunters in particular are coloured by bathos and nostalgia.

A modern version of this pessimism is heard from the prophets of doom who see in every innovation the seeds of fatal change. Critics of industrialization draw often and effectively upon visions of disaster. Once machinery has reached out to the remotest corners of the world, its presence and effects are everywhere to be seen and heard. The noise of an internal combustion engine breaks into rural and Arctic silence. Roads disgorge at new and sudden terminations the effluent paraphernalia of a new, different, and intrusive world. If the eye and ear anticipate these signs of implied disaster, then at each new change there are cries of alarm — and the cry, also, that isolated, innocent, nonindustrial peoples are doomed.

Fatalism about the overpowering momentum of industrial society is revealed as an extreme and widespread reaction to the world's energy crisis. Any restraint upon the search for, and exploitation of, oil and gas reserves is held to be mistaken, futile, or simply unimaginable. We no longer believe that national interests, still less the needs of even a majority of an electorate, can much influence large oil and gas corporations. We are lured into being fatalistic about the very possibility of politics that mean anything to ordinary people, and about any prospect for control over our everyday lives.

Having lost long-standing beliefs in our own political processes, we are more than skeptical about any such possibilities for groups that are small, marginal, and disadvantaged. Any attempt by Indians to modify the pace or direction of the energy industry's activities can hardly be taken seriously. Hunters of the North who depend upon lands now at the centre of an energy frontier are thus condemned. The several rhetorics combine to deprive them of an economic future. Any voice on their behalf is likely to be heard as a whisper in a wilderness.

The politics of the possible future for the hunters of northeast British Columbia can make sure progress only if fatalism is avoided. We may then see beyond ingrained preoccupations to what people need. Listening is difficult; hearing, even more so. But listening is not always helped by unqualified belief in Indian claims. Support for them necessarily appeals to an undeniable history and points, with quite warrantable fervour, to the scale of injustice that has been done. In the end, though, it is all too easy to slip onto a rhetorical highroad which also leads to despair and inaction.

Here the difficulties worsen. The alternative to rhetoric usually comes in the shape of here-and-now social engineers who congratulate themselves on being down-to-earth and realistic. They have the capacity, they say, to get things done. Yet they reduce people to numbers, and cultures to short-term options. They express the possible with indifference to the desirable. Thus the self-styled pragmatists disregard the Indian interest with the help of a mistaken and distasteful insistence on social programmes, mitigations, or formulae with which to calculate dollar compensation for cultural loss. Nor are these quite as altruistic and *ad hoc* as they might appear. They are practical in the short run because they fit into the policy makers' and frontier developers' ideas of what is good for themselves in the longer run. Their programmes and policies, or lack of them, duly create both social and natural conditions which fail to meet the Indians' needs. This brings the rhetorician and the pragmatist into the same arena, as servants — however unwittingly — of the same economic and political interests. On the one hand, the world of the aboriginal or the Indian or Joseph Patsah is reproduced as a fading sepia tint. On the other hand, we are urged to get on, in a realistic and pragmatic way, with an adequate job and not to bog down in concern with what people say or feel. Either way nothing remains but survival in the most literal sense.

In northeast British Columbia, hydroelectricity is exported to the south by inundating large tracts of Indian land. Coal will be delivered to Asian markets by mining Indian hunting areas. Oil and gas is developed by making inroads into the farthest reaches of Indian territories. Discussion of the Alaska Highway pipeline — the supposed apotheosis of the frontier — has now spawned all the rhetorics and idioms that would seem to affirm everything except a basis for dealing with the region's Indians. There is talk of the inevitable destruction of the Indians of northeast British Columbia. At the same time, government officials and others discuss terms and conditions, mitigative measures: more social workers, a native development corporation, payments to trappers whose traplines are damaged, suitable construction schedules, reseeding of rights-of-way, Indian representation on committees that will monitor impacts . . .

In turning to the future, then, I am faced with the problem of vernacular: how is it possible to point towards solutions — as one must — without slipping into a self-defeating or unacceptable idiom? There may be no single answer. Perhaps one can never do justice both to Joseph Patsah's dreams and to the planner's need for useful maps. Yet there is a middle ground to which everything I have been describing, in both the odd and even chapters, now points.

The crucial facts are simple and clear. Stereotypes and fatalists notwithstanding, the Indians of northeast British Columbia have survived. They say that their right to the lands and resources upon which their survival has depended is guaranteed in a treaty. Their economic system has withstood violation of the Treaty, and their use of and dependence upon hunting and trapping territories are undeniable. This continuing economic strength has been facilitated by two factors. On the one hand, the region's frontiers have left large areas of unoccupied Crown lands in which the Indians can hunt, trap, and fish. On the other hand, the Indians' system has proved flexible enough to avoid or accommodate frontier activity and intrusion. Both these factors have limits beyond which the existence of the Indian economy and frontier development would be irreconcilable. The simple fact here is that these limits have not been reached and, in the relevant term, need not be. Even with national economic needs and international pressures at present levels, the Indian economy could exist as a strong and important part of the frontier for the next fifty years. Beyond then, to the distant economic future, it is hardly possible to see.

In almost every way the region's Indians have been accommodating, and they continue to be so. They now say that one option — their culturally and economically distinctive option — must be guaranteed in the future, and that their hunting territories therefore should be recognized and protected. This is not to suggest that they withdraw into some bizarre and insular domain of their own. The territories are what they use now.

Recognition and protection of these territories would mean that stands of mature forest are left as a basis for fine fur species; pipeline construction is carried out at times of year when there is the least possibility of environmental damage; access roads are routed in consultation with Indians; extensions of ranching are limited; and, most important of all, sports hunting is banned. The Fort Nelson Reserve has proposed that access roads be closed to sports hunters, or — if no longer needed by those who built them — destroyed. Some bands have suggested restrictions on routing of access roads. Others have made proposals about the routing of major pipelines. In the absence of a hunting territory that guarantees these rights and limits destructive intrusion onto Indian lands, many Indians have demanded that all oil and gas development be halted. The hunting territory can secure an economic stake for Indians in the future. It represents what they have, need, and want.

This demand that hunting territories be recognized is not a land claim in the normal sense of the term; nor is it a demand for Indian sovereignity in northeast British Columbia. It is not even an unqualified rejection of frontier developments. Nor does it amount to a hopeless idealism. The Indians' point of view does not necessarily entail a drastic collision between their present needs and the interests of the oil and gas industry. Insofar as the Alaska Highway pipeline has given rise to discussion of terms and conditions for its construction, the Indians' proposal that the lands they use be established as hunting territories occupies the middle ground that is usually so hard to find between grand rhetoric and *ad hoc* pragmatism. The Indians are sure that their demand is just, sensible, and could easily be met. Yet it is a proposal that either falls on deaf ears or is rejected out of hand. They might as well be demanding the abolition of Canada.

Why do government officials, lawyers, and British Columbians generally react in this way to a seemingly uncontentious idea? Part of the answer is general. British Columbia has an expanding economy which looks to the northeast region for great strength in the future. It may not always be clear what activities will generate this strength, but the ubiquitous hope for a continuing economic boom is encapsulated in belief in the limitless northern frontier. Major economic interests and impassioned fantasy both play their parts in, and are nourished by, this hope. The developers have many dreams: new mines, sudden energy bonanzas, endless oil and gas reserves at deeper and deeper levels in the ground, possibilities for more and bigger and grander hotels. They dream of restless, expanding, and remunerative activity in a place that, because of its distance from where developers actually live and its history, seems to have no limits. Such dreams are the most established carcinoma of the North American imagination.

An imprecise but overriding economic interest both helps to

spawn, and then reinforces, the popular ideology that has shaped ideas about all the frontiers of the New World. Governments that depend on an electorate with a sizeable proportion of would-be outdoorsmen are reluctant to suggest that Crown lands are not, in some ill-defined way, up for grabs. But the actual grabbing in northeast British Columbia is done by large corporations, a relatively small number of skilled men who earn good money in the oil and gas business, and the provincial government's treasury. Indian claims to special rights on the frontier appear as intolerable interference and restriction. Sports hunting is upheld far more widely, and with much greater conviction, than is the Indians' right to land that is their home and upon which they depend for their livelihoods. Developers and politicians, when countenancing Indian demands in northeast British Columbia, express a sense of economic claustrophobia. The Indians' maps are in the way of the white men's dreams.

A far more specific form of resistance to Indian rights to exclusive hunting territories might be found in local business interests. Tourism is a significant part of the region's economy, especially along the Alaska Highway. Sports hunters provide a part of the tourist business. Any restriction of the hunters would therefore be against the interests of some local businessmen. They have not said as much. Demands for limitations on sports hunting have not even become articulate enough for anyone to oppose them. This hypothetical resistance would become real, however, if the idea were so much as mentioned, even as a mere possibility, by officials of the provincial government.

This leads to an even more specific reason why a simple idea encounters complex obstacles. The provincial government has jurisdiction over Crown lands. Since the Indians' territories are almost entirely situated on Crown lands, their proposals for hunting rights would seem to belong with provincial officials. But the federal government has responsibility for all matters concerning Indians. Perhaps in a wish to avoid treading on jurisdictional toes, as well as in a more general reflection of the obstacles I have already described, the federal government's 1979 report on terms and conditions for the construction of the Alaska Highway pipeline makes no mention of hunting territories. This report, aptly titled "Forgotten Land, Forgotten People," is based on hearings at which Indians again and again expressed their right to and need for such territories. Yet the provincial government very rarely agrees to negotiate with Indians or their representatives, and refused to participate in the hearings in the northeast region. The demand for hunting territories thus falls between jurisdictional stools, and it is all too easy for each government to find in this separation of responsibilities an overwhelming reason for inaction. When this jurisdictional difficulty is reinforced by a vague but intense frontier ideology, hunting territories appear as an ambitious, daring, and idealistic scheme. They are not a panacea for all the Indians' ills; but neither do they deny the future of the white man's economy. Yet a simple and good idea is regarded as extreme, and is obstructed by bureaucratic niceties and socioeconomic mythologies.

Sub-Arctic forest and the Rocky Mountain foothills: a terrain where white frontiersmen can make no profit from the clearing and ploughing of land; an area rich in wildlife; an Indian population that is accommodating, flexible, yet economically and culturally tenacious. All this in Canada, a country proud of a great northern wilderness, of its place among the wealthiest nations of the world, and of its liberal political heritage. In this setting a frontier that moves in bursts and booms but with good sense and some firm policy for its activities could leave much land and wildlife undestroyed. All the conditions exist for a real social and economic pluralism, in which an imaginative but tough-minded state might fulfil its obligation to Indian people.

Joseph, Atsin, and all the other Indians of northeast British Columbia express surprise, dismay, and indignation when their needs and demands go unheeded. They know, as no one else can, about the extent of the land, the condition of animal populations, and their own social and economic limits. They also know that the government has local, regional, and national offices, all staffed by well-paid officials.

Yet when it comes to the people's real problems, there appears to be no one with either the will or the means to make changes. Given the historical and geographical background, the Indians' feelings of puzzlement and outrage are perfectly understandable. In fact, Canada could achieve something in its North that no country has ever done.

The obstacles to this achievement are not trivial. A change in the pace of energy development in northeast British Columbia would also mean a change in the rate at which tax revenues increase. The plans of some powerful corporations would be checked, and visions of new towns in areas Whites have thought of as underpopulated could fade. These obstacles might be insurmoutable if the advantages of rapid development of all the region's energy potential were clear — but that is not the case. British Columbia is a rich province, whose economy, with drastically inflated real estate values, already bears the mark of overheating. Its tax base is solid enough; the province enjoys sizeable budgetary surpluses. Meanwhile the energy frontier is in place; and no one proposes that it be dismantled. The need for resources is already well met by oil, gas, and hydroelectricity on tap in British Columbia. At the same time, large-scale capital-intensive projects entail a heavy reliance on short-lived and unstable growth. This is the economic cause of local boom-bust cycles that result in so much damage.

Hard questions can also be asked about the advantages of a fast-moving energy frontier in British Columbia for Canada, and even for North America as a whole. Does it really make economic sense to export limited and unprocessed resources to the most wasteful society there has ever been? Is this rush for northern oil and gas and coal in the interests of Canada? The resources of the North are economically marginal, and their development requires public subsidy — sometimes on an immense scale. Would not the interests of the many be better served by leaving these resources undeveloped, at least until they are no longer economically marginal? Who is the northern frontier really for? The Alaska Highway natural gas pipeline, a project that serves American demands for energy, at its present estimated cost of $35 billion is of doubtful real value even to the United States economy. The northern frontier dream is in part a hoax: its proponents nurture wild optimism in order to keep development going. We are all urged to share their belief in the future. No room is left for doubt; no place for skepticism about the dreamers' economic sense. Great fortunes are to be made, from construction and speculation — so long as we all continue to believe in the urgency of northern resource development. For this reason, all such development is trumpeted as a great challenge; and its progress, whatever the costs, is celebrated as a new and unquestionable triumph. But heady talk about national expansion has all too often, in the history of many countries, been a brightly coloured smokescreen behind which minority rights, local needs, economic interests of the majority, and destruction of the land itself have all been conveniently concealed. Future generations will wonder at the dominance of the few and the gullibility of the many.

Resources left in the ground are saved, not lost. The rapacious frontier in northeast British Columbia is not in anyone's long-term interests. A questionable economic urgency is being allowed to overwhelm the needs of the Indians for whom the northeast corner of the province is both a home and an economic base that has lasted more centuries than the energy frontier might last years.

The obstacles to a recognition of Indian hunting territories, when viewed alongside both the possibility in northern Canada for genuine economic pluralism and the people's history, become clearer: outworn frontier myths, the idea that sports hunting is a privilege of citizenship, the interests of small numbers of local businessmen, squabbles about federal-provincial jurisdiction. This failure to seize the opportunity in the North for real and lasting solutions to the problem — a problem that has blighted all the fine ideas of freedom and justice in the New World — is familiar and dismaying. Meanwhile, the uncompromising frontier in northeast British Columbia, flexible only in its quick eye for new financial fortunes, will go unmodified even by the conciliatory proposals and long-standing needs of the Indian societies within its compass. And the Indians will continue to be, as Edward Curtis remarked in the early 1900s, "the most visible sign that something was wrong with the American dream."

I shall be told, as I have been told before, that prolonged participation in the lives of small and remote bands of Indians results in romantic and idealistic shortsightedness. The details of the small picture, close at hand, obscure the large, real world of harsh politics and social necessity. The critics who would be realists say that no Indian group can withstand the pressure of the white man's frontier. Nowhere in the world is there an example to be found of an Indian economic system that survived intensive settlement and development of Indian lands. So, they say, it is naive — and wasteful of time if not of resources — to pretend that by some unusual method the inevitable can, in the end, be arrested.

In the end the prophets of doom — with Joseph Patsah perhaps among them — might turn out to be right. Hunting territories cannot survive being flooded by hydroelectric projects, and maybe every last river and creek will eventually be turned into the bays and arms of artificial lakes. Perhaps in the long term the whole of northern British Columbia will become an industrial wasteland or a huge conurbation. But these apocalyptic prospects are distant and no more inevitable than several other possibilities. For the relevant term, which means for the lifetimes of the children now growing up in the area, the possible ultimate devastation of their lands is not a very good reason for denying them what they need now.

The total number of Indians in northeast British Columbia is no more than 3,500, and this number includes persons who consider themselves to be Indian but do not live on reserves and are not legally recognized as Indians. Insofar as there is a conflict of interest in the area, therefore, it is between this small group of people and an energy frontier whose economic advantages are, to say the very least, questionable. If we also consider the nature of the Indian peoples' claim to the resources that they have always harvested, then there is every reason to pay attention to their maps and dreams.

Joseph Patsah, Atsin, and many others of the region's Indians say that Whites in northern British Columbia are ruthless to the point of complete destructiveness. With the support of detailed description of the animals' westward movements, Joseph sometimes anticipates the loss or ruin of the land he has dreamed and mapped. Yet this need not be so. Again and again people have said that one or another Indian society was dead or dying — only to discover, sometimes fifty years later, that it was still alive. Indians in northeast British Columbia have shown just how resilient a society can be.

What Joseph Patsah knows, and what leads him to make his own pessimistic prophecy, is that the resilience of even his people has its limits. The coming years will show whether or not the frontier will push them beyond those limits. The outcome is not decided, which is why fatalists are wrong, and hunting territories are right. Fatalism can be the only quality that Joseph Patsah shares with those who, in a mindless if enthusiastic acceptance of the frontier, have the means but not the need to bring an end to his world.

Bibliography

Throughout the book I have avoided footnotes. This bibliography, then, gives all the works that are referred to in the text and also identifies books, articles, reports and other sources of information and ideas that have been of help. It is not an attempt to list everything that has been written about northeast British Columbia in particular or northern hunting societies in general.

Bellrose, F.C. *Ducks, Geese, and Swans of North America*. Harrisburg, Pa.: Stackpole Books, 1976.

Berger, T.R. *Northern Frontier, Northern Homeland: The Report of the Mackenzie Valley Pipeline Inquiry*. 2 vols. Ottawa: Ministry of Supply and Services, 1977.

Bowes, G.E., ed. *Peace River Chronicles*. Vancouver: Prescott Publishing, 1963.

Brice-Bennett, Carol, ed. *Our Footprints are Everywhere: Inuit Land Use and Occupancy in Labrador*. Ottawa: Queen's Printer, 1977.

Canada. Parliament. Sessional Papers. Ottawa. 1870-1900.

Canada. Parliament. Senate. Journal. Ottawa. 1888.

Canada. Parliament. Annual Report of the North West Mounted Police. 1897.

Chamberlin, J.E. *The Harrowing of Eden*. Toronto: Fitzhenry & Whiteside, 1975.

Coutts, M.E. *Dawson Creek Past and Present*. Dawson Creek, B.C.: Dawson Creek Historical Society, n.d.

Community Information Research Group. Research results reported as Chapter 1, in "Final Submission on the Northeast British Columbia Land Use and Occupancy Study." See entry under Union of British Columbia Indian Chiefs.

————. Statement in Evidence to the Northern Pipeline Agency Public Hearings, Fort St. John, 13-14 December 1979. Transcript vol. 16, pp. 1671-1712 and vol. 17, pp. 1827-31.

Cowan, Ian M., and Guiguet, C.J. *The Mammals of British Columbia*. 3rd ed., rev. Provincial Museum Handbook, no. 11. Victoria: Queen's Printer, 1965.

Cumming, Peter A., and Mickenberg, Neil H., eds. *Native Rights in Canada*. 2nd ed. Toronto: The Indian-Eskimo Association of Canada in association with General Publishing, 1971.

Daniels, R. "Research Papers on the Implications of Treaty 8." Edmonton: Indian Association of Alberta, n.d.

Eklund, C.R. "Fur Resource Management in British Columbia." *Journal of Wildlife Management* 10(1946):29-33.

Engler, Robert. *The Brotherhood of Oil: Energy Policy and the Public Interest*. Chicago: University of Chicago Press, 1977.

————. *The Politics of Oil*. Chicago: University of Chicago Press, 1961.

Farley, A.L. *Atlas of British Columbia: People, Environment and Resource Use*. Vancouver: University of British Columbia Press, 1979.

Feit, H. "The Ethno-ecology of the Waswanipi Cree; or How Hunters Can Manage Their Resources." In *Cultural Ecology: Readings on the Canadian Indians and Eskimos*, edited by B. Cox. Toronto: McClelland & Stewart, 1973.

Footner, H. "Travelling Down the Peace." In *Peace River Chronicles*, edited by G.E. Bowes. Vancouver: Prescott Publishing, 1963.

Freeman, Milton, ed. *Inuit Land Use and Occupancy Project: A Report*. 3 vols. Ottawa: Ministry of Supply and Services, 1976.

Fumoleau, René. *As Long As This Land Shall Last: A History of Treaty 8 and Treaty 11, 1870-1939.* Toronto: McClelland & Stewart, 1976.

Godfrey, W.E. *The Birds of Canada.* Ottawa: National Museums of Canada, 1966.

Godsell, Phillip H. *Arctic Trader: The Account of Twenty Years with the Hudson's Bay Company.* 1943. 6th rev. ed. Toronto: Macmillan of Canada, 1946.

Gordon, Rev. D.M. "From Fort McLeod to Fort St. John." In *Peace River Chronicles,* edited by G.E. Bowes. Vancouver: Prescott Publishing, 1963.

Hanke, Lewis. *All Mankind Is One: A Study of the Disputation Between Bartolomé de Las Casas and Juan Ginés de Sepúlveda in 1550 on the Intellectual and Religious Capacity of the American Indians.* Dekalb: Northern Illinois University Press, 1974.

————. *Aristotle and the American Indian: A Study in Race Prejudice in the Modern World.* Bloomington: Indiana University Press, 1970.

Harper, James. Presentations to the Northern Pipeline Agency Public Hearings, Fort St. John, 13-14 December 1979. Transcript vol. 16, pp. 1671-78, 1685-93, 1697-98, 1704-12, and vol. 17, pp. 1829-31.

Haworth, P.L. "On the Headwaters of Peace River." In *Peace River Chronicles,* edited by G.E. Bowes. Vancouver: Prescott Publishing, 1963.

Hawthorn, H.B., ed. *A Survey of the Contemporary Indians of Canada.* 2 vols. Ottawa: Queen's Printer, 1966 and 1967.

Hawthorn, H.B.; Belshaw, C.S.; Jamieson, S.M. et al. *The Indians of British Columbia: A Survey of Social and Economic Conditions: A Report to the Minister of Citizenship and Immigration.* 3 vols. Vancouver: University of British Columbia Press, 1955.

Horetzky, C. "The First Railway Survey." In *Peace River Chronicles,* edited by G.E. Bowes. Vancouver: Prescott Publishing, 1963.

Innis, Harold A. *The Fur Trade in Canada.* Toronto: University of Toronto Press, 1956.

Jackson, Michael. Presentations to the Northern Pipeline Agency Public Hearings, Fort St. John, 13-14 December 1979. Transcript vol. 17, pp. 1927-42.

Jamieson, Kathleen. *Indian Women and the Law in Canada: Citizens Minus.* Ottawa: Ministry of Supply and Services, 1978.

Jochim, M.A. *Hunter-Gatherer Subsistence and Settlement: a Predictive Model.* New York: Academic Press, 1976.

Johansen, Bruce, and Maestas, Roberto. *Wasi'chu, the Continuing Indian Wars.* New York: Monthly Review Press, 1980.

Josephson, Matthew. *The Robber Barons: the Great American Capitalists, 1861-1901.* New York: Harvest, 1962.

Laxer, James. *Canada's Energy Crisis.* Toronto: James Lewis and Samuel, 1974.

Loggie, I. *Interview with Joseph Apsassin.* Calgary: Glenbow Alberta Institute, 1956.

Mackenzie, Alexander. *Voyages from Montreal on the River St. Laurence Through the Continent of North America to the Frozen and Pacific Oceans in 1789 and 1793.* Edmonton: Hurtig, 1971.

————. "The Discovery of the Canyon." In *Peace River Chronicles,* edited by G.E. Bowes. Vancouver: Prescott Publishing, 1963.

Mair, Charles. *Through the Mackenzie Basin: A Narrative of the Athabasca and Peace River Expedition of 1899.* London, 1908.

Mair, W. Winston. *Forgotten Land, Forgotten People: A Report on the Alaska Highway Gas Pipeline Hearings in British Columbia.* Ottawa: Northern Pipeline Agency [1980].

Manuel, George. Presentations to the Northern Pipeline Agency Public Hearings, Fort St. John, 13-14 December 1979. Transcript vol. 16, pp. 1655-66 and vol. 17, pp. 1942-53.

Moberly, H.J. "The Monopoly is Broken." In *Peace River Chronicles,* edited by G.E. Bowes. Vancouver: Prescott Publishing, 1963.

Moodie, Inspector J.D. "Blazing a Trail to the Klondike." In *Peace River Chronicles,* edited by G.E. Bowes. Vancouver: Prescott Publishing, 1963. Extracted from Reports of Northern Patrols, Canadian Sessional Papers, no. 15, vol. 33, no. 12, 1899, Ottawa.

Northern Pipeline Agency. *Alaskan Highway Gas Pipeline.* British Columbia Public Hearings. 18 vols. Vancouver and Calgary: Northern Pipeline Agency, 1980.

Ormsby, Margaret A. *British Columbia: a History.* Toronto: Macmillan of Canada, 1971.

Overstall, Richard. Presentations to the Northern Pipeline Agency Public Hearings, Fort St. John, 13-14 December 1979. Transcript vol. 16, pp.1668-75, 1694-97, 1699-1703, and vol. 17, pp. 1827-29.

Patterson, R.M. "The Sikanni Chief River." In *Far Pastures.* Sidney, B.C.: Gray's Publishing, 1963.

Peterson, R.L. *North American Moose.* Toronto: University of Toronto Press, 1955.

Richards, John, and Pratt, Larry. *Prairie Capitalism: Power and Influence in the New West.* Toronto: McClelland & Stewart, 1979.

Ridington, R.R. *The Duneza Prophet Tradition.* Mercury Series. Ottawa: National Museum of Man, 1978.

————. *The Environmental Context of Beaver Indian Behaviour.* Ph.D. dissertation, Harvard University, n.d.

————. "The Medicine Fight: An Instrument of Political Process Among the Beaver Indians." *American Anthropologist* 70, no. 6 (1968).

Robertson, W.F. "The Provincial Mineralogist Reports." In *Peace River Chronicles,* edited by G.E. Bowes. Vancouver: Prescott Publishing, 1963.

Robin, Martin. *Pillars of Profit: The Company Province 1934-72.* Toronto: McClelland & Stewart, 1973.

Sahlins, Marshall. "The Original Affluent Society." In *Stone Age Economics.* London: Tavistock, 1974.

Simpson, George. *Journal of a Journey to the Peace River Country 1820-23.* London: Hudson's Bay Company, 1926.

Stefánsson, Vilhjálmur. *Not By Bread Alone.* New York: Macmillan, 1956.

Union of British Columbia Indian Chiefs. "Final Submission on the Northeast British Columbia Land Use and Occupancy Study." Vancouver, 1980.

Usher, Peter. *The Bankslanders: Economy and Ecology of a Frontier Trapping Community.* 3 vols. Ottawa: Department of Indian Affairs and Northern Development, 1971.

Vreeland, F.K. "An Expedition to Laurier Pass." In *Peace River Chronicles,* edited by G.E. Bowes. Vancouver: Prescott Publishing, 1963.

Weinstein, Martin. "Hares, Lynx and Trappers." *The American Naturalist* 3, no. 980 (July-August 1977):806-08.

————. "Indian Land Use and Occupancy in the Peace River Country of Northern British Columbia." Vancouver: Union of British Columbia Indian Chiefs, 1980.

————. Presentations to the Northern Pipeline Agency Public Hearings, Fort St. John, 13-14 December 1979. Transcript vol. 16, pp. 1726-37 and vol. 17, pp. 1775-1805.

————. *What the Land Provides: An Examination of the Fort George Subsistence Economy.* Montreal: Grand Council of the Crees, 1976.

Williams, M.Y. "Fauna of the Former Dominion Peace River Block, British Columbia." In *Report of the Provincial Museum of Natural History of the Year 1932.* British Columbia Sessional Papers, vol. 1 (1934):14-22.

Winterhalder, B.P. "Canadian Fur Bearer Cycles and Cree-Ojibwa Hunting and Trapping Practices." *American Naturalist,* forthcoming.

Index